The History of
TENSE/ASPECT/MOOD/VOICE
in the Mayan Verbal Complex

The History of
Tense/Aspect/Mood/Voice
in the Mayan Verbal Complex

JOHN S. ROBERTSON

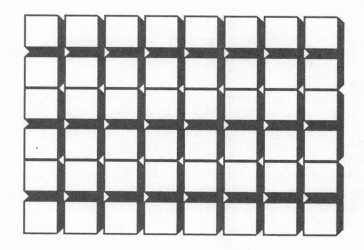

UNIVERSITY OF TEXAS PRESS   AUSTIN

For reasons of economy and speed this volume has been printed from camera-ready copy furnished by the author, who assumes full responsibility for its contents.

Copyright © 1992 by the University of Texas Press
All rights reserved
Printed in the United States of America

First edition, 1992

Requests for permission to reproduce material from this work should be sent to:

> Permissions
> University of Texas Press
> Box 7819
> Austin, Texas 78713-7819

⊗ The paper used in this publication meets the minimum requirements of American Nati‹ Standard for Information Sciences—Permanence of Paper for Printed Library Materials, A Z39.48–1984.

Library of Congress Cataloging-in-Publication Data

Robertson, John S., date
  The history of tense/aspect/mood/voice in the Mayan verbal complex
/ John S. Robertson.
      p.   cm.
  Includes bibliographical references and index.
  ISBN 0-292-72075-0
  1. Mayan languages—Verb phrase. 2. Mayan languages—Grammar,
Comparative. 3. Linguistic change. I. Title.
PM3963.R54 1992
497' .415—dc20

                                                                                    92-17

To
Barbara, Christian, Jacob, James, Kirsten, Jennifer, and Matthew
and to
Steven, Debbie, Ruth, and John

Contents

Abbreviations

<	derived from
>	becomes
1	first person
2	second person
3	third person
ABS	absolutive
AFF	affix
AGNT	agent
ANTI	anti (e.g. antipassive)
ASP	aspect
C	consonant (in CVC, etc.)
CAUSE	causative
COMP	completive
CONSERV	conservative
CONT	continuative
DAPD	double argument predication declarative
DAPO	double argument predication optative
DEPEND	dependent
DIST	distant (past, future)
DU	dual
DV	directional verb
ERG	ergative
EXC	exclusive
FUT	future
GEN	genitive
IMPER	imperative
INC	incompletive
IND	indirect
INNOV	innovative
INTRANS	intransitive
LOC	locative
MALE	male
N	noun
NEG	negative
NOM	nominative

NOMLZR	nominalizer
OBJ	object
OPT	optative
PASS	passive
PL	plural
PRED	predicate
PREP	preposition
PROG	progressive
PROX	proximate (past, future)
REL	relative
SAPD	single argument predication declarative
SAPO	single argument predication optative
SG	singular
SUFF	suffix
TAMV	tense/aspect/mood/voice
TRANS	transitive
TRANSTVZR	transitivizer
v	verb
V	vowel (in CVC, etc.)
V-INIT	verb-initial
V$_{IN}$	intransitive verb
V$_T$	transitive verb

Preface

In the late summer of 1967, just before I took my first linguistics course, fifteen or so other students and I drove in several cars from Provo, Utah, through Mexico to Patzicía, Guatemala. Robert Blair had incited our interest, and as a twenty-four-year-old with only a year of beginning Spanish, I was ready to learn everything I could about Kaqchikel Mayan in this temporally abbreviated, 6,000-mile odyssey. As it worked out, I was able to consult with a Kaqchikel speaker only a few hours a day during the short two-week stay, but it was enough to convince me that if this was what linguists did, I wanted to spend my whole life doing it. It would be a lifelong hobby for which I would get paid. I do not think I slept much, because my mind raced through paradigms with holes, conjuring up questions whose answers might fill those paradigmatic holes. I resented having to lie so long in my sleeping bag in the dark before being able to resolve the burning questions that I wanted so much to find the answer to. Subsequent work on other Mayan languages grew from this briefly planted seed into comparative historical research, for what I had learned about the Kaqchikel verbal system was readily transferable to other Mayan language families. Indeed, a master's thesis, a Ph.D. dissertation, a number of publications, and this book directly resulted from this short but moving introduction to Mayan languages.

Robert Blair gave me substantial opportunity to learn more about Mayan languages by turning over to me the project of producing a Mam pedagogical grammar during my graduate work at BYU; he was a good teacher, and is now a dear friend and colleague. Calvert Watkins' classes at Harvard and his considerable help during the writing of my dissertation are at the core of the work I have done and will do, since the comparative historical method, as a method, will never be dated. I sat in on Linda Waugh's seminars and classes on Jakobson during my year of teaching at Cornell, and these discussions stimulated my thinking and clarified my understanding of the nature of language. Lyle Campbell, who participated in the 1967 trip mentioned above, has always been a great help in my career. Charles Sanders Peirce's semiotic is the product of perhaps the greatest American mind ever, and I have found his thinking to be of inestimable value in understanding the life of language. Those scores of Mayan-language speakers with whom I have worked in the more than two decades since my first introduction have showed remarkable patience and insight. A recent rereading of Edward Sapir, showing his sensitivity to the knowledge and intuition of the native speaker, reconfirmed my constant inclination to depend upon the linguistic wisdom of Mayan speakers in my fieldwork. All of these people directly or indirectly influenced the writing of this book. (None is responsible, of course, for any infelicities.) To all of them I owe a great debt, and without them I would be much poorer.

In writing this book, I received significant help from Joseph Martineau with his careful and thoughtful work in proofing and cleaning up the manuscript. Tim Hiatt, Jennifer Rey, and Julie Thornton have also read various drafts and have helped improve its quality. I would also like to thank Karen Crowther for her work on the cover design, and Elizabeth Gold for her significant help on copy-editing.

At the administrative level, my Department Chairs, Rey Baird, Harold Madsen, and Mel Luthy, have been supportive, not only in giving me time to research and write, but in giving me the means to conduct research and writing. The support has taken the form of time off, generous travel help, and computer support. It has been a pleasure to work under such positive circumstances.

Clearly, my interests have widened since the 1967 trip to Guatemala, but my love for understanding the nature of language has never flagged. My initial intuition about being paid for a full-time hobby has been born out in these subsequent years.

The History of
TENSE/ASPECT/MOOD/VOICE
in the Mayan Verbal Complex

Chapter 1. **Introduction**

This book does not present a series of successive arguments, one connected to another in a long train. Instead, it presents a set of interconnected arguments, related through the context of the several different Mayan languages, and all growing out of the same reconstructed system of TENSE/ASPECT/MOOD/VOICE (TAMV) common to all the languages. This approach to historical linguistics agrees completely with Peirce's approach (5.265) to philosophy,[1] which

> ought to imitate the successful sciences in its methods, so far as to proceed only from tangible premises which can be subjected to careful scrutiny, and to trust rather to the multitude and variety of its arguments than to the conclusiveness of any one. Its reasoning should not form a chain which is no stronger than its weakest link, but a cable whose fibers may be ever so slender, provided they are sufficiently numerous and intimately connected.

Because the very method of comparative linguistics inclines to proceed "from tangible premises which can be subjected to careful scrutiny," it is certainly true that explanations of language change growing out of a reconstruction either confirm that reconstruction or force improvement of it. Therefore, reconstructed systems may be constantly growing in their accuracy, reflecting more and more faithfully the state of the original system that existed in time-gone-by. And it is the multitude of explanations which naturally flow from such well-informed reconstructions which constitute the kind of Peircian "cable whose fibers are ever so slender," but at once are "numerous and intimately connected."

As a consequence of the inevitable growth to which all reconstructions are subject, the reader must assume—contrary to the author's fondest wishes—that there will be some mistakes, in the form of logical lapses, and more mundane errata; there will be some hypotheses and associated arguments which are only partly accurate, and others which will be wrong, despite the best intentions and efforts. As a matter of course, such hypotheses must be cheerfully discarded, either partially or wholly, in accordance with more reasonable and accurate ones as they present themselves.

---

[1] In keeping with the traditional way of referencing Charles Sanders Peirce's *Collected Papers* (1931–1966), I will use the format 8.232, where the digit preceding the period refer(s) to the volume number and the digits following the period, the paragraph number.

But with such healthy pruning and discarding comes the firm reminder that the real business of reconstruction is not to throw out, but to render intelligible; not to discard, but to clarify; for the purpose of reconstruction is to achieve as clear an understanding as possible of *how* each language came to exist in its attested state. Furthermore, like any scientist, the comparatist must assume that reconstructions and explanations of change are infinitely refinable, genuinely growing in intelligibility with the combined efforts of the community of scholars. Each reconstruction contributes to a more refined understanding of the common language, with each clarification of the several paths which brought the descendent languages from their unattested ancestor to their later, attested state.

While it is true that our inherited Cartesian tradition generally favors the shallow, chain-type reasoning referred to by Peirce above, which promotes the notion that a single counterexample can render the whole suspect, and that single counterarguments can topple entire theories, the real truth is that the kind of argumentation that genuinely carries weight in the comparative historical tradition is strands-to-cable, as suggested above. Weighty arguments—arguments that stand the test of time—are always subject to further elaboration and amplification; consequential arguments are never thrown out on the basis of a single counterexample.

Therefore, the reconstructions and explanations presented in this book will inevitably be reconsidered and revised. New data will be born of future research on the modern languages and of yet-to-be-discovered Colonial documents. Revisions will also come in reconsidered analysis of data already at hand, Colonial and modern. But it must never be forgotten that the purpose of reconstruction—and the purpose of this book—is to render observed facts intelligible by giving reasonable arguments which show a possible evolution from the postulated, unattested ancestral system to those systems found in the attested daughter languages.

The Comparative Historical Method in the Context of the Mayan Languages

Mayan languages lend themselves nicely to the comparative historical method because of their number, because of their territorial integrity, and because there are so many materials that date from Colonial times. The classification of these languages has a long history, which is summarized in Campbell (1977). Kaufman (1974) gives a recent, authoritative grouping, to which the writing of this study has forced some modifications: First, Tojolabal has been moved from the Q'anjob'alan to the Tzeltalan subgrouping (p. 189, n. 1); second, Awakatek has been moved from Ixilan to Mamean (p. 119); third, Choltí is proposed to have been the Colonial ancestor of Chorti' (p. 169); next, Huastec is proposed to have come from the Western Branch and not directly from the common language (p. 221); and finally, Q'anjob'alan is proposed to have come directly from the common language via a Central Branch. The justifications for such modifications are more conveniently given in the course of this study, since they are a part of the very warp and woof out of which this book is written. For visual convenience, the groupings are listed in tree form in Figure 1.1.

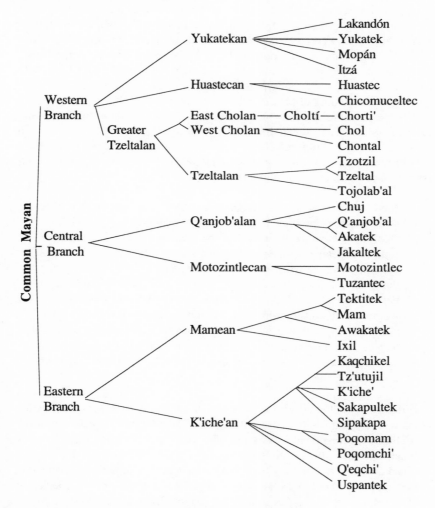

Figure 1.1. Mayan subgroups listed in tree form.

It is, in fact, the relationships that exist among these languages which provide the impetus for defining comparative reconstructions in the first place, for a cross-comparison of equivalent linguistic facts not only yields expected similarities, but more importantly results in certain unexpected differences. The surprise of such differences compels the researcher to seek the reasons for such unexpected variation.

Indeed, the vitality and stability of these languages and the richness of Colonial documents put Mayan linguists in a great laboratory of experimentation, allowing for rich explanation of the changes that occurred in the several languages. They use three steps common to all scientific inquiry: First, they makes hypotheses (reconstructions); second, they see by deduction where such hypotheses must lead (applying logical schemata to the reconstructions); and third, they inductively compare these deductive results with the actual data, thereby refining such hypotheses further, ever clarifying not only the general understanding of Mayan, but also of language itself.

While a casual reader may mistakenly infer from the title of this book that its primary aim is to reconstruct the system of Common Mayan TAMV, it must be clarified at the outset that reconstruction (hypothesis) is merely a part of the purpose of this book. As Watkins (1973:101) rightly points out (speaking of common Indo-European),

> reconstruction is not our fundamental object, as it would be if we were writing a descriptive grammar of a known language.... Even if we were, by some miracle, handed a complete grammar of Common Indo-European as spoken somewhere in, say, 4000 B.C. (the date is meaningless), the work of the Indo-Europeanist would scarcely be done. In fact, it would be barely begun. For his task would be, then as before, to relate the facts vouchsafed him to the facts of attested languages: to construct hypotheses, and to demonstrate precisely how it is possible, within a linguistic tradition or traditions, for a language to pass from one system at one point in time to another system at a later point. The position of the specialist in Romance languages offers a clear analogue.

Unfortunately, too much of the work in comparative Mayan linguistics stops with hypothesis (i.e., reconstruction). Some linguists apparently think their linguistic responsibility is completed with the pronouncement of a reconstruction, ignoring the explanatory steps of deduction and induction outlined above. Hypothesis without justification is scientifically unacceptable; reconstruction without explanation, no matter how accurate, is as intellectually irrational today in linguistics as it was in ancient times in science:

> Accordingly, it appears that the early scientists, Thales, Anaximander, and their brethren, seemed to think the work of science was done when a likely hypothesis was suggested. (Peirce 7.202).

Reconstruction, therefore, is merely part of the means to an important end. The end, simply put, is *explanation,* for without explanation one can never put to rest the questions that naturally arise from the comparison of equivalent linguistic structures. The intrinsic need to explain and thereby understand is appropriately characterized in the following definition by Peirce (7.192):

> What an explanation of a phenomenon does is to supply a proposition which, if it had been known to be true before the phenomenon presented itself, would have rendered that phenomenon predictable, if not with certainty, at least as something very likely to occur. It thus renders that phenomenon rational—that is, makes it a logical consequence, necessary or probable.

The explanation which furnishes the rationalizing proposition referred to above rests upon the three-legged stool of hypothesis, deduction, and induction. Consequently, this book is set up on those three legs. The principles of deduction (which for purposes of this book logically precede even hypothesis) involving theory, definition, classification, and exemplification of certain principles of linguistic change, in Mayan and more generally in language, are given in Chapter 2. The hypothesis is given with the reconstruction of the system of the TAMV of the verbal complex of Common Mayan, and constitutes Chapter 3. The remainder of the book, Chapters 4–11, forms the third explanatory leg, where factual data from the several languages are inductively compared to the outcome of applying the deductive principles of change to the reconstructed form.

If the facts of the several languages are consistent with the prediction given by the deductive principles, as applied to the reconstruction, then the proposition is assumed to be rational, and the job is done. The aim is "to construct hypotheses, and to demonstrate precisely how it is possible...for a language to pass from one system at one point in time to another system at a later point" (Watkins 1973:101), by the deductive and inductive procedures outlined above. Whether that aim conduces to the proposed end can only be judged by the staying power of the explanations presented in this book.

Chapter 2. Deductive Principles of Language Change

The purpose of this chapter is to furnish theory, definition, classification, and exemplification of those principles which, when applied to the reconstructed system of the common language, anticipate outcomes ideally coincidental with the facts of both the Colonial and the modern languages.[1] The process of deduction in the comparative-historical method, which can be defined here as the application of principles to the reconstructed system for the purpose of predicting ideal results, permits the inductive comparison of attested facts of language with deductively secured, ideal results. And it is these three concepts taken together—hypothesis (reconstruction), deduction (prediction of results based on principles of language change), and induction (comparison of actual linguistic forms to the expected deductive outcomes)—which underwrite the chief aim of this book: to supply the propositions necessary to render intelligible the changes that brought the TAMV of Common Mayan to the TAMVs of the several Colonial and modern languages. Otherwise, without the careful application of the comparative-historical method, the phenomena of language change would remain unexplained or, perhaps worse, unnoticed.

The explanation of these deductive principles requires a foundational discussion of several basic concepts: first, the definition of *sign*; second, an explanation of how signs are organized into *systems of signs*, particularly grammatical systems; and third, the role of the Peircian notions of *icon, index,* and *symbol* in such grammatical systems. These definitions allow a systematic discussion of the deductive principles referred to above, which are *influence, reverse influence (markedness reversal), introductive change,* and *displacement.*

The Peircian Notion of Sign

One of many definitions that Peirce (8.343) gave of the sign is as follows:

> I define a *Sign* as anything which on the one hand is so determined by an *Object* and on the other hand so determines an idea in a person's

---

[1]The Colonial languages, it turns out, act as "reconstructed forms" to which the deductive principles of language change can be applied and the result inductively compared to the modern languages.

mind, that this latter determination, which I term the *Interpretant* of the sign, is thereby mediately determined by that Object.

The notions *Sign, Object,* and *Interpretant* are indispensable to an understanding of the above definition. First, at least part of what is meant by *Sign* is the perceptible carrier of information: in language, the phonological entity—what Jakobson would call the *signans*. Thus, at least part of what is meant by the sign *chair* is the three associated phonemes, čɛr. The other two parts of the Sign will be discussed below.

Second, there are technically two Objects: the Dynamical Object, which is not a part of the Sign, and the Immediate Object, which is. The Dynamical Object corresponds to the Object that is what "Dynamical Science (or what at this day would be called 'Objective' science) can investigate" (8.183). The Dynamical Object of the sign *sun*, for example, would be the gaseous, heat- and light-emitting body that is open to scientific measurement and observation. "It is the 'real,' (but more accurately, the existent) object represented by the sign" (5.473). It is the "really efficient but not immediately present Object" (Peirce 8.343).

The Immediate Object, on the other hand, *is* a part of the Sign, by virtue of its being the "mental representation" (Peirce 5.473) that constitutes the origin of the Sign, the motivating source of the speaker-encoded message. Simply stated, the Immediate Object is what wants to get said. The reality of the Immediate Object is readily apparent in consideration of, say, a student who raises his hand, but when called on says, "Oops, I forgot what I was going to say." It is what he was going to say—what he forgot—that constituted the Object. Had he remembered the Object, his speaking would have been its significant product. The Object is the source for encoding. Or, when someone says "That's not quite what I meant to say; what I really mean is...," it is what the person "really means" that is the Object. It is of no small consequence that the speaker is able to compare what was actually said with the prior "mental representation" (Peirce 5.473) that constitutes the Immediate Object. In summary, the Object is that part of the Sign that determines what gets said, including the phonemes referred to above.

The Interpretant, on the other hand, has three parts: the Immediate Interprant, the Dynamical Interpretant, and the Final Interpretant. The Immediate Interpretant can be described as "all that is explicit in the sign itself apart from its context and circumstances of utterance" (5.473). It is "the Interpretant represented or signified in the Sign" (8.343). Those acquainted with Roman Jakobson's work will recognize that Peirce's Immediate Interpretant corresponds to the Jakobsonian notion of *Gesamtbedeutung*, or general/invariant meaning, which figured so prominently in his seminal "*Beitrag zur allgemeinen Kasuslehre...*" (Jakobson 1971d).

The Dynamical Interpretant involves an interpretive act, based on the Immediate Interpretant and resulting in an interpretation which takes into account the context and circumstances of the utterance. This is closely related to the Jakobsonian notion of contextual variant. Ideally, the interpretive result is equivalent to the Immediate Object which first determined the production of the Sign by the speaker. Thus, when someone says something, motivated by the Immediate Object, the Immediate Interpretant emerges in the mind of the interpreter, and a specific interpretation is made (the Dynamical Interpretant) according to the circumstances of the utterance. Such experientially located objects—based upon the Immediate Interpretant—would in effective communication correspond to the Immediate Object spoken of above. This correspondence between the interpretation of the interpreter and the Object of the originator of the Sign is given by Peirce (4.531) in another discussion of the Sign. A sign is "anything which, being determined by an object, determines an interpretation to determination, through it, by the same object."

The Final Interpretant is the inferential result(s) that comes of the interpretational act. If one hears the sign *Fire!* its inherent Immediate Interpretant would result in an interpretation where one would look for the referential fire (Dynamical Interpretant); he then would think of what he would have to do to bring himself and others to safety. Those subsequent thoughts which logically follow from the dynamically interpreted object would all be part of the Final Interpretant.

What is of particular interest to this book, however, is the Immediate Interpretant, since, as will be shown in detail below, it constitutes the positive information that underlies all grammatical and lexical paradigms. For purposes of this book, let us further define the Immediate Interpretant as that general set of instructions associated with the Sign telling the interpreting mind either, first, how to find Objects in the world of experience (the lexical function), or second, how Objects exist in time and/or space, or even how they exist with respect to each other (the grammatical function). In language, all Immediate Interpretants have either a lexical or a grammatical function, or, most often, a combination of both in varying degrees. In contrast to the Object, the Immediate Interpretant is general and below conscious awareness. Thus, for example, the sign *išoq-iʔ* 'women' addresses a Kaqchikel-speaking interpreter, instructing that interpreter (by the Immediate Interpretant) to look out into the existential world or at least the world of Kaqchikel experience, and identify more than one (the suffix *iʔ* 'plural' grammatical function, how the Object exists in space) woman (*išoq* 'woman' lexical function, Object).

The linguistic sign, therefore, has a lexical or grammatical function, and systems of signs exist in both. In their lexical function, signs exist as thesaurus-like systems: *go, walk, run, trot, gallop, hop, skip, jump,* and so forth. In their grammatical function, signs form paradigmatic sets: *eat, will eat, have eaten, be eating, be eaten, will have eaten, will have been eating,* and so on. The grammatical systems of signs incline more toward binary, dyadic systems, as will be shown explicitly below, while lexical systems seem to emphasize gradation and variation, although there is no absolute distinction between the two types of systems. Furthermore, the most pure form of grammatical sign is compulsory (e.g., the plural in English, or gender in Romance languages), while the lexical sign is selectional (e.g., *The boy/lad/young man went to town*). Since this book focuses on the grammar of Mayan TAMV and thus the paradigms of the Mayan verbal complex, the following discussion is aimed at showing how grammatical (not lexical) systems are organized.

The Organization of Linguistic Signs into Grammatical Systems

The organization of paradigmatic, grammatical systems is based on the notion of *opposition*, defined as follows: an opposition is a compound in one, where the compound consists of two members, separate but indissolubly linked, resulting in a single system. An example would be the oppositional pair *eat, ate*, where the appearance of *ate* calls up *eat*, and vice versa, although, as will be explained below, there is an important asymmetry.

Systems of Oppositions

It is important to note that all oppositions are *systems of oppositions,* with each member standing in a particular, mathematically defined relationship to all other members of that system. Careful illumination of such organizational relationships makes possible the definition and classification of the deductive principles of grammatical change, given below, which underlie diachronic explanation, not only in Mayan but more generally in language. The structure of grammatical (paradigmatic) systems is determined by the logical combination of the *Immediate Interpretants* of the Signs in question, according to the formula 2^m. It is important to recognize that the formulations given below are means of categorizing the members' grammatical systems—means of showing the classes (categories) to which the elements of a paradigmatic set belong.

In establishing such systems of relationships it is essential to understand that the systems are organized around the Immediate Interpretants. In theory, a system of oppositions can consist of the presence or absence of a single Immediate Interpretant (2^1), two Immediate Interpretants (2^2), three Immediate Interpretants (2^3), etc. A system with one Immediate Interpretant, 2^1, is understood to have a single Immediate Interpretant and two categories, with the Immediate Interpretant present in one () and absent in the other, as shown in Figure 2.1.[1]

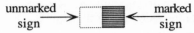

Figure 2.1. Example of a paradigmatic 2^1 system.

A system with two Immediate Interpretants, 2^2, has four categories, one unmarked for both Immediate Interpretants, two singly marked for each Immediate Interpretant (▤ and ▥), and one doubly marked (▦) containing both Immediate Interpretants taken together, as seen in Figure 2.2.

Figure 2.2. Example of a paradigmatic 2^2 system.

A system with three Immediate Interpretants, 2^3, has eight categories: one unmarked, three singly marked, three doubly marked, and one triply marked, as seen in Figure 2.3.

Figure 2.3. Example of a paradigmatic 2^3 system.

A quadruple opposition has sixteen signs, with the possible combinations found in Figure 2.4.

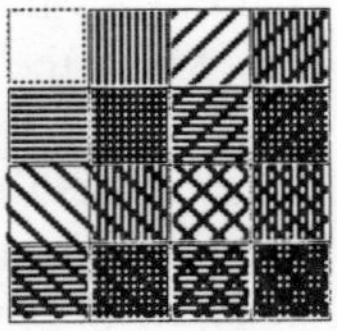

Figure 2.4. Example of a paradigmatic 2^4 system.

---

[1]Notice that each category *can* be filled with a sign, but the unmarked category is often empty. In any case this is considered to be the unmarked category in the Praguian sense.

Opposition and Classification

It is important to note here that the systems resulting from the logical combination of Immediate Interpretants are nothing more nor less than classificatory systems which allow for an explanatory power which is otherwise unattainable, since by definition "explanation consists in bringing things under general laws or under natural classes" (Peirce 5.289).

All natural classification consists of three elements, two of which are obvious and well known, and a third which is less obvious and almost always ignored, but of capital importance. First, the classificatory process implicates Objects to be grouped into kinds. Second, certain *qualities* of the Objects constitute the categories for that classification.[1] These two elements of classification are obvious. The third focuses on the theory of how classificatory qualities are chosen in the first place, for it is the appropriate choice of qualities that provides explanatory power, or in Peircian terms, *natural classes*. *How* the classificatory qualities are chosen must be based on final cause, as Peirce (1.231) so clearly states:

> All classification, whether artificial or natural, is the arrangement of objects according to ideas. A natural classification is the arrangement of them according to those ideas from which their existence results. No greater merit can a taxonomist have than that of having his eyes open to the ideas in nature; no more deplorable blindness can afflict him than that of not seeing that there are ideas in nature which determine the existence of objects. The definitions of Agassiz will, at least, do us the service of directing our attention to the supreme importance of bearing in mind the final cause of objects in finding out their own natural classifications.

As suggested above, I will here take *final cause* to be defined as ideas, or better, laws which determine the existence of Objects. In the case of grammatical categories as existing Objects, their raison d'être is best understood in their final cause: the communicative need of showing how lexical items exist in time or space or with respect to each other. This particular communicative necessity determines the existence of such grammatical Objects (morphemes) that mark genuine grammatical categories. For instance, the very idea of the communicative process requires a grammatical sign whose Interpretant results in referencing the speaker—hence the universality of FIRST PERSON—and the need of an interpreter of the sign—hence the universality of SECOND PERSON. Each language has grammatical categories that are particular to it, as, for

---

[1] For linguistic systems, such qualities are the Immediate Interpretants of the Sign.

example, the verb phrase of English, but it is the communicative necessity of modality, tense, aspect, and voice in the context of predication which determine the existence of such grammatical categories in the first place.

It is therefore the grammatical qualities (Immediate Interpretants) of the paradigm in question that determine the logical, categorical organization of the grammatical morphemes in question. A more concrete, linguistic example of a sixteen-place grammatical system can be found in the organization of the English verb phrase of Figure 2.5. Structurally, it contains the unmarked category *eat*; the four singly marked categories *have eaten, will eat, be eating, be eaten*; the six doubly marked categories *will have eaten, will be eating, will be eaten, have been eating, have been eaten, be being eaten*; the four triply marked categories *will have been eating, will have been eaten, will be being eaten, have been being eaten*; and the single, quadruply marked category *will have been being eaten*.

The classificatory system in Figure 2.5 demonstrates that the English verb phrase is not a random agglomeration of linguistic facts, but a well-defined, hierarchically organized system, whose members stand in a complex but logical oppositional relationship to each other.

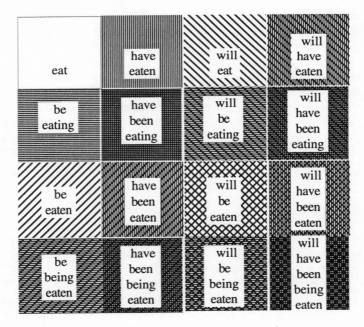

Figure 2.5. Paradigm of the English verb phrase, a 2^4 system.

It must never be forgotten that the system itself exists for its communicative raison d'être. Although the grammatical systems of the Mayan languages discussed below are not as complex, they are nonetheless logical systems of the kind described above.

A Definition of *Index, Icon,* and *Symbol*

Up to this point the discussion has focused on the organization of signs into hierarchically defined grammatical systems, based on the interrelationships of Interpretants per se, but nothing has been said regarding the relationships between the Signs and their Objects.[1] This relationship was perspicaciously defined by Peirce in his celebrated classificatory trichotomy *icon, index,* and *symbol,* whose definitions are based on the notions *similarity, contiguity,* and *habit,* respectively. For Peirce (8.335) these three categories are defined in accordance with their relationship to the Dynamical Object: "In respect to their relations to their dynamic objects, I divide signs into Icons, Indices, and Symbols."

Put into linguistic terms, an aural comparison between the English sign *moo* [mu·] and its Dynamical Object (the sound the cow makes) reveals a *similarity* between the Sign and its associated Object. Thus, *moo* is primarily iconic, based on the similarity that exists between the Sign and its Dynamical Object. Such instances of onomatopoeia are important, but more interesting (for the purposes of this book) are the relationships based on similarity which exist among the members of grammatical systems, as defined below.

The sign *here* [hir], on the other hand, is primarily an indexical sign signaling a relationship of contiguity between the Sign and its Dynamical Object. That is, *here* contains instructions telling the interpreter to locate some object in the physical vicinity of the sign as it is uttered by the speaker, that object being in some sense contiguous with (i.e., not perceptually separate from) the speaker. A disembodied voice coming from all directions that said "Look over *here* for the book," for example, could not be interpreted appropriately, since the interpreter would not be able to identify the book because of not being able to identify the location of the speaker.

A symbol, unlike an icon or an index, has a relationship between the Sign and its Dynamical Object that is founded on habit. There is nothing iconic in the phonemic ensemble *sun* [sən], for example, that tells the hearer to look for a Dynamical Object that looks like it sounds up in the sky, nor is there anything indexical, that tells one to locate the object by means of contiguity. Rather, the interpreter of the message *sun* knows by habit where and how to look for the object.

---

[1]More accurately, it is the relationship between the Sign and its Dynamical Object.

The Trichotomy *Conformative, Reciprocal,* and *Constructive* in Grammatical Systems

As shown above, the relationship between the Sign and its Dynamical Object can fruitfully be classified as icon, index, and symbol, but it is also true that this trichotomy is analogically valid for classification of the relationships *among the signs of* 2^m *grammatical systems*. With respect to the purpose of this book, the chief value of such classification is in its logical outcome, which leads to the definition of those principles of language change which yield ideal reconstructions. Actual Mayan linguistic facts can be compared with these reconstructions. Simply put, classification leads to explanation in historical linguistics.

It is therefore of great merit to extend the notions of icon, index, and symbol to the classification of the relationships that exist among the signs of grammatical systems. The classification of the relationships among the categories of a grammatical system (2^m system) does not fit under Peirce's strict definitions of icon, index, and symbol, which are based on the relationship between the Sign and its Dynamical Object. What is being defined here is something different: the interrelationships of signs to each other in a hierarchically defined, grammatical system. Therefore, in an attempt not to stretch Peirce's original definitions of icon, index, and symbol beyond the original intent (part of a much larger classificatory system), I am here compelled to give different names to the three relationships that exist among the categories of the grammatical systems described above: *conformative, reciprocal,* and *constructive*.[1]

Those signs of a grammatical system are *conformative* which are related by a similarity of signs,[2] as in, for example, **gyrate, gyrated; big, bigger.** Those signs are *reciprocals* whose reference to other signs within the grammatical system is dyadic, given by the notion of self-returning pairs. For example, in the system of kinship the terms **child** and **parent** are reciprocals, as are *I* and *you* in the pronominal system. These kinds of relationships are like indices in that they point to other categories of the system. The rules governing reciprocals form a mathematical group, but their definition goes beyond the scope of this book.[3] Finally, those signs of a grammatical system are *constructive* which are interrelated by habit, but are dissimilar in their signs, as in the pairs **go, went; good, better.**[4] The focus in this book

---

[1] These are analogous to *icon, index* and *symbol*.

[2] Note that they are by definition already similar in Immediate Interpretant, since they are members of the same 2^m system.

[3] There are a series of rules constituting a mathematical group that predict reciprocals in language, as defined in Robertson (1984a).

[4] This relationship is commonly known as suppletion.

will be on the *conformative* and the *constructive* relationships that exist among the members of paradigmatic systems. The *reciprocal* relationship plays a less fundamental role in governing language change.

These classificatory definitions now provide a means of discussing readily observable facts of grammatical systems. Perhaps the most significant and far-reaching observation is this: the signs of those categories that contain a lesser amount of interpretable information (i.e., that contain the fewest Interpretants, or, in other words, the signs of the less-marked categories) tend toward constructive relationships, whereas the terms of those categories that contain the most interpretable information (i.e., that contain the most Interpretants, or, in other words, the more-marked categories) tend to show conformative relationships. This is readily documented and universally present in all languages.

The above distribution of constructive and conformative relationships is in some ways a simple observation, but as will be shown in the rest of the book, the consequences are far-reaching. For example, the English verb *be* contains the least information of all verbs, and as suggested above, the interrelationship of its members in the several grammatical categories is highly constructive—*am, is, are, was, were, be, been.* Similarly, the slightly more marked verb *go* is strikingly constructive:—*go, goes, went, go, gone*—although it has fewer categorical realizations. Finally, an information-packed verb like *gyrate* is conformative, as in *gyrate, gyrates, gyrated.* It is no accident that suppletion strongly occurs in languages of the world with those lexical items whose Immediate Interpretants have little instructional information.

In the system of cardinal and ordinal numbers it is always true that the members of the least-marked categories—one, two, and three, for example—tend to be constructive, while the members of the most marked categories are conformative:

English		**Spanish**		**Tzotzil**	
one	first	uno	primero	jun	sba
two	second	dos	segundo	chib	schibal
three	third	tres	tercero	oxib	yoxibal
four	fourth	cuatro	cuarto	chanib	schanibal
five	fifth	cinco	quinto	jo'ob	yo'obal
six	sixth	seis	sexto	vaquib	svaquibal
seven	seventh	siete	séptimo	jucub	sjucubal
eight	eighth	ocho	octavo	vaxaquib	svaxaquibal
nine	nineth	nueve	noveno	balunib	sbalunebal
ten	tenth	diez	décimo	lajuneb	slajunebal
eleven	eleventh	once	undécimo	buluchib	sbuluchibal
twelve	twelfth	doce	duodécimo	lajchaeb	slajchaebal
thirteen	thirteenth	trece	decimotercero	oxlajuneb	soxlajunebal
fourteen	fourteenth	catorce	decimocuarto	chanlajuneb	schanlajunebal
fifteen	fifteenth	quince	decimoquinto	jo'lajuneb	sjo'lajunebal
sixteen	sixteenth	dieciseis	decimosexto	vaclajuneb	svaclajunebal
seventeen	seventeenth	diecisiete	decimoséptimo	juclajuneb	sjuclajunebal
eighteen	eighteenth	dieciocho	decimoctavo	vaxaclajuneb	svaxaclajunebal
nineteen	nineteenth	diecinueve	decimonoveno	balunlajuneb	sbalunlajunebal
twenty	twentieth	veinte	vigésimo	jtob	sjtobal

Although this is not a 2^m system[1]—and not all language systems are 2^m, though almost all *grammatical* systems are—it is nonetheless true that the interrelationships among these counting forms bear out the observation above that the forms of the least-marked categories tend toward constructive relationships, whereas the more-marked forms show conformative relationships. For example, the least marked of all the forms is *one,* and its relationship to its cardinal is always constructive: *one/first, uno/primero, jun/sba.* On the other hand, as more information is present in the more-marked categories, the relationship becomes conformative: *eighth/eighteenth, octavo/decimoctavo, svaxacibal/svaxaclajunebal.* Furthermore, the numbers between one and ten are constructive (although one sees slight conformation in higher numbers), and the numbers, between twelve and twenty, are highly conformative. It is important to note that the lower numbers between ten and twenty are relatively more constructive, whereas the higher numbers are conformative, as in *ten, eleven, twelve* (constructive), *thirteen* (conformative); *diez, once, doce...quince* (constructive), *dieciseis* (conformative); *lajuneb, buluchib* (constructive), *lajchaeb* (less constructive), *oxlajuneb* (conformative).

It is of particular interest to look at the digitally closing numbers ten and twenty, which are unmarked with respect to the other numbers, and the semiclosing numbers five and fifteen, which are slightly more marked. Ten and twenty are always constructive, and in fact form the basis for the more-marked conformatives that appear later in the system.

The distribution of constructives and conformatives is readily found in 2^m grammatical systems as well. A good example of a 2^4 system is given in the pronominal systems of Tojolabal, Tzeltal and Tzotzil, as seen in Figure 2.6, which system has the following four Interpretants:[2] (a) ERGATIVE, whose absence implies ABSOLUTIVE; (b) PLURAL, whose absence implies SINGULAR; (c) SECOND PERSON, whose absence implies THIRD PERSON when occurring in a category without the positive presence of FIRST PERSON; (d) FIRST PERSON, whose absence implies THIRD PERSON when occurring in a category without the positive presence of SECOND PERSON. Careful comparison of the categories of the above system confirms the observations that (a) there is a strong tendency for the less-marked categories to exhibit constructive relationships, whereas the more-marked categories tend to exhibit conformative relationships, and that (b) there is also a strong tendency for syncretism—where two or more logically implied categories share a single sign—to occur in the more-marked portion of such a system. In fact, in the context of grammatical

---

[1]The Tzotzil data are taken from Delgaty and Sánchez (1978:458–460).

[2]The Tojolabal and Tzeltal data are mine; the Tzotzil data are from Delgaty et al. (1960), Larrainzar dialect.

paradigms, syncretism might best be seen as a kind of homophony, which is the ultimate conformative relationship.

	(ERG) (PLUR) (2ND) (1ST) **ABS3SG**	(ERG) PLUR (2ND) (1ST) **ABS3PL**	(ERG) (PLUR) 2ND (1ST) **ABS2SG**	(ERG) PLUR 2ND (1ST) **ABS2PL**
Tojolab'al	Ø	-e?	-a	-eš
Tzeltal	Ø	-ik	-at	-eš
	Ø	-ik	-ot	-ošuk

	ERG (PLUR) (2ND) (1ST) **ERG3SG**	ERG PLUR (2ND) (1ST) **ERG3PL**	ERG (PLUR) 2ND (1ST) **ERG2SG**	ERG PLUR 2ND (1ST) **ERG2PL**
Tojolab'al	s-	s-...-e?	a-	a-...-eš
Tzeltal	s-	s-...-ik	a-	a-...-ik
Tzotzil	s-	s-...-ik	a-	a-...-ik

	(ERG) (PLUR) (2ND) 1ST	(ERG) PLUR (2ND) 1ST **ABS1EXC**	(ERG) (PLUR) 2ND 1ST **ABS1DUINC**	(ERG) PLUR 2ND 1ST **ABS1PLIN**
Tojolab'al	-on	-otikon	-otik	-otik
Tzeltal	-on	-otkotik	-otik	-otik
Tzotzil	-un	-unkutik	-utik	-utik

	ERG (PLUR) (2ND) 1ST **ERG1SG**	ERG PLUR (2ND) 1ST **ERG1EXC**	ERG (PLUR) 2ND 1ST **ERG1DUINC**	ERG PLUR 2ND 1ST **ERGPLINC**
Tojolab'al	h-	s-...-tikon	h-...tik	h-...tik
Tzeltal	h-	s-...-kotik	h-...tik	h-...tik
Tzotzil	h-	s-...-kutik	h-...tik	h-...tik

Figure 2.6. Paradigm of the pronominal system of Tojolab'al, Tzeltal, and Tzotzil.

It is noteworthy that the least marked category, ABS3SG, which has no positive Interpretant present, also has no formal marking, whereas those categories that have a positive presence of one or more Interpretants have signs which exhibit varying degrees of constructive/conformative relationships.

The relationships of the signs of the categories with one Interpretant present are constructive. These simple categories, ABS3PL, ABS2SG, ERG3SG, and ABS1SG, have the following dissimilar signs for Tojolab'al: -e?, -a, s-, and -on.

The categories with two Interpretants begin to exhibit conformative relationships, but in the main, the relationships are constructive. Thus, ABS2PL, ERG2SG, ERG1SG, and ABS1INC are constructive, *-eš, a-, h-, -otik*, whereas only ERG3PL and ABS1EXC, *s-...-e?* and *-otikon*, are conformative.

The categories with three or more signs exhibit one of two characteristics: either they are conformative, as in ERG2PL, *a-...-ik*, and ERG1EXCL, *h-...-kotik*, or they are syncretic, where two logically implied categories have but a single sign, as in ABS1INC, *-otik*, and ERG1INC, *h-...-tik*. Syncretism is really a kind of super conformatism.[1]

Principles of Diachronic Change

This discussion of 2^m systems along with classification of their attendant signs into conformative, reciprocal and constructive relationships now permits the further definition of important principles of language change.

Influence

The most powerful, pervasive, and important principle, which is the diachronic consequence of the synchronic observations made above (*unmarked* emphasizes constructive relationships, *marked* emphasizes conformative relationships), is what might be termed *influence*. Influence occurs when the signs of the more-marked categories of the paradigm tend to become more like the signs of the less-marked categories, thus reinforcing paradigmatic conformative relationships. When the sign of a grammatical system is affected by change, that sign will belong to a marked category, assimilating characteristics of signs belonging to less-marked categories.[2]

This conformative influence can take many forms. It can be a simple influence, possibly of a phonological distinctive feature. For example, in pre-Tzotzil, the more-marked sign for ABS2PL, **ešik*, was influenced by rounding

---

[1]The syncretic categories, labeled ABS/ERG1INC, which are really two logically possible categories collapsed into one—one dual inclusive (combination of FIRST and SECOND PERSON), and the other plural inclusive (combination of FIRST, SECOND, and PLURAL)—are distinguished in the San Quintín dialect of Yukatek Maya. See Robertson (1983) for a complete discussion.

[2]These observations are behind Kurylowicz's (1966:164) so-called second law of analogy, which states, "the so-called analogical actions follow the direction: unmarked → marked, where the relationship is given by their range of reference." It is obvious from ulation of this "law" that it is not based on the notion of Interpretant, yielding the paradigmatic, hierarchical structure proposed here; rather, it is based on the "range of reference," which is, in effect, the interpretation of the Interpretant. The disadvantage of the Kurylowiczian theory is that it is based on a secondary effect, not on the primary cause.

the vowel of the less-marked sign ABS2SG, *ot,* to go from **ešik* to the attested, modern *ošuk,* as illustrated in Figure 2.7.[1]

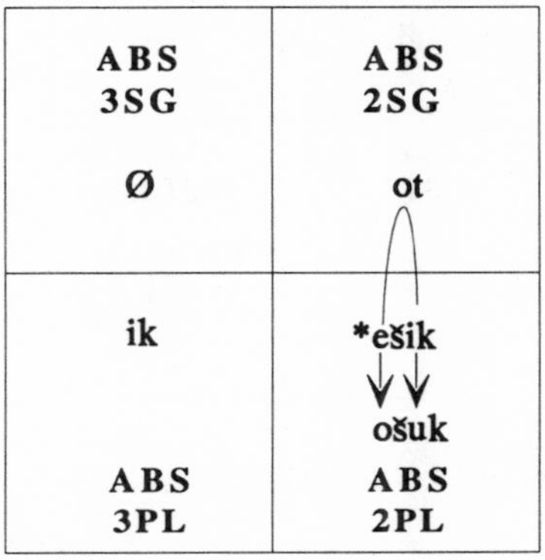

ABS 3SG	ABS 2SG
Ø	ot
ik	**ešik* ošuk
ABS 3PL	ABS 2PL

Figure 2.7. Paradigm of Tzotzil ABS2, ABS3, showing influence.

Thus, in this particular 2^2 paradigm, where ABS3SG is unmarked both for PERSON and NUMBER (and literally has no sign), but where its opposite, ABS2PL (**ešik*), is marked both for SECOND PERSON and for PLURAL, it is exactly in the most marked section that the constructive-to-conformative change occurs, since, for example, *-ošuk* more closely resembles *-ot* than did its ancestral form, **-ešik.*

The above is a simple example of how a phonologically distinctive feature (ROUNDING) of a less-marked sign influences the sign of a more-marked category. By that same influence of less-marked on more-marked, an entire sign may simply attach itself to a more-marked sign. For example, at an earlier point in the history of the same Tzotzil paradigm, the original Common Mayan sign for ABS2PL, **-eš,* was augmented by the ABS3PL, *-ik,* yielding the form **-ešik,* as shown in Figure 2.8.

The assimilative influence can go beyond distinctive features or even attachment of entire morphemes—it is not uncommon to have a total replacement of the sign of a more-marked category by the signs of less-marked categories. For example, Figure 2.9 shows that in Q'eqchi', the Common Mayan sign for the more-marked ERG3PL, **ki-,* was replaced by the less-marked ABS3PL, *-eb²,* and the less-marked ERG3SG, *š-.* Once again in this 2^2 system the pronouns are hierarchically organized, where the pronoun of the most marked category has as its Interpretant ERG3PL, which is the logical combination of the Interpretants ABS3PL and ERG3SG.

---

[1]See Robertson (1982).

ABS 3SG Ø	ABS 2SG ot
ABS 3PL ik	ABS 2PL *eš ↘ *ešik ošuk

Figure 2.8. Paradigm of Tzotzil ABS2, ABS3.

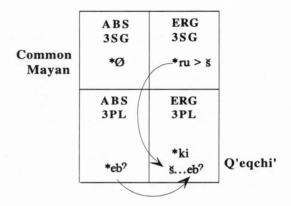

Figure 2.9. Paradigm of Q'eqchi' ABS3.[1]

In addition to the kinds of changes shown above, it is important to note that some changes can be both highly systematic and extensive, as seen in Figure 2.10 comparing the non-first-person portion of the Common Mayan and Tojolab'al PERSON paradigms.[2]

The most radical possible outcome of influence is syncretism (paradigmatic homonymy), where the more-marked sign becomes so much like the sign from a less-marked category that they become indistinguishable, with the sign of the less-marked category totally replacing the sign of the more-marked

---

[1]The shift from *ru- to š- took place with the loss of the *u of *ru- with its subsequent devoicing of the *r- in its immediate, preconsonantal position.

[2]For an extensive explanation of pronominal change in the Mayan languages, see Robertson 1984b.

category. In other words, if two categories collapse, leaving but a single sign for both categories, the sign of the less-marked category will prevail, resulting in syncretism. This is illustrated in comparing Castilian Spanish (where the distinction between POLITE and FAMILIAR is realized in both SINGULAR and PLURAL) with Latin American Spanish (where that distinction has been neutralized in the PLURAL), as seen in Figure 2.11.

	ABS3SG	ERG3SG	ABS2SG	ERG2SG
Common Mayan	*Ø	*ru	*at	*a
Tojolab'al	Ø	s	a	a

	ABS3PL	ERG3PL	ABS2PL	ERG2PL
Common Mayan	*eb?	*ki	*eš	*e
Tojolab'al	e?	s...e?	eš	a...eš

Figure 2.10. Paradigm of Tojolab'al ABS3, ABS2.

In Castilian Spanish, the sign *vosotros* occupies the most-marked category, since its Interpretant signals PLURAL (whose absence implies SINGULAR) and FAMILIAR (whose absence implies POLITE), which is the logical combination of the Interpretant FAMILIAR of *tú* and the Interpretant PLURAL of *ustedes.* And it is precisely the unmarked form of the opposition POLITE/FAMILIAR, *ustedes,* which replaces *vosotros* in Latin American Spanish, through influence.

An equivalent change took place in Mam, not only in the plural, as in Spanish, but in the singular as well, with the less-marked POLITE taking over the more-marked FAMILIAR.[1] It is remarkable that two such unrelated languages,

---

[1]In this regard, it would be well to note that

in recent decades throughout most of Europe and parts of Latin America the FAMILIAR seems to be displacing the POLITE. However, I know of no language where the formal marker of the FAMILIAR has thoroughly displaced the marker of the POLITE. On the other hand, as shown in the examples below and as documented by Head (1978:161, 194), there are many examples of the reverse, where the 'plural pronouns used formerly in polite address of individuals have acquired general usage in address, losing both their earlier social meaning and their original numbers....' This is not to say that what is the European FAMILIAR will not ultimately displace the POLITE. It is just that it has not happened yet in modern Europe, nor is there one Indo-European and the other Mayan, should undergo such similar changes independently of each other. The best possible candidate for explaining this type of identical but genetically unrelated type of shift is the theory of markedness set forth earlier.[1]

Castilian Spanish		Latin American Spanish	
2SG POLITE usted	2PL POLITE ustedes	2SG POLITE usted	2PL ustedes
2SG FAMILIAR tú	2PL FAMILIAR vosotros	2SG FAMILIAR tú	

Figure 2.11. Comparison of POLITE/FAMILIAR pronouns in Castilian Spanish and Latin American Spanish.

Careful consideration of a related Mamean language, Awakatek, sheds more light on the process of change. Although both Awakatek and Mam almost surely developed the POLITE/FAMILIAR distinction long after they separated as languages, it is nonetheless true that Awakatek is structurally equivalent to premodern Mam. By the time of the conquest, Mam had lost the POLITE/FAMILIAR distinction, as illustrated in Figure 2.12.[2]

Up to this point several kinds of change due to *influence* have been noted, where the more-marked categories of a grammatical system are conformatively related in their signs. These changes are *reinforcement* (part of the sign from a less-marked category is incorporated into a sign of a more-marked category), *replacement* (a sign of a less-marked category totally replaces a sign of a

---

evidence that it ever has happened anywhere else in the world, at least up to this point. To the contrary, the POLITE has displaced the FAMILIAR so consistently that Head has proposed it as a language universal. (Robertson 1987a:82)

[1]That these changes were independent of each other is evidenced by the fact that Mam of Reynoso (1644) shows the change already to have taken place. Furthermore, the polite/familiar distinction is an areal phenomenon in the Mayan family, probably starting with Mam, and spreading to Awakatek and bordering dialects of K'iche'.

[2]Notice, incidentally, that the 17th-century English distinction between the POLITE *you* and the FAMILIAR *thou* was lost in favor of the POLITE *you*.

more-marked category), and *syncretism* (the collapse of two categories into one, where the sign of the less-marked category wholly replaces the other). These are all instances of influence, where signs of more-marked categories absorb part or all of the characteristics of contiguous, less-marked categories.

Markedness Reversal

In the examples given above, the signs of the less-marked grammatical categories tend to influence the signs of the more-marked grammatical categories. But there is a certain, well-defined circumstance where the opposite is true—the more-marked category *can* influence less-marked categories. That is, influence flows from what normally would be taken to be the more-marked to the less-marked categories of the paradigm. This phenomenon is traditionally known as *markedness reversal*.

Awakatek **Mam**

2SG POLITE t...uʔ	2PL POLITE kʸ...uʔ	2SG POLITE t...e	
2SG FAMILIAR aw-	2PL FAMILIAR it...uʔ	2SG FAMILIAR aw-	2PL kʸ...e

Figure 2.12. Paradigm comparing Awakatek and Mam prevocalic POLITE/FAMILIAR pronouns.

Although linguists have historically taken markedness reversal to be a capricious mystery, it turns out that such reversals are neither mysterious nor capricious. They are, rather, straightforward in their explanation.

The necessary conditions for the occurrence of markedness reversal are defined by the process of *augmentation*: Through this process, two signs having Interpretants belonging to the same class are brought into contiguity, on either the syntagmatic or the paradigmatic axis. The contextual co-occurrence of near-synonymous terms provides the conditions under which markedness reversal can take place.

Examples of such semantic assimilation are readily observable in such common syntagmatic expressions as *two twins, more better, irregardless,* and the like. In all these instances, each member of each pair shares a semantic value belonging to the other member of the pair.

A brief investigation of the pair *thaw/un-thaw* will illustrate. Usually, the morpheme *un-,* when prefixed to a verb, causes the interpreter to view the arguments of that verb as having returned to their original state—the state that existed before the verbal action was first effected on those arguments, as in, e.g., *un-lock the door, un-snap the snaps, un-cover the table.* Hence, *un-* normally does not occur with such verbs as *paint/un-paint, wash/un-wash* and the like, since the action described by the verb is irreversible. But, contrary to the usual interpretational value of *un-,* with *thaw, un-* simply augments the meaning, as in, for example, "Let's unthaw the meat," which has a meaning equivalent to "Let's thaw the meat." Of course, this usage is colloquial, but it is real and commonly occurring, and the propensity to say it cannot be ignored. It seems reasonable to assume that such an augmentative interpretation occurs because the Interpretants for both *un-* and *thaw* belong to the same class; there is synonymy between the two morphemes. The Interpretant of *thaw* contains a set of instructions asking the interpreter to do something like the following: "Look for a process of frozen liquid returning to its original prefrozen state," which is roughly synonymous with, though obviously more specific than, the meaning of *un-* as explained above, which also requires an interpretation of absolute reversal. Hence, both *thaw* and *un-* share the meaning 'return to originality,' and what emerges, therefore, by adding *un-* to *thaw,* is an augmentation, and *not* a reversal of the meaning of *thaw.* The difference between adding *un-* to, say, *snap* and adding it to *thaw* is that *un-* and *snap* do not share meanings belonging to the same class, whereas *un-* and *thaw* do.[1]

Examples of such augmentation are readily found in the Mayan languages. There are instances in the pronominal systems where the preconsonantal pronouns tend to prefix themselves to their prevocalic counterparts. In Akatek, for example, the preconsonantal ERG3SG is *s-,* while the corresponding prevocalic pronoun is *y-.* It is not uncommon to find instances of words which occur with either the simple prevocalic *y-* or the augmented *sy-,* as in *y-etbi/sy-etbi* 'his friend.'[2] In Cunén K'iche' a similar phenomenon exists. Note that *in-*

---

[1]Other examples of augmentation are typically seen in the NEGATIVE, as in some English dialects: "I don't want no apples."

[2]It might be suggested that this is not augmentation, but a misinterpretation of the root—that *-yetbi* was taken to be the root, thus necessitating the addition of the preconsonantal *s-.* This is unlikely, since *-etbi* can appear either with *y-* functioning as the pronoun or with both *s-* and *y-.* The speakers must know what the root is. This necessity, coupled with the fact that augmentation readily occurs in languages of the world, suggests that augmentation and not misinterpretation is the more likely explanation.

(1SG) and *u*- (3SG) are preconsonantal, optionally augmenting the prevocalic forms, which are *w*- and *r*-:

AUGMENTED	SIMPLE	
kàti·nw -ǐlo	katw -ǐlo	'I see you'
ki·nw -ǐlo	kw -ǐlo	'I see him'
kǐši·nw -ǐlo	kǐšw -ǐlo	'I see you-guys'
kʔei·nw -ǐlo	kʔew -ǐlo	'I see them'
kna·w-ǐlo	—	'you see me'
ka·w-ǐlo	—	'you see him'
qòxa·w-ǐlo	—	'you see us'
qʔea·w-ǐlo	—	'you see them'
kǐnu·r -ǐlo	kinr- ǐlo	'he sees me'
kàtu·r -ǐlo	katr -ilo	'he sees you'
ku·r -ǐlo	kr -ilo	'he sees him'
qòxu·r -ǐlo	qoxr -ǐlo	'he sees us'
kǐšu·r -ǐlo	kišr -ilo	'he sees you-guys'
kʔèu·r -ilo	kʔer -ilo	'he sees them'

It is of capital importance to observe that augmentation can *only* occur where the Interpretants of both morphemes share elements that are equivalent to each other—where the semantic value of one morpheme is reinforced by another near-synonymous morpheme. It is precisely such semantic similarity which provides the necessary condition for markedness reversal.

A patent example of such a reversal can be found in Frisian, as reported by Tiersma (1982), and examplified in figure 2.13.

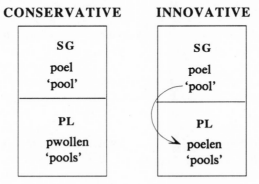

Figure 2.13. Paradigm showing Frisian SINGULAR influencing the PLURAL.

Briefly, a historically conservative form exists where the plural is marked by both a change in syllabic diphthong and a suffix, *-en*: *hoer/hworren* 'whore/whores,' *poel/pwollen* 'pool/pools.' The innovative forms, however, are, except for the cases listed below, based on the singular: *hoer/hoeren* 'whore/whores,' *poel/poelen* 'pool/pools' (834). Notice that, as shown in Figure 2.13, the unmarked singular influenced the more-marked plural, as expected.

On the other hand, there are instances where the plural influences the singular. For example, historically conservative pairs such as *earm/jerman* 'arm/arms,' *goes/gwozzen* 'goose/geese,' *kies/kjizzen* 'tooth/teeth,' *trien/trjinnen* 'tear/tears' have given way to these comparable innovative forms: *jerm/jerman* 'arm/arms,' *gwos/gwozzen* 'goose/geese,' *kjizze/kjizzen* 'tooth/teeth,' *trjin/trjinnen* 'tear/tears.' Notice that in Figure 2.14 the plural influences the singular, and not vice versa.

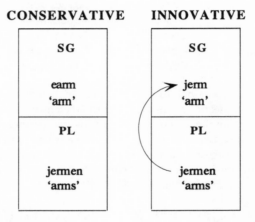

CONSERVATIVE   INNOVATIVE

Figure 2.14. Paradigm showing Frisian PLURAL influencing the SINGULAR via markedness reversal.

The reason for this and all other markedness reversals in Frisian plurality results from the fact that the Interpretant PLURAL is twice present in all the markedness reversal morphemes, once as part of the lexical meaning of the word itself, and again in the grammatical markers. With *jermen*, for example, the lexical Interpretant instructs the interpreter to look for more than one arm (since single arms normally do not occur in nature), while the grammatical morphology, in this case both the vowel change and *-en*, similarly instructs the interpreter to see more than one arm. This amplification of plurality is an instance of augmentation, as discussed above. It is important to reemphasize, in contrast with the previous example (*poelen* 'pools,' where lexical plurality is not present), the Interpretant of *jerm* 'arm' positively instructs the hearer to look for more than one arm. In other words, certain lexical items in

Frisian whose meaning is 'arm,' 'goose,' 'tooth,' 'tear,' and the like are inherently plural, and these most naturally co-occur with the markers for plurality. It is precisely with such nouns, and only such nouns, that markedness reversal took place in Frisian.

A good example of marked overtaking unmarked can be found in English, where formerly the word for *chicken* was *chick,* and the word for *chickens* was *chicken.* The change involved a synonymy in augmentation, where a new plural, *-s,* augmented the old plural, *-en,* yielding *-ens,* with the original plural taking over the singular, and the new plural occupying the originally most marked category, as illustrated in Figure 2.15.

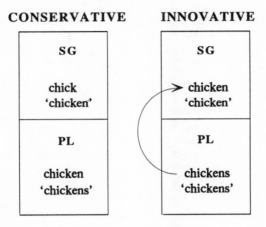

CONSERVATIVE   INNOVATIVE

Figure 2.15. Paradigm showing English PLURAL influencing the SINGULAR via markedness reversal.

Similarly, in Japanese, the old word for 'child' was *ko,* and for 'children,' *ko-domo;* today, 'child' is *kodomo,* and 'children' is *kodomo-tati,* as seen in Figure 2.16.

In these instances, where one plural augments another, markedness reversal occurs, and the original plurals become singulars. The impetus for such a reversal, for such "backward" replacement, is due to augmentation, where a sign with an Interpretant of a given class is added to another sign of that same class.

A Mayan example of such augmentation by synonym resulting in markedness reversal can be seen in the Tzeltalan and bordering Cholan language families. Figure 2.17 illustrates what happened to the Chol absolutive first-person pronouns from Common Mayan times.[1]

---

[1]The reason for the emergence of the INCLUSIVE/EXCLUSIVE *we* in Mayan is

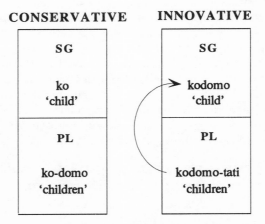

Figure 2.16. Paradigm showing Japanese PLURAL influencing the SINGULAR via markedness reversal.

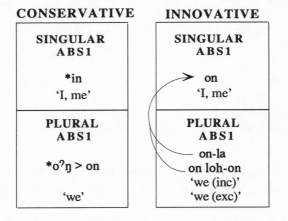

Figure 2.17. Paradigm showing Chol ABS1PL influencing the ABS1SG via markedness reversal.

What happened with Chol is another example of markedness reversal, where the old plural **on* was augmented by another plural (*la* and *lohon*), and as a consequence, the old marked plural became a singular, unmarked form with respect to the new plural.

A more complete way of looking at markedness reversal can be seen in

---

discussed in Robertson (1983).

Figure 2.18, where the notion of *paired opposites* plays an important role. Paired opposites are those members of a 2^m system whose Interpretants are complements of each other. Thus, in the Frisian system of plurality the paired opposites are indicated as follows, where the words for 'pool/pools' stand for the general class of morphemes not subject to markedness reversal, and the words for 'arm/arms' stand for those that are.

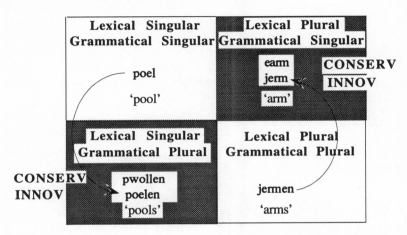

Figure 2.18. Paradigm illustrating forward and reversed influence for Frisian plural.

The paired opposites are (a) the unmarked pair—categories that have two singulars and two plurals (the ungreyed categories in Figure 2.18)—and (b) the marked pair—the mixed categories (the greyed categories in Figure 2.18).[1]

Other examples are readily found. In a most insightful article, "Genitive and Plural of Russian Nouns," Roman Jakobson (1971c:151) points out that both the NOMINATIVE SINGULAR and its complement, the GENITIVE PLURAL are typically marked with either a null (Ø) or a desinence, while the NOMINATIVE PLURAL and its complement, the GENITIVE SINGULAR, "coincide with each other and may be differentiated, if at all, merely by the place of stress."

It is important to note that this is a 2^2 system whose Interpretants all share the presence or absence of a common value: QUANTIFICATION. That is to say,

---

[1]It is important to note that the notion of markedness reversal with paired opposites is central to phonological analysis as well. In the following example, the phonological Interpretants, GRAVE/ACUTE and FLAT/NONFLAT, belong to the same class: TONALITY. In other words, the interpreting mind is attending to pitch in distinguishing these diffuse, vocalic speech sounds.

the NOMINATIVE is unmarked for QUANTIFICATION, whereas its oppositional counterpart, the GENITIVE, is marked; the SINGULAR is unmarked for QUANTIFICATION whereas the PLURAL is marked. Here, QUANTIFICATION is taken to mean 'partitive,' where part of a whole is indicated. On interpreting the GENITIVE, as in, for example, *a piece of cloth,* one looks for a piece, a portion, a segment from the greater whole. Furthermore, plurality has the same notion of segmentability, but in the context of countability, where each countable item is a subset or part of the same class. Note that the GENITIVE tends toward noncountability, with plurality tending toward countability, but both share QUANTIFICATION. For convenience in reference, the GENITIVE and the PLURAL will be said to be different "degrees of the same kind"; In this case, both belong to the supercategory of QUANTIFICATION. The paradigmatic structure which is postulated for Russian is illustrated in Figure 2.19.

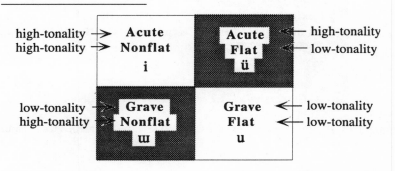

Note that in this classificatory system, there are four categories which divide into opposite pairs, one paired opposite consisting of "pure tonality" (high/high or low/low) and the other of "mixed tonality" (high/low or low/high). Thus, the ACUTE, NONFLAT category (both high-tonality) and the GRAVE, FLAT categories (both low-tonality) are complements. Because their Interpretants belong to the same class, they are paired opposites. Similarly, the ACUTE, FLAT category (high vs. low tonality) and the GRAVE, NONFLAT categories (low vs. high tonality) are also complements of each other—paired opposites—because their Interpretants belong to different classes.

This 2^2 system with Interpretants belonging to the same class (in this case both GRAVE/ACUTE and FLAT/NONFLAT are of the class *tonality*), like the others shown below, results in a markedness reversal. Such reversal is evidenced by the fact that both *i* and *u* are unmarked and almost universally present in phonological systems of languages of the world—in contrast to the more marked ɯ and *ü*, which occur much less frequently. Thus, *i/u* belong to the unmarked axis, while ɯ/*ü* belong to the marked axis. This example is one of many in phonology that can be explained by the principle of markedness reversal. Although much work remains to be done in the area of phonology, I have found many instances of similar markedness relationships which, without taking into account "degrees of the same kind" (yielding the type of markedness reversal shown above), would remain mysterious and unexplained.

The diachronic aspect of Figure 2.19 is that "the GENPL desinences -*ov* and -*ej* were generalized in the declension of those nouns which have a zero desinence in NOMSG" (Jakobson 1971c:150) and that "the -*a* declension shows a gradual extension of stress alternation in the GENSG and NOMPL" (1971c:152).

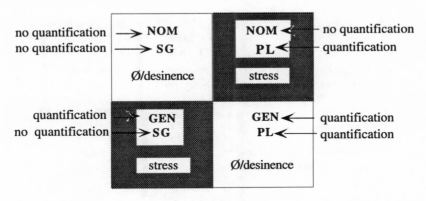

Figure 2.19. Paradigm illustrating paired opposites in part of the Russian case system.

Another instance of markedness reversal, this time from Mayan, can be found in a shift starting with late Colonial Tzeltal and ending with the modern language. The system was 2^2, where the Interpretants were (a) TRANSITIVE vs. INTRANSITIVE verb, and (b) INCOMPLETIVE vs. COMPLETIVE aspect, resulting in classification of four morphemes: (1) COMPLETIVE, INTRANSITIVE, *u*-, (2) INCOMPLETIVE, INTRANSITIVE, *š*-, (3) COMPLETIVE, TRANSITIVE, *la*-, and (4) INCOMPLETIVE, TRANSITIVE, *š*-. Figure 2.20 shows that the paired opposites, the COMPLETIVE, INTRANSITIVE, *u*-, and the INCOMPLETIVE, TRANSITIVE, *š*-, both became unmarked by modern times, losing their formal markers.

While in the Russian example QUANTIFICATION was the shared value, in this example, there is a shared value here called CONTINUITY. CONTINUITY is found both in TRANSITIVE verbs and in the INCOMPLETIVE aspect. For transitive verbs, one sees an unbrokenness in action carried from the agent, the originator of the verbal action, to the patient, the recipient of that action. There is a difference, for example, between saying *I saw John* and *I looked at John, I ate the pie* and *I ate at the pie*. There is a directness, an immediacy, between subject and object with transitive sentences which is not necessarily there with intransitives with their objects of prepositions. Similarly, for the INCOMPLETIVE, there is a parallel notion of continuity in the sense that the verbal action is ongoing, as against, say, the COMPLETIVE, where that action is broken off and a part of time-gone-by, or as against the FUTURE or OPTATIVE, where the action has never yet been a part of experiential reality—nor can it be, since the instant it is, it will be COMPLETIVE. Thus the reason for the change in the paired opposites is due to the fact that both marked Interpretants, TRANSITIVE and INCOMPLETIVE, share the common value CONTINUITY; they are two different degrees of the same kind.

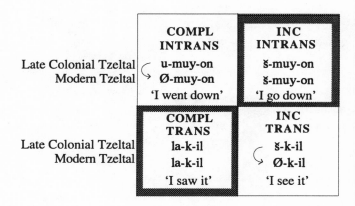

Figure 2.20. Paradigm illustrating language change based on paired opposites in part of the Tzeltalan verbal system.

The structural logic of so-called markedness reversal resides in the notion of "degrees of the same kind." A transparent example of this can readily be seen in those types of adjectives that are antonyms, such as *good/bad, hot/cold, light/dark*. Thus, it is true that *not good* roughly means *bad,* and conversely that *not bad* quite closely corresponds to *good.* In this case, the negation of an opposite is accomplished either lexically, by its antonymal counterpart, or syntactically, by prefixing *not.* Figure 2.21 shows the structure of such a system of paired opposites to be similar to what has heretofore been observed.

This example typifies all instances of the kind of structure referenced in this section: where degrees of the same kind occur—in this case two kinds of negation, one lexical and the other syntactic—then the complementary pairs of the logical system will come to resemble each other. The pairs will resemble each other either semantically, as in the antonymal example above, or conformatively, as in the Russian, Tzeltalan, and Frisian examples shown earlier. All instances of markedness reversal that I have seen up to this point share the common phenomenon of degrees of the same kind.

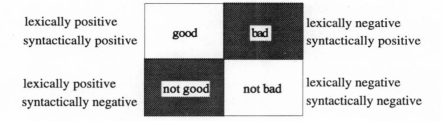

| lexically positive
syntactically positive | good | bad | lexically negative
syntactically positive |
| lexically positive
syntactically negative | not good | not bad | lexically negative
syntactically negative |

Figure 2.21. Paradigm illustrating the structural logic of paired opposites.

The Hierarchical Status of Syntagmatic Combination and Paradigmatic Cumulation

It was earlier observed that the relationships among elements of unmarked categories could be defined as constructive relationships (e.g., *go, went*), whereas such relationships tend to be conformative in the more-marked categories of hierarchically defined systems (e.g., *gyrate, gyrated*). With the above discussion of markedness reversal, it is now possible to explain *why* such a paradigmatic distribution should exist universally among the languages of the world, and furthermore, what effect such relationships have on language change.

The explanation rests on two factors: syntagmatic vs. paradigmatic combinations on the one hand, and simplicity vs. complexity of the Interpretant on the other. The asymmetry of the above relationships comes into focus in consideration of relative interpretative difficulty. That is, relationships based on syntagmatic combination are more readily accessible for interpretation than relationships based on paradigmatic cumulation. Thus, for example, by inspection, the relationship between *eleven* and *eleven-th* is self-evident, whereas there is no such superficial self-evidence in *one* and *first*.

More generally, it is the transparent, syntagmatic combination that is more immediately accessible than the opaque, paradigmatic cumulation. For example, owing to the general knowledge of the linguistic code, *male witch* is more generally accessible for interpretation than *warlock* because more people have both *male* and *witch* in their lexical store than *warlock*. In going from the known to the unknown, it is always a patent syntagmatic sequence (known to the interpreter) that stands for the opaque word (unknown to the interpreter): *Hookybob* means 'to be pulled on one's feet on a snowy road holding on to an unsuspecting driver's rear bumper.' In any definition it is an assumption on the part of the speaker, universal to all languages that both speaker and hearer hold the defining words of the predicate in common, whereas the subject of the definition is known only to the originator of the message. This is the premise of all dictionary making. The defined word is the repository of much information, whereas the defining words are the syntagmatic sequencing of more generally known words containing approximately equivalent information. Thus, syntagmatic constructions, because they are more generally interpretable, are less marked than their lesser-known paradigmatic counterparts.

But even for the type of interpretation that is inherent in originating a message, it is true that the syntagmatic is more accessible than the paradigmatic. For example, it is a fact of the encoding process that when one cannot come up with the right word, one can—even must—resort to the iconism of syntax: *Get the uhm...the funny looking thing over there on the table.* Encoding then becomes an interpretive act of equivalency, where the equivalent is syntagmatic and not the difficult, lost paradigmatic cumulation.

With this discussion of the variables it is now convenient to diagram their relationships, in Figure 2.22, where the classificatory degrees of the same kind have to do with simplicity and complexity, and the preferred axis is the mixed portion of the system.

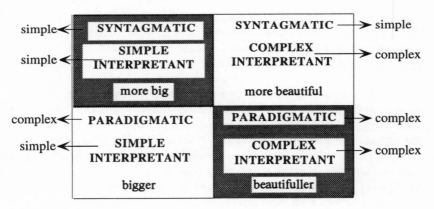

Figure 2.22. Paradigm illustrating the structural logic of paired opposites in the context of syntagmatic combination and paradigmatic cumulation.

Those categories that have both simplicity and complexity are the categories to which language systems gravitate. Two degrees of simplicity or two degrees of complexity are systematically avoided by language. Thus, the simple *big* has a paradigmatically cumulative comparative as against the more complex *beautiful,* whose comparative is syntagmatic. Also, the Latin ACTIVE has a paradigmatic cumulation (e.g., *legit* 'he reads') as compared with the semantically more complex PASSIVE (e.g., *lēctus est* 'it is read'). That is, it is *not* the norm for simple relationships of syntagmatic combination and simple meaning to co-occur, any more than it is normal for a relationship of both paradigmatic cumulation and complex meaning to exist simultaneously. This system of paired opposites sheds light on the reason for the earlier observation that there should be constructive relationships in the unmarked categories of a 2^m system (a tendency toward paradigmatic cumulation) and conformative relationships among the more-marked categories (a tendency for syntagmatic combination).

In the context of the above observations, the implications for language change are profound. In those abnormal instances where there are syntagmatic combinations with simple Interpretants, they tend to become paradigmatic, and in those instances where there are complex, paradigmatic cumulations, they become syntagmatic.

A good example of how the latter—PARADIGMATIC with COMPLEX INTERPRETANT—becomes SYNTAGMATIC is seen in the Common Mayan ERG3PL **ki-* which becomes SYNTAGMATIC in Q'eqchi' *š...eb²*, where the new, conformative form partakes of ERG3SG, *š-*, and ABS3PL, *-eb²*, as illustrated earlier (in Figure 2.9). In fact, the general notion of INFLUENCE as discussed above is often, though not always, an instance of syntagmatic combination's taking the place of paradigmatic cumulation.

On the other hand, examples abound, both lexical and grammatical, of the opposite, where SYNTAGMATIC with SIMPLE INTERPRETANT becomes PARADIGMATIC. For example, the English lexicon is a virtual graveyard of syntagmatic sequences that have become paradigmatic: *not* < **na* + **wiht* 'no' + 'man, thing'; *world* < **wer + aldh* 'man' + 'age', *warlock* < *wær + loga* 'oath' + 'liar.'[1] It is also common to see syntagmatic complexes collapsing into paradigmatically simple structures. Perhaps one of the most dramatic examples from Mayan happened in Huastec, where the Common Mayan PROGRESSIVE, which is the syntagmatic combination

$$*\text{PROG} + \text{ABS PREP} (*t^y\tilde{\imath}) \text{ERG} - \text{VT} + \text{PASSIVE} + \text{NOMINALIZER} (*-V_L)$$

came to be reinterpreted as a paradigmatic cumulation of the INCOMPLETIVE as

$$t - \text{ABS} - \text{ERG} - \text{VT} - \text{el}$$

as shown in detail on page 212.

Another manifestation of this same phenomenon can be seen in Witkowski and Brown's (1983) observation that at the time of the conquest, the Tzeltal word for 'deer' was *čih,* and that the introduction by the Spanish of sheep

---

[1] These examples were taken from the *American Heritage Dictionary of the English Language* (1975).

elicited the syntagmatic name *tunim čih* 'cotton deer.' When tame sheep became culturally central and wild deer peripheral, the syntagmatic combination vs. paradigmatic cumulation switched: sheep came to be called simply *čih*, and deer came to be called *te?ikil čih* 'wild sheep.' Using the terms of this discussion, when a form that is SYNTAGMATIC with a COMPLEX INTERPRETANT (*tunim čih* 'sheep' in Colonial times) comes to have a simpler Interpretant (*čih* 'sheep' in modern times), then it moves to a paradigmatic status. When a form that is PARADIGMATIC with a SIMPLE INTERPRETANT (*čih* 'deer' in Colonial times) comes to have a more complex Interpretant (*te?ikil čih* 'deer' in modern times), then it moves to a syntagmatic status.

Sapir (1949:95) observed this phenomenon long ago when he suggested that it often happens that language erects

> a bold bridge between the two basically distinct types of concept, the concrete [syntagmatic constructions] and the abstractly relational [paradigmatic accumulations], infecting the latter, as it were, with the color and grossness of the former. By a certain violence of metaphor the material concept is forced to do duty for (or intertwine itself with) the strictly relational.

Introductive Change

The examples of systematic change observed up to this point have been instances in which constructive signs become conformative signs, which is in keeping with the observation made on page 15 that in grammatical systems the more-marked categories of the paradigm tend to be conformative. The corollary to that observation—that the less-marked categories tend to be relatively more constructive—also has its diachronic consequences. First, it is almost always true that when something new is added to the system, it will be added first to the unmarked category of that system. It is for this reason that THIRD PERSON, which is unmarked compared with first or SECOND PERSON, is in constant flux, relative to its more-marked counterparts. For example, the unmarked Mayan numeral for 'twenty,' which was historically **k?al*, has been replaced by *winaq* 'man'; however, the more-marked 'sixty' **oš-k?al*, literally 'three twenty,' remained intact:[1]

pre-Kaqchikel		Colonial Kaqchikel		
*xun-k?al	lit. 'one tie'	*hu-vinak*	lit. 'one man'	'twenty'
*oš-k?al	lit. 'three ties'	*ox-ɉal*	lit. 'three ties'	'sixty'

---

[1]For a thorough discussion of this phenomenon in light of the reconstruction of the Common Mayan system of counting, see Robertson 1986.

In other words, with respect to the relationships existing among the members of a logical linguistic system, the constructive relationship is emphasized and the conformative deemphasized, because newly introduced elements in the system tend to occur in the unmarked categories.

A good illustration of introductive change is found in Kaqchikel, which was changing at the time of the Conquest and duly recorded by the Colonial grammarians. It nicely illustrates an instance of a new sign being introduced into the least-marked category of a 2^m system.

The Kaqchikel ABS1SG and ABS2SG pronouns changed from Common Mayan *in* and *at* to *i-* and *a-* before consonant-initial intransitive verbs and before the ERG3SG, but remained *in* and *at* before all other ERGATIVE pronouns, and before vowel-initial intransitive verbs. On the face of it, such a shift seems arbitrary and capricious, but careful formulation of the 2^m system into which these linguistic facts categorize themselves reveals a well-defined logic governing this change.

First, the reason for the change from *in* and *at* to *i-* and *a-* is clear-cut. Closed syllables tend to become open syllables in languages of the world; that is, CVCCV... > CVCV.... Thus, *š-in-war* > *š-i-war* COMPL-ABS1SG-sleep 'I slept,' and *š-at-war* > *š-a-war* COMPL-ABS2SG-sleep 'you slept,' but *š-in-oˑqʔ* COMPL-ABS1SG-cried 'I cried,' and *š-at-oˑqʔ* COMPL-ABS2SG-cried 'you cried.' Intransitive verbs changed in a straightforward, phonological way: C → Ø/__C.

š-i-war	COMP-ABS1SG-sleep	'I slept'
š-in-oˑqʔ	COMP-ABS1SG-cry	'I cried'
š-a-war	COMP-ABS2SG-sleep	'you slept'
š-at-oˑqʔ	COMP-ABS2SG-cry	'you cried'

No amount of phonological reasoning, however, can explain the shift from *in* to *i-* and *at* to *a-* before ERG3SG *ru-*, but not before any of the other consonant-initial pronouns, ERG3PL *ki-* or ERG1PL *qa-*. The explanation of the change in question is clearly *not* strictly phonological.

š	-i	-ru-čʔey	COMP-ABS1SG-ERG3SG-hit	'he hit me'
š	-a	-ru-čʔey	COMP-ABS2SG-ERG3SG-hit	'he hit you'
š	-in	-ki-čʔey	COMP-ABS1SG-ERG3PL-hit	'they hit me'
š	-at	-ki-čʔey	COMP-ABS2SG-ERG3PL-hit	'they hit you'
š	-at	-qa-čʔey	COMP-ABS2SG-ERG1PL-hit	'we hit you'

The explanation, rather, goes beyond phonology to include grammatical meaning.[1] Careful analysis reveals a 2^3 paradigm, whose three constitutive

---

[1] The form *-čʔey-* 'to hit' originally had a short *a,* which is preserved in some

elements are made up of both phonological *and* semantic attributes: consonant-vs. vowel-initial verbs, singular vs. plural, and PERSON (FIRST or SECOND) vs. NONPERSON (THIRD PERSON). The markedness relationships in each of these oppositional pairs emerge through careful consideration.

First, without exception, all Mayan languages have a significant grammatical distinction between consonant- and vowel-initial verbs and substantives, as evidenced by the fact that every Mayan language has two sets of ergative pronouns, the unmarked set occurring before consonant-initials, and the marked set occurring before vowel-initials. Given this important opposition in Kaqchikel, consonant-initial roots (along with their prefixed set of ergative pronouns) are the unmarked member of the set, as evidenced by their commonness of occurrence, as well as their adherence to the universal syllable type CV... (as against V...).

Second, given NUMBER as a grammatical category, SINGULAR is unmarked over PLURAL, as suggested by the range of reference of the two sets. For example, the Kaqchikel singular *išoq* 'woman' has a broader range of reference since it can refer to one or more women, whereas *išoq-iʔ* must refer only to more than one woman.

Finally, PERSON, which is the marked member of the set, includes both the initiator of speech (FIRST PERSON) and the interpreter of that speech (SECOND PERSON), whereas NONPERSON is unmarked, making no comment concerning deixis of PERSON. Thus, NONPERSON could be interpreted as third person, or anything else *not* marked for PERSON. It is important to note that the unmarked member of the set is simply that: NON-VOWEL-INITIAL is normally interpreted as consonant-initial; NONPLURAL as SINGULAR; and NONPERSON as THIRD PERSON.

Figure 2.23 unambiguously and exhaustively classifies those morphemes that follow the ABSOLUTIVE pronouns *in* and *at,* including intransitive verbs (in their function as subjects) and the ERGATIVE pronouns (in their function as direct objects).Thus, for example, the seemingly disparate morphemes *war* 'to sleep' and *ru-* ERG3SG meet the three qualifications which classify them as unmarked members of this particular 2^m system: (a) both are NONPERSON since neither refers to the initiator (FIRST PERSON) or interpreter (SECOND PERSON) of speech, (b) neither is VOWEL-INITIAL, and (c) neither signals plurality. In other words, by default, both *war* and *ru-* are unmarked. And it is precisely in this unmarked area of the paradigm that the change from **in* to *i-* and **at* to *a-* took place. This exemplifies what was said earlier, that *when new changes enter the system, there is a strong tendency for those changes to occur in the least-marked area of the paradigmatic system.*

---

dialects. In Tecpan, however, the form has been raised to *e.* Also, the form *š-at-nu-čʔey* alternated with *š-at-in-čʔey* 'I hit you' in Colonial times, as seen in the grammar of Guzmán's *Compendio* (1704:198), where he has " *catnucamahih* [k -at-nu-kamaxix]...I serve you."

This classificatory explanation is further strengthened by the fact that in a grammar of Kaqchikel by Torresano (1692), the loss of the *n* was extended from the unmarked NONPLURAL, NONPERSON, NON-VOWEL-INITIAL to PLURAL, NONPERSON, NON-VOWEL-INITIAL:

> Nota que la *n* del acusativo de la primera persona de singular se pierde i quita quando la persona es de la tercera persona singular—o plural como *quirucoɛ-oh Padre* el padre me ama *quiquiloɛoh utzilah vinak* los buenos me aman.

> Note that the n of the accusative of first person singular is lost (or left off) when the person is third singular—or plural, as *k-i-ru-koq²-ox Padre* [INC-ABS1SG-ERG3SG-love-DAPD father] 'the Father loves me' *k-i-ki-loq²-ox uɕilax winaq* [INC-ABS1SG-ERG3PL-love-DAPD good man] 'the good men love me.'[1]

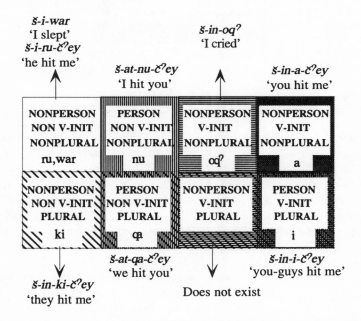

Figure 2.23. Paradigm illustrating the categorization of the linguistic elements following the ABSOLUTIVE (object) pronouns in Colonial Kaqchikel.

---

[1]Although to my knowledge this dialect has not been attested in modern times, there is no reason to doubt that it accurately represents grammatical fact.

Figure 2.24 shows that the elision of the *n* is undergoing a logical spread from the unmarked to the more-marked portions of the system.

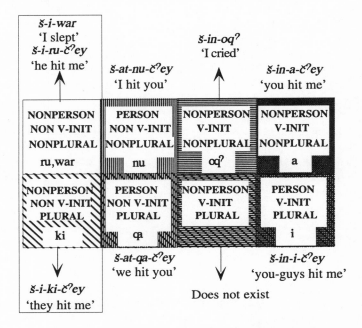

Figure 2.24. Paradigm illustrating the categorization of the linguistic elements following the ABSOLUTIVE in a dialect of Colonial Kaqchikel.

Therefore, the correct definition of the 2^3 system allows systematic explanation of what would otherwise be a mere observation, for "what an explanation of a phenomenon does is to supply a proposition which, if it had been known to be true before the phenomenon presented itself, would have rendered that phenomenon predictable, if not with certainty, at least as something very likely to occur" (Peirce 7.192). In this instance, the proposition is this: that the change in the ABSOLUTIVE pronouns takes place in the least-marked category of the 2^3 system, where the three elements are (1) universal syllable type (CV...), (2) PERSON, and (3) NUMBER. Such a proposition is at the heart of explanation, without which one could only observe that the change took place before consonant-initial verbs and before the ERG3SG pronoun.[1]

---

[1]It is also worth noting that such explanation would be impossible if one really went on the premise that phonological considerations should be separate from semantic considerations, for here the phonological consideration of universal syllable type is no more or less important than the semantic considerations of

Displacement

With respect to introductive change, we have observed that when a new sign is introduced into a grammatical system, that introduction tends to occur in the least-marked category. One of the consequences of introductive change is that the new sign will occupy the least-marked category and the Immediate Interpretant of the old sign will take on more information, creating a new, more-marked category.[1] This phenomenon is here called *displacement*.

Put differently, displacement is a kind of change where the introduction of a new sign into a given category will result in a division of that category into a marked and an unmarked category, with the new sign occupying the least-marked, and the old sign occupying the more-marked category.

A good example of this phenomenon can be seen in the shift from the pre-Romance to the modern Romance languages in the PERFECTUM. The Spanish PRETERITE, for example, is the reflex of the Latin PERFECTUM, whose Dynamical Interpretants included what is today both the PRESENT PERFECT and the PRETERITE, as evidenced by the fact that a translation of Spanish back into Latin would see, in the main, both the Spanish PRETERITE and the PRESENT PERFECT as the Latin PERFECTUM. What happened from Latin to Spanish is that a new form based on *haber* + PARTICIPLE was introduced into the category PERFECTUM, which had the effect of bifurcating the category, with the new form *haber* + PARTICIPLE occupying the unmarked category and the old reflex of the PERFECTUM occupying the PRETERITE. Thus, the old Latin category PERFECTUM was subdivided into two categories, where the new form became the unmarked category, and the old form took on the specialized meaning of marking completed action in time-gone-by.

Although the examples of language given up to this point have been in terms of paradigmatic 2^m systems, displacement—perhaps more than the other principles of change—finds broad application in the lexicon. To illustrate, several lexical examples follow.

The Common Mayan word for 'kill' is **kam-isa*[2] as evidenced by the reflexes of this form in such diverse languages as Yukatek Maya (*kim-s*) and Kaqchikel (*kam-isa*). In Mam a new sign, *kub⁷-b⁷iy* [lit. 'down-hit'], was introduced into the category of *ka·m-sa·*, the reflex of **kam-isa·*, 'kill'. This divided the category in two. The new sign occupied the least-marked category.

---

person and number.

[1]This is a recasting of Kurylowicz's (1966:169) so-called Fourth Law of Analogy, which he formulated as follows: "When as a result of a morphological transformation a form undergoes differentiation, the new form corresponds to its primary function (*forme de fondation*), and the old form is restricted to its secondary function (*forme fondée*)."

[2]The *-isa* suffix is a causative attached to the root *-kam* 'die.'

The original sign occupied the more-marked category, which came to mean, roughly, 'the experience of letting an incurably sick kinsman die through neglect.' Graphically, such change is represented in Figure 2.25.

A similar semantic change occurred independently in Tzotzil, except that specialization was slightly different. In Figure 2.26 the original word, *čam-es,* was replaced by a new word, *mil.* Then, *čam-es* took the specialized meaning 'murder, kill people'[1].

Figures 2.25 and 2.26 are instances of simple changes that result in binary oppositions.

Stage I	Stage II
sign: ka·m-sa· 'kill, let die, …' *original category*	sign: kub^ʔ b^ʔiy 'kill, …' *original category*
	sign: ka·m-sa· 'let die' *new category*

Figure 2.25. Paradigm illustrating displacement in Mam.

Tzotzil

Stage I	Stage II
sign: čam-es 'kill, murder, …' *original category*	sign: mil 'kill, …' *original category*
	sign: čam-es 'murder' *new category*

Figure 2.26. Paradigm illustrating displacement in Tzotzil.

There are other examples of more complex changes, resulting in chain displacements: Figure 2.27 compares the lexicon of Ixchiguan Mam with the lexicon that is generally found in Mam.[2] In the common vocabulary, these words occur:

> *nim* 'big, a lot'
> *ti·x* 'old'

In Ixchiguan a series of three words occurs:

---

[1]It still means 'to kill' in ritual speech. For details see Laughlin (1975).

[2]For a similar occurrence in Latin, see Anttila (1972:147).

nim 'too big, too much'
ti·x 'big, a lot'
ma·ʔ ti·x 'old'

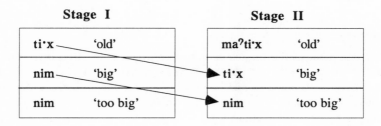

Stage I		Stage II	
ti·x	'old'	maʔti·x	'old'
nim	'big'	ti·x	'big'
nim	'too big'	nim	'too big'

Figure 2.27. Paradigm illustrating chain displacement in Mam.

Thus, for example, in other dialects of Mam the word for river is *nim ʔaʔ* 'big water', whereas in Ixchiguan it is *ti·x ʔaʔ.* On the other hand, *nim ʔaʔ* in Ixchiguan means 'too much water, surfeit of water.' In standard Mam the phrase *ti·x ṣi·naq* means 'old man,' while in Ixchiguan *ma·ʔ ti·x i·chin* means the same.[1]

There is an abundance of this kind of chain shift in the TAMV system of the several Mayan languages. One illustrative instance is represented in Figure 2.28.

	Pre-Choltí	Choltí	Gloss
PROGRESSIVE	*wal u-wan-el	??	'I am sleeping'
INCOMPLETIVE	*š-wan-on	wal u-wan-el	'I sleep'
FUTURE	*la-wan-on	š-wan-ik-on	'I will sleep'
NEG FUTURE	*ma la-wan-on	el-wan-on	'I will not sleep'

Figure 2.28. Paradigm illustrating chain displacement in Choltí.

In Common Mayan the form for the FUTURE was *la-,* while the form for the INCOMPLETIVE was *k(i)-* (which in Cholan became *č-* and ultimately š-); the form for the progressive was a syntactic construction something like 'continue ERG-sleep.' In this example, the progressive displaced the INCOMPLETIVE to the

---

[1]A similar change is observed in the English *flesh, meat, food,* where *flesh* originally meant 'meat,' and *meat* originally meant 'food.'

FUTURE, which caused displacement of the original FUTURE to a specialized meaning, NEGATIVE FUTURE. This phenomenon is represented in Figure 2.28[1] (See also p. 171).

Chain displacement is illustrated over and over again in the investigation below of the TAMV in the Mayan languages.

Summary

This treatment of the linguistic sign—with its organization into systems of signs—allows for the postulation of the deductive principles necessary for the kinds of explanations which render intelligible the shift from Common Mayan to its several daughter languages. The discussion of how the particular languages changed constitutes Chapters 4–10. Up to this point, only the deductive principles have been presented; nothing has been said about the hypothesis—the reconstruction—from which ideal results are predicted. The next chapter's purpose is to lay out the reconstruction of Common Mayan TAMV.

The deductive expectations based on hypothesis, however, are not—nor can they ever be—equivalent to absolute, mechanical prediction, any more than weather forecasting can be a mechanical, perfunctory certainty. A more modest goal is to render linguistic change comprehensible and explainable, if not mechanically predictable. It is reasonable to suppose, for example, that (a) with a given 2^m system, linguistic change is more apt to be initiated in the unmarked portion of that paradigm, *if* the change is to take place; (b) with an opposition constituted of two signs, the less-marked sign influences the more-marked sign, *if* any influence is to take place; (c) with Interpretants of a 2^m system belonging to the same class, markedness reversal is a likely outcome of change, *if* there is to be a change; and (d) with the displacement of one sign by another, the new sign will take over the Interpretant of the older, leaving the older sign with a more restricted Interpretant which denotes a more specific Object, *if* a change is to take place at all. What is *not* predictable, however, is whether the process of change will take place at all; more certain is the direction that the change will take, if it does occur.

Kurylowicz (1966:174) once said that knowledge of the drainage system of a courtyard can assure reasonable inference of the direction the water will flow in the event of rain; it's just the foreknowledge of the rain's appearance that is incalculable. Knowledge of the structural organization of a grammatical system is equivalent to knowledge of the courtyard's drainage system—the

---

[1]For purposes of comparison, I made up the form for the Choltí NEGATIVE FUTURE given the fact that there are no intransitives attested in the Morán grammar. There are many transitive examples, however. Also, I have no record of the PROGRESSIVE of Stage II.

"lay of the land" which determines the direction the change will take—but it would be naive to presume to know beforehand whether a change is going to occur, much less the exact form the change will take.

Chapter 3. The System of TAMV in the Common Language

This chapter, because it is the chapter of hypothesis, has a smaller and a greater purpose. The smaller purpose is partitive and involves the reconstruction of the TAMV of the common language, but the greater purpose is holistic. The hypothesis itself (the reconstruction) is given to make possible the deductive predictions and the inductive comparisons necessary to render the changes from the common language to the modern languages understandable.

The lesser purpose referred to above (the reconstruction of the TAMV of the common language) is in fact a highly exacting task, for two reasons. First, it requires a thorough understanding and general exposition of the grammatical systems common to the several Mayan languages. Second, in order to understand that system, it requires a careful definition of terms and concepts, often both in their Mayan-particular as well as in their general language sense. These include, among others, *proposition, argument, transitivity, ergative vs. absolute, split-ergative, inherent (transitive, intransitive verbs) vs. reductive voice (passive, antipassive), relative vs. nominative voice, object incorporation, substantival transitivity,* and *voice, mood,* and *aspect/tense.*

The system which is common to all the modern languages, as reconstructed here, is a 2^3 system, where there are three Interpretants: (1) VOICE VS. MOOD, (2) SYNTAGMATIC VS. PARADIGMATIC, and (3) PARTICULAR VS. GENERAL. The system can be represented by the diagram of Figure 3.1. The explanation of that system will proceed first with the explanation of the COMPLETIVE, IN-COMPLETIVE, OPTATIVE, and FUTURE, which form the PARADIGMATIC portion of the cube (Figure 3.2), after which an explanation of the syntagmatic system (Figure 3.3) will follow. Before either of these can be discussed, however, it is necessary to define and discuss the terms mentioned above.

Predicates and Arguments

At the very root of all Mayan grammar is the proposition, from whence grows all the rest: the pronominal system, the vast system of TAMV, the system of transitivity, and more generally the verbal complex, whose branches reach out to touch all aspects of the grammar. The proposition is constituted of two unequal, but intimately intertwined parts: the predicate, which mediates the argument(s), and the argument(s), which relies on the predicate to show its mode of being. When the predicate with its arguments are brought into unity, that unity is a proposition.

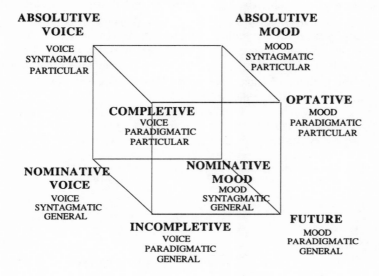

Figure 3.1. TAMV structure common to all modern Mayan languages.

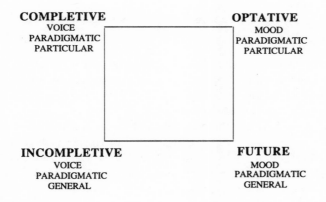

Figure 3.2. Paradigmatic portion of the TAMV structure common to all modern Mayan languages.

A predicate is a general category whose chief office is to characterize the being or action of any argument it might call up. An argument of a predicate, by contrast, is a particular category through which the general class of behavior or being of the predicate is manifested (instantiated) in the world of experience. For example, *bark* is the predicate and *the dog* is the argument of the proposition *the dog barked.* By itself, *bark* (which is general) can never be attested; by itself it must remain forever unheard. To be heard—to have existence—it, like any predicate in any system of signs, must instantiate itself through an argument, a particular entity. In the case of the above example, the particular instantiating symbol is *the dog*—in this case, the argument called up by the predicate.[1]

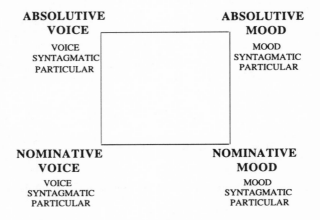

Figure 3.3. Syntagmatic portion of the TAMV structure common to all Mayan languages.

By their very nature, therefore, predicates are generals and arguments are particulars. Even when the argument is generalized, such as, *dogs,* in *dogs bark,* the barking can only exist through an existential instance of a case of the argument (via its referent) that calls up the referent.

The asymmetry between the predicate and its arguments is due to their general and particular nature, as is illustrated in Hopper and Thompson's observation (1984:745–746) that languages "seem to be able to derive predicates productively from either nominal or verbal roots, while generally requiring nominalizing morphology to derive a N [noun] from a verbal root." The reason for this inequality is straightforward, since "a nominalization names an event taken as an entity," whereas a "'verbalization' does not name an entity taken as an event." Thus, if a verb is used as a noun, it must be

---

[1]Of course it is the existential referent of *the dog* that provides the hearable bark.

particularized semantically, usually by an accompanying derivational affix, whereas nouns recruited as verbs lose their particular nature in favor of the necessarily general nature of the verb:

> *The resulting mixture is shaped into balls.* Here the nominalization in fact refers to a concrete entity, but there still must have been an event of mixing. But suppose we say *We squirreled away the money.* The V *squirrel away* reports an event, and has nothing to do with any squirrel. Its relationship with the N *squirrel* is in fact very loose, depending on an assumed property of this class of rodents (Hopper and Thompson (1984:745–746).

It is important to note that with propositions, which bring into unity the predicate and its argument(s), verbs tend to be predicates and nouns tend to be arguments of predicates, although all degrees of gradation between the two do exist. Thus, predicates, which are summarized and generalized being or action, most often correspond to the notion *verb,* and arguments, which are particulars through which predicative behavior or being is specified, generally correspond to the notion *noun*. But even where nouns are used as predicates, they are, of necessity, general, owing to their predicative function. This is compellingly apparent in the seemingly tautologous proposition *boys are boys,* where the interpreter sees a particular set of boys as the referent of the argument *boys,* but sees only the most nonspecific quality of boyness (possibly doing something mischievous, among innumerable other things) in the predicate *are boys.*[1]

Finally, because predicates manifest themselves through their associated entities—their arguments—they virtually call up their arguments. Thus, by itself, the sign *hit* is a general whose Interpretant calls up two arguments, one an active doer of the hitting, and the other the passive receiver of that action. *Sleep,* on the other hand, calls up but a single argument. Nonetheless, in languages of the world, it is important to note that the determination of who is doing the action to whom is not determined by the predicate itself, but by syntax, morphology, and in some cases by the relationship that is experientially most obvious. All the verb does in its general mode of being is to call up arguments.

Voice and Transitivity

This calling up of arguments is related to the ancient notion of VOICE, which here is generally defined as the calling up by the predicate of a

---

[1]An important discussion of this can be found in Peirce 2.315 ff.

specified number of arguments. This definition permits the classification of intransitive verbs as predicates that call up single arguments, and transitive verbs as predicates that call up two arguments. In many languages of the world, there is no nonarbitrary way to draw a firm distinction between transitive and intransitive verbs based on the Interpretants of verbs by themselves. Virtually any verb can be used transitively, as in English, *we sleep six kids in that room,* or *he cried giant crocodile tears.* On the other hand, a transitive verb can have the character of an intransitive with no object present, as in *the lion kills for sport.* Syntax partly takes on the function of indicating transitivity in English, as it does in many of the world's languages, although it is still keenly felt that the transitive use of *sleep* (or the intransitive use of *kill*) is an accident of syntax—that, inherently, *sleep* still calls up a single argument, and *kill,* two arguments.

Languages do exist, however, where the distinction between the transitive and intransitive is unambiguously present in the morphology of the grammar. Mayan is one of these, since *all* Mayan verbs are unconditionally classed either as inherently intransitive (calling up only one argument), or as inherently transitive (calling up two arguments). Transitivity is not an accident of syntax, but an inherent, grammatical fact of the Interpretant associated with the verb. Therefore, the mode of being of every verb in the Mayan languages is either transitive or intransitive, in much the same way that in Romance languages every substantive must exist with inherent gender, masculine or feminine. Transitivity, which has its roots in the notion of *proposition*, is the most pervasive of all grammatical features common to Mayan languages, affecting virtually every aspect of the language, from substantive to aspect and from mood to voice, as shown below.

It is important to note, however, that the two arguments called up by the transitive verb have different functions, one agentive—here called the active argument—and one yielding—here called the passive argument. These notions are put into perspective in the following diagram, where verbs such as *sleep* and *die,* which call up a single argument, are inherently intransitive, and where verbs such as *hit, kill,* and *see,* which call up two arguments (one active, the other passive) are inherently transitive—although, as will be shown below, transitive verbs can be inflectionally reduced to a single argument by means of a rich system of VOICE. Figure 3.4 illustrates VOICE in Mayan.

Arguments of Predicates and Prepositions

For clarity, note what a predicate can and cannot call up. The predicate can call up one argument for intransitives and two for transitives; it cannot call up objects of prepositions. For example, in the proposition *John went to town,* the verb *go* has only one argument, *John,* while the substantive *town* is an argument of the preposition *to,* and not an argument of the predicate *went.* Similarly, the verb *hit* of the proposition *I hit John with a stick* has two arguments, *I* and *John,* while *stick* is an argument of the preposition *with.* Prepositional and other adverbial modifiers are peripheral to the sentence, while the verb and the arguments it calls up constitute the core of the sentence. Such a view of core vs. periphery is crucial to pronominal distribution, as will be seen below.

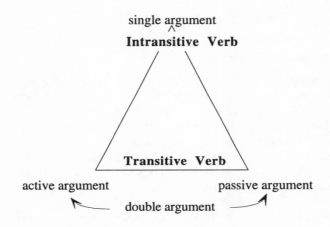

Figure 3.4. Illustration of VOICE in Mayan.

Finally, Common Mayan had two types of transitive verbs, one whose syllable structure was monosyllabic, (C)VC, and the other, polysyllabic. The polysyllabic type tends to be derived, whereas the monosyllabic type is not derived, and is sometimes called "root transitive." The major focus in this work, unless otherwise stated, will be to reconstruct the morphology for the monosyllabic, (C)VC transitives.

Aspectual vs. Nonaspectual Predication

Common Mayan, which like most languages of the world did not have a "to be" verb (though all Mayan languages do have an existential verb), had two kinds of predication, ASPECTUAL and NONASPECTUAL. The difference between these predicational types is simply that verbal predication takes the markers of TENSE/ASPECT/MOOD/VOICE; nonverbal predication does not. Nonverbal predication involves the association of the ABSOLUTIVE pronoun to nouns, adjectives, or participles; ASPECTUAL predication involves TAMV. Here are some examples of nonverbal predication from K'iche':

> winaq le šwan   'John is a person'
> winaq   'he is a person'
> kʸaq   'it is red'

In Common Mayan there was a form, **-inaq,* for participial predications of a single argument, and another, **-Vˑm,* for participial predications of two arguments. K'iche' exemplifies these two forms:

> in-warinaq   'I have slept'
> at-nu-čʔay-oˑm   'I have hit you'

ERGATIVE and ABSOLUTIVE Pronouns

Intimately associated with the Common Mayan system of grammatical transitivity described above was a system of ergativity, involving the affixation of certain ERGATIVE and ABSOLUTIVE pronouns to the verb. The referents of the ERGATIVE included the active argument (subject) of the transitive verb, as well as the possessor substantives, as demonstrated in modern K'iche': *š-u-čʔay-oh* COMPL-ERG3SG-hit-DAPD 'he hit him,' and *u-laˑq,* ERG3SG-clay.bowl 'his clay bowl.' The referents of the ABSOLUTIVE pronouns, on the other hand, are again twofold: the argument of the intransitive verb and the passive argument of the transitive. For example, in K'iche', *š-at-in-čʔay-oh* COMPL-ABS2SG-ERG1SG-hit-DAPD 'I hit you.' The pronominal distribution described above is summarized in Figure 3.5, and the explanation of the verbal suffixes is given on page 62 with an accompanying footnote.

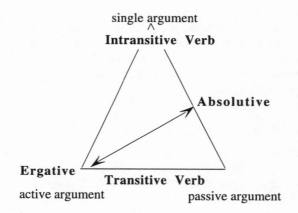

Figure 3.5. Illustration of verbal pronominal distribution in Mayan.

The reconstruction for the Common Mayan ABSOLUTIVE and ERGATIVE pronouns is shown in Figure 3.6.[1] The ERGATIVE (marked) pronouns in Common Mayan were always prefixed. The ABSOLUTIVE (unmarked) pronouns were either prefixed or suffixed: prefixed when aspectual predicate markers were present, and otherwise suffixed.[2]

ABSOLUTIVE		ERGATIVE Before Consonants		ERGATIVE Before Vowels	
3SG:	—	3SG:	*ru-	3SG:	*r-
2SG:	*-at	2SG:	*a-	2SG:	*aw-
1SG:	*-in	1SG:	*nu-	1SG:	*w-
3PL:	*-eb?	3PL:	*ki-	3PL:	*k-
2PL:	*-eš	2PL:	*e-	2PL:	*er-
1PL:	*-o?ŋ	1PL:	*qa-	1PL:	*q-

Figure 3.6. Reconstruction of Common Mayan pronouns.

Split Ergativity

Some time after the breakup of Common Mayan, certain languages (starting with Yukatekan and Cholan, and followed later by other languages influenced by these) changed the above system of pronominal inflection into a so-called split-ergative system. This modification, as implied by the name *split-ergative*, involves *two* systems, where one is directly descendent from the old ERGATIVE/ABSOLUTIVE found in Common Mayan, and the other is innovative. Languages such as Mam, Q'anjob'al, and Huastec changed differently, and each is discussed in its appropriate chapter. Yukatek Maya, perhaps the most striking example of split ergativity, is characterized by the expected ERGATIVE/ABSOLUTIVE as well as by a kind of NOMINATIVE/ACCUSATIVE, as explained below. The office of these two oppositional pronominal systems is aspectual. The original system (with ERGATIVE marking the subject of transitives and ABSOLUTIVE marking both the active argument of transitives and the single argument of intransitives) came to signal 'COMPLETIVE aspect.' The newly

---

[1]For several discussions on the nature of change of the pronominals, see Robertson (1982, 1983, 1984b).

[2]Chuj, and Q'anjob'alan more generally, probably come closest to preserving the Common Mayan pronominal system.

formed NOMINATIVE/ACCUSATIVE system (in which the ERGATIVE marks both the active argument of transitives and the single argument of intransitives, while the ABSOLUTIVE only marks the passive argument of the intransitives) came to mean 'INCOMPLETIVE aspect.' The split-ergative system is shown in Figure 3.7.

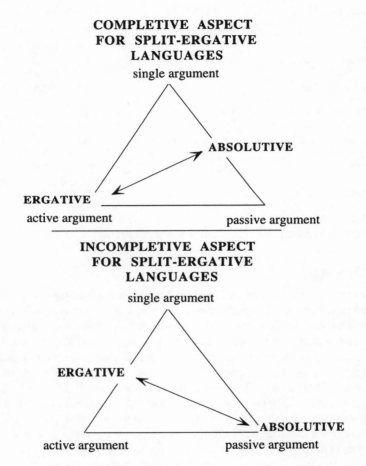

Figure 3.7. Split-ergative system in Mayan.

The INCOMPLETIVE above has the same pronominal distribution as NOMINATIVE/ACCUSATIVE languages such as European languages, since the ERGATIVE, like the NOMINATIVE, marks the subject of the transitives and intransitives, while the ABSOLUTIVE, like the ACCUSATIVE, marks the object of the transitives.

The history of this particular shift from a purely ergative to an innovative split-ergative system is found on page 203. The TAMV of Common Mayan contains structural motivation for the shift from simple to split ergativity, in all its varieties, as will be explained throughout this book.[1]

INHERENT VS. REDUCTIVE VOICE

Another related consequence of the TRANSITIVE/INTRANSITIVE grammatical distinction discussed above is the elaboration of VOICE. It will be recalled that VOICE was defined as a calling up by the predicate of a specified number of arguments, with intransitive predications calling up a single argument and transitive predications calling up two arguments. This is termed INHERENT VOICE. There is another kind of VOICE, called REDUCTIVE VOICE, defined as follows: either the active or the passive argument called up by the transitive verb is proscribed, excluding that argument from grammatical consideration, thus leaving the transitive verb with but a single argument. Such proscription makes two types of VOICE possible, depending on whether it is the active or passive argument that is suppressed. Figure 3.8 exhibits the PASSIVE VOICE with its suppression of the active argument.

PASSIVE VOICE
single argument

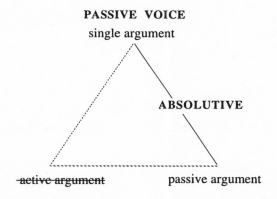

active argument   passive argument

Figure 3.8. PASSIVE VOICE and suppression of the active argument.

Despite this reduction of the active argument, the interpreter still recognizes the inherent transitivity of the verb, and that underneath it all, the verb still has two arguments. Nonetheless, only one of them, the passive argument in this case, is to be viewed in these interpretive circumstances as a part of the

---

[1]This system of split ergativity is the most well-known and generally used system among languages of the world. Other Mayan languages such as Mam have a different kind of split ergativity, and will be discussed below.

grammatical and interpretable picture. Consequently, the construction now becomes grammatically equivalent to an intransitive construction, owing to the fact there is but one argument. The consequence of this—that there is now but a single argument—is that, as with intransitives, the ABSOLUTIVE and not the ERGATIVE is the inflected verbal pronoun, for the Interpretant of the ERGATIVE instructs the interpreter to find two arguments present. Thus, for example, K'iche' has *š-at-qa-č'ay-ok* COMPL-ABS2SG-ERG1PL-hit-DAPD 'we hit you' in the ACTIVE VOICE, where ERG1PL marks the active argument (subject) and ABS2SG marks the passive argument (object). But for the PASSIVE, with the proscription of the active argument, the ABSOLUTIVE marks the single remaining argument associated with the verb: *š-at-č'a·y-ik* 'you were hit.'

The remaining possibility of the REDUCTIVE VOICE is the interdiction of the passive argument, leaving only the single active argument, resulting in the so-called ANTIPASSIVE, as shown in Figure 3.9.

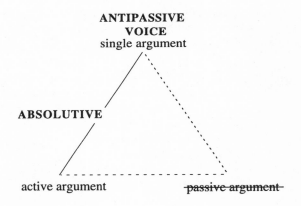

Figure 3.9. ANTIPASSIVE VOICE and suppression of the passive argument.

The meaning, as can be deduced from the above structure, is that the subject is doing something, but without knowing, or at least not saying, on whom or what the action is manifest. The action described by the verb has no expressed object. The K'iche' example, *š-at-č'ay-on-ik* COMPL-ABS2SG-hit-ANTIPASS-SAPD 'you hit,' expresses agentive hitting without saying what or whom was hit. This kind of ANTIPASSIVE is found in K'iche'an, Mamean, Q'anjob'alan, Yukatekan, and in part of Tzotzilan (Zinacantan dialect), but not in the rest of Tzeltalan, nor in Cholan. It surely goes back to Common Mayan times.

OBJECT INCORPORATION

OBJECT INCORPORATION is similar to the ANTIPASSIVE in that it also interdicts the passive argument of the transitive verb.[1] But the interdiction is different in that OBJECT INCORPORATION is defined by the occurrence of a direct object so totally free from modification and therefore so general as to be considered a part of the verbal action itself, and therefore conceptually a part of the predication. In other words, the general, unmodified passive argument, unlike its particular and modified counterpart, has no status as an *argument* of the predication, but is, rather, a part of the predication itself. As with the ANTIPASSIVE, where there is but a single remaining argument (the active argument), so with OBJECT INCORPORATION the construction is grammatically equivalent to intransitive constructions, resulting in the affixation of the ABSOLUTIVE (and not the ERGATIVE) as the inflected verbal pronoun of the inherently transitive verb.

Thus, for example, the Mam generic passive argument, *qʔoˑqʔ* 'squash,' is lost with its incorporation into the predicate, leaving but one argument, the active argument, which results in the inflection of the ABSOLUTIVE (not the ERGATIVE) pronoun to mark the active argument:

> ma-čin-lo-:n-e qʔoˑqʔ maˑkyʔ
> PROX.PAST-ABS1SG-eat-AFF-ABS1SG squash today
>
> 'I ate squash today'

On the other hand, if the passive argument loses its generality by any kind of modification, remaining a grammatical argument, then the ERGATIVE marks the active argument of the predication:

ma-či ʔ-n-lo-ʔn-e t-loʔ-ye qʔoˑqʔ maˑkyʔ
PROX.PAST-DV.go-ERG1SG-eat-AFF-ABS1SG ERG2SG-fruit-ERG2SG squash today
'I ate your squash today'

To my knowledge, there are instances of OBJECT INCORPORATION in Mam, Q'anjob'alan, Q'eqchi',[2] and Yukatekan. It is difficult to be sure that it was a part of the common language, but its far-flung distribution suggests the possibility. On the other hand, Mithun (1984) proposes a natural process of evolutionary development for OBJECT INCORPORATION, and it is possible that it could have developed independently in Yukatekan but not in Mam and Q'anjob'alan. For Mam and Q'anjob'alan, shared cross-language borrowing is not an unattractive possibility since they seem to have developed along

---

[1] For an important discussion of the general process of OBJECT INCORPORATION, see Mithun (1984).

[2] I would like to thank Joe Martineau for pointing this out to me.

similar lines elsewhere. Phonologically, Mam influenced Q'anjob'alan toward retroflection—only the northernmost Chujean dialects do not have it. Syntactically, both have a highly developed process of directional verb incorporation; Q'anjob'alan seems to have influenced Northern Mam and Ixil toward noun classification. Both groups lost raising and passivization—as did Yukatekan, interestingly. Even though the processes are different, one still senses a mutual influence. In light of Mithun's observation that OBJECT INCORPORATION comes later, it might be that it did not exist in the common language, and that it is somehow related to the fact of the loss of raising, thus developing independently in the three languages.

Substantival Transitivity

One of the remarkable facts of the system of Mayan transitivity discussed above is its extension even beyond the verbs to the substantives, as shown in Figure 3.10.

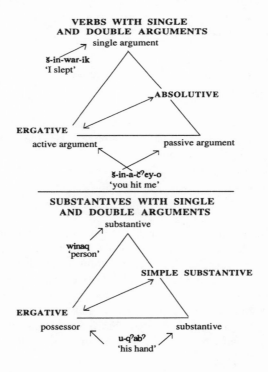

Figure 3.10. Substantival transitivity in Mayan.

Thus, just as the Mayan languages have two principal classes of verbs, so they have two principal classes of substantives. Moreover, just as one of those verbal classes (intransitives) has but a single argument, so there is a class of simple substantives; and just as the other verbal class (transitives) has two arguments, one transitively imposing the behavior described by the predicate on the passive argument, so there is a class of substantives with two "arguments," one transitively imposing possession on the other. Furthermore, it is no coincidence that the ERGATIVE pronoun governs both the active argument of the predicate and the possessive argument of the substantive. These parallels as seen in Figure 3.10 use K'iche' as the illustrating language.

The "transitive" class of substantives referred to above is a class whose Interpretant requires an interpretation of contiguity, with the effect that these substantives never appear without the ERGATIVE pronoun. Typically, substantives of this class refer to objects like body parts and kin names, which are existentially always associated by contiguity with the body or with next of kin, as in, e.g., *ru-qʔabʔ* 'his arm,' *nu-xoloˑn* 'my head,' *ru-kʔaxoˑl* 'his son.' Unlike other substantives, these *must* be possessed.

Substantival "Voice"

There is a further similarity between predicational and substantival transitivity based on the notion of voice, as showin in Figure 3.11.

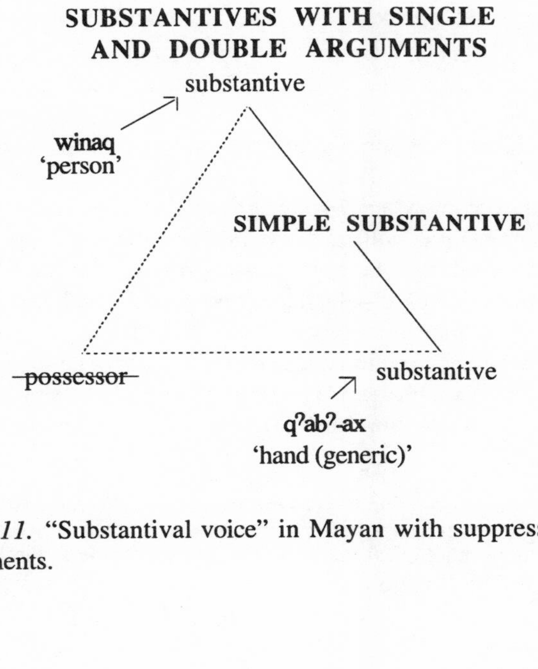

SUBSTANTIVES WITH SINGLE AND DOUBLE ARGUMENTS

Figure 3.11. "Substantival voice" in Mayan with suppression of one of the arguments.

Thus, just as voice amounts to interdiction of argument with transitive verbs, so there is interdiction of the ERGATIVE argument of inherently possessed, "transitive" substantives. And just as the passive or ANTIPASSIVE affix accompanies such predicational interdiction, so there is a generic suffix, *-(b²)ax* (which goes back at least to Mamo-K'iche'an and probably to the common language), which accompanies substantival interdiction, as in, for example, Kaqchikel *q²ab²-ax* 'hand (without saying whose hand).'

Although the system of substantival voice is not as extensive as predicational voice, it is nonetheless there, analogically reflecting voice of the predicational system.

It is therefore here proposed that Common Mayan had a system of transitivity which defines its major grammatical systems, both predicationally and substantivally, as can be seen as a 2^m system in Figure 3.12.

SUBSTANTIVE	SUBSTANTIVE CONTIGUITY
winaq 'person'	u-q²ab² 'his hand'
VERB	VERB CONTIGUITY
š-in-war-ik 'I slept'	š-in-u-č²ey-o 'he hit me'

Figure 3.12. Illustration comparing VOICE in verbs and substantives.[1]

There were in the common language two major classes of verbs, one transitive and the other intransitive, with ERGATIVE marking the active argument of the transitive verb. Similarly, there were two primary classes of nouns, one simple and the other complex—obligatorily possessed—with ERGATIVE marking the possessor. It is therefore not by chance that the ERGATIVE of Common Mayan should have occurred in both contexts, for although they are different (subject of transitives vs. possessive pronoun), there is but a single Interpretant, which is based on the notion of contiguity. The transaction of the active

---

[1]Although I am here referring to Mayan, there is a universal tendency for there to be a feeling of contiguity for both possession and the active verbal transaction. I suspect that the morphological manifestation of this fact is at the bottom of the ERGATIVE-ABSOLUTIVE typology.

agent of a transitive verb is to manifest whatever action is described by that verb onto the passive argument, and all this is done by contiguity. Similarly, all possession is given by contiguity, as is particularly evident in inherent possession.

The Reconstruction of the Markers for Single and Double Arguments

Another system growing out of the transitivity under discussion is a paradigm of morphemes which signal to the interpreter one of four things: (1) the presence of one argument associated with the predication in a declarative mode, (2) the presence of two arguments associated with the predication in a declarative mode, (3) the presence of one argument associated with the predication in an optative mode, or (4) the presence of two arguments associated with the predication in an optative mode. In Common Mayan these four morphemes are reconstructed as shown in Figure 3.13, where the double-argument predication is of the CVC type.

SINGLE-ARGUMENT PREDICATIONS DECLARATIVE	DOUBLE-ARGUMENT PREDICATIONS DECLARATIVE
*-ik	*-O
SINGLE-ARGUMENT PREDICATIONS OPTATIVE	DOUBLE-ARGUMENT PREDICATIONS OPTATIVE
*-oq	*-Aʔ

Figure 3.13. Reconstruction illustrating the paradigm of MOOD and VOICE in Common Mayan.

K'iche' essentially preserves the Common Mayan system:

   k-in-war-ik INC-ABS1SG-sleep-SAPD[1] 'I sleep'

---

[1]Hereafter, the abbreviations for indexing the morphemes will be as follows: single-argument predication, declarative = SAPD; single-argument predication, optative = SAPO; double-argument predication, declarative = DAPD; double-argument predication, optative = DAPO.

k-at-in-č'ay-o INC-ABS2SG-ERG1SG-sleep-DAPD 'I hit you'
k-in-war-oq INC-ABS1-sleep-SAPO 'would that I sleep'
k-at-in-č'ay-a? INC-ABS2SG-ERG1SG-sleep-DAPD 'would that I hit you'

The capitalization of the *-O* of the double-argument predication stands for a kind of vowel harmony, whose quality is determined by the root vowel. A skeletal outline of how this vowel harmony works in some representative languages follows:

K'iche'		Jakaltek		Mam	Choltí
DECLAR	OPT	DECLAR	OPT	FUT<OPT	FUT<OPT
CiC-o	CiC-a?	CiC-a	CiC-a?	CiC-a?	?
CeC-o	CeC-a?	CeC-a	CeC-a?	CeC-a?	?
CaC-o	CaC-a?	CaC-a	CaC-a?	CaC-a?	?
CoC-o	CoC-o?	CoC-o	CoC-o?	CoC-o?	CoC-o?
CuC-u	CuC-u?	CuC-u	CuC-u?	CuC-u?	CuC-u?

Thus, K'iche' takes this form:
    š-in-muq-u COMP-ERG1SG-bury-DAPD 'I buried it,'
    k-a-muq-u? INC-ERG2SG-bury-DAPO 'bury it,'
but
    š-in-b?an-o COMP-ERG1SG-do-DAPD 'I did it,'
    k-a-b?an-a? INC-ERG2SG-do-DAPO 'do it';

and in Jakaltek,
    č-in-mux-u INC-ERG1SG-bury-SAPD 'I buried it,'
    č-in-mu-u? INC-ERG1SG-bury-DAPO 'I will bury it,'
but
    š-in-č'ah-a COMP-ERG1SG-wash-DAPD 'I washed it,'
    č-in-č'ah-a? INC-ERG1SG-wash-DAPO 'I will wash it';

and in Mam,
    k-t-il-a? FUT-ERG3SG-see-DAPO 'he will see him'
    ok-t-mq-ú? FUT-ERG3SG-bury-DAPO 'he will bury it'

and in Choltí,
    x-ca-toh-o [š-ka-čoh-o?] INC-ERG1PL-pay-DAPO 'we will pay it.'

In the common language, as is now the case in modern K'iche'an and Q'anjob'alan, the declarative morphemes of the above paradigm, *-ik* and *O,* only appear at the end of a breath group. Thus in Cunén K'iche', for example, one says *š-in-war-ik* 'I slept,' but *š-in-war tla?* 'I slept over there.'

This system of affixes, as pointed out above, signals what is here termed only appear at the end of a breath group. Thus in Cunén K'iche', for example, one says *š-in-war-ik* 'I slept,' but *š-in-war tla?* 'I slept over there.'

This system of affixes, as pointed out above, signals what is here termed *single-argument predication,* and *double-argument predication.* Single-argument predication results from (1) intransitive predications, which call up only a single argument, and (2) transitive predications of the passive, ANTIPASSIVE, and object INCORPORATIONAL voice, all of which have but a single argument. All of the single-argument predications in the common language took **-ik* in the declarative and **-oq* in the optative, and all the double-argument predications took declarative **-O* and optative **-A?*.

The Four Major Prefixal Categories

Just as there are four principal categories of suffixes reconstructed above for the common language based on VOICE and MOOD, so there are also four major prefixal categories. These are based on the differences between PARTICULAR and GENERAL, on the one hand, and between REALIS and IRREALIS on the other. The paradigmatic system is given in Figure 3.14. The discussion that follows takes its sequence from Figure 3.14: first the COMPLETIVE/INCOMPLETIVE, then the OPTATIVE, and finally the FUTURE.

PARTICULAR REALIS	PARTICULAR IRREALIS
COMPLETIVE	OPTATIVE
GENERAL REALIS	GENERAL IRREALIS
INCOMPLETIVE	FUTURE

Figure 3.14. Paradigm illustrating the system of Common Mayan ASPECT.

COMPLETIVE/INCOMPLETIVE

The terms *particular* and *general* help distinguish the COMPLETIVE and the INCOMPLETIVE, respectively. The COMPLETIVE aspect means, in the simplest terms, that the action described by the verb is a particular, existential fact, a fait accompli; it instantiates potential verbal action into the actual, experiential world of existence. Thus, in Kaqchikel, the sentence *š-kam ri Pedro* (COMPL-die the Pedro) translates into the English PAST TENSE, 'Pedro died,' since both the

Mayan COMPLETIVE and the English PAST convey interpretive instructions to see the predicational manifestation as definite facts of existential, experiential reality. The difference between the two is the difference between ASPECT and TENSE, where aspectual markers define the character of verbal predication itself, while tense markers place such predication in time with respect to the here-and-now of the speech situation. The reason there is such a tenacious overlap between PAST TENSE and COMPLETIVE in languages of the world is the fact that PAST TENSE has the effect of placing such action *before* the here-and-now (i.e., in time-gone-by), whose mode of being is *esse in praeterito,* thus rendering it a fait accompli. With similar effects, the instructional value of the Interpretant for the COMPLETIVE is simply to see the verbal action as a particular, existential fact—again, a fait accompli. More will be said of this overlap below with respect to Common Mayan.

Peirce (2.147) captures the nature of an action whose mode of being is existential:[1]

> It cannot be generalized without losing its essential character. For it is an actual passage at arms between the non-ego and the ego. A blow is passed, so to say. Generalize the fact that you get hit in the eye. And all that distinguishes the actual fact, the shock, the pain, the inflammation, is gone. It is anti-general. The memory preserves this character, only slightly modified. The actual shock, etc., are no longer there, the quality of the event has associated itself in the mind with similar past experiences. It is a little generalized in the *perceptual fact.* Still, it is referred to a special and unique occasion, and the flavor of anti-generality is the predominant one.

On the other hand, the Mayan INCOMPLETIVE has an Interpretant that asks the interpreter to see the verbal action as *generally or habitually occurring.* Thus the Kaqchikel expression *ni-kam ri winaq* (INC-die the people) would normally translate into English as 'people die.' This overlap between the Mayan INCOMPLETIVE and the English PRESENT TENSE results from the presence of an Interpretant that describes a predication that is generally or habitually occurring. The difference between the Mayan INCOMPLETIVE and the English PRESENT TENSE is, again, an aspectual vs. atemporal distinction, and therefore, the above English translation is injurious to the understanding of the real meaning of the Mayan INCOMPLETIVE. A more complete appreciation of the meaning would be 'people habitually (by nature) die': 'were dying,' or 'are sleeping,' or 'will be dying,' where temporality (TENSE) is factored out. Any

---

[1] This belongs to the Peircian category of Secondness.

textual inspection of any Mayan language shows that the INCOMPLETIVE describes the action not temporally, but as ongoing and habitual, regardless of whether the action is past, present, or future—hence the aspectual name INCOMPLETIVE.

Peirce (2.147) again cogently describes the generality inherent in the INCOMPLETIVE and the PRESENT TENSE:[1]

> There is a sort of picture in your imagination whose outlines are vague and fluid. You do not attach it to any definite occasion, but you think vaguely that some definite occasion there is, to which that picture does attach itself, and in which it is to become individualized. You think that at present its state of being consists in the fact that either in your will or in somebody else's, or somehow in something analogous thereto in the nature of things, some rule is determined, or nearly determined, which will probably govern the individual event when it occurs.

Figure 3.15 summarizes the above discussion of the COMPLETIVE/INCOMPLETIVE and the PAST/PRESENT.

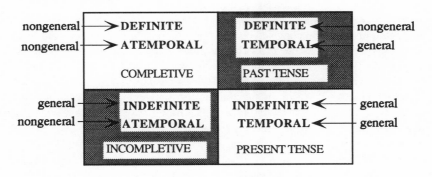

Figure 3.15. Paradigm comparing ASPECT and TENSE.

The markedness relationships that hold in the above diagram are particularly important to this discussion of TENSE and ASPECT. Notice that for the system COMPLETIVE/INCOMPLETIVE the COMPLETIVE is unmarked, whereas for the system PAST/PRESENT it is the PRESENT that is unmarked. This markedness reversal occurs because the characteristics "indefinite" and "temporal" are both degrees of the same kind—both belong to the order GENERAL. The generality of habit is self-evident, and anything to do with temporality presupposes sequential

---

[1]This belongs to the Peircian category of Thirdness.

occurrence; even the mere recognition that elements occur in an order is a significant kind of generalization.

It should come as no surprise, therefore, that in Common Mayan the form for the COMPLETIVE was literally unmarked, *∅, while the form for the INCOMPLETIVE was *k(i)- for all persons but 1 PL, where it was *q-.[1] The Common Mayan conjugation for 'to sleep' is shown in the following:

COMPLETIVE		INCOMPLETIVE	
*war ik	'he slept'	*ki war-ik	'he sleeps'
*war at	'you slept'	*k-at war-ik	'you sleep'
*war in	'I slept'	*k-in war-ik	'I sleep'
*war eb⁷	'they slept'	*k-eb⁷ war-ik	'they sleep'
*war eš	'you-guys slept'	*k-eš war-ik	'you-guys sleep'
*war o⁷ŋ	'we slept'	*q-o⁷ŋ war-ik	'we sleep'

The Relationship between COMPLETIVE Aspect and PAST Tense

Because the chief characteristic of the COMPLETIVE as well as of the PAST is factual accomplishment, as pointed out above, it is easy to see how such existential instantiation comes to be interpreted in relation to the here-and-now, deictically anchored to the current instant, thus being viewed as time-gone-by; in this way the interpretation moves from aspect to tense. My inclination is to assume that Common Mayan was in the process of making the distinction between TENSE and ASPECT in the distinction between PROXIMATE PAST and COMPLETIVE, so that at the division of the common language this distinction was essentially formed. To be more specific, PROXIMATE PAST usually had reference to past time of today, although it sometimes translates 'already.' Such a distinction is found in Q'anjob'alan (reconstructible), and in the Colonial and modern languages of Mamean (p. 98) and K'iche'an (p. 176), reconstructible to *iš.[2] There is some indirect evidence that it also existed prehistorically in Tzeltalan (p. 183). Furthermore, in Colonial times Yukatek

---

[1]The postulation of *q- for 1 PL is made necessary by the fact that it is present in both poqomchi' *q-ox-wir-ik* INC-ABS1PL-sleep-SAPD 'we sleep'; Colonial Kaqchikel *q-ox-pe* INC-ABS1PL-come 'we come' (modern only in the imperative); Colonial (but not modern K'iche') *koxwarik [q-ox-war-ik]* INC-ABS1PL-sleep-SAPD 'we sleep' (Anleo n.d.); vestigially in Mam *n-q-o-b⁷e·t* INC-INC-ABS1PL-walk 'we walk.' Because the *ki- changed to č- in the lowland languages, it is likely that the original Common Mayan *q- was analogically replaced by *k> č-, as Colonial K'iche' was k- was replaced by č- in modern times. If *q- were not postulated, it would be difficult to account for it in the Mamo-K'iche'an branch.

[2]For a justification of this reconstruction see Robertson (1975).

Maya had a morpheme for the PROXIMATE PAST, *t-* (p. 207). In Choltí (Morán 1695) the PROXIMATE PAST existed only as a clitic: *winikilesbʔil iš* '(man) was already created'/*u-korpes iš* 'he already saved him.' Similarly, in Tzeltal *iš* is a suffixed clitic that means PROXIMATE PAST. Thus, in the category COMPLETIVE, there was at least in late Common Mayan times an apparent PROXIMATE PAST probably referring to past time of today.[1] There is, incidentally, an equivalent morpheme of tense, **a-*, that may have also existed in the Cholan languages, as discussed for Choltí and Poqomam below (p. 189).

The reconstruction with PROXIMATE PAST, at least for Q'anjob'alan, Mamean, and K'iche'an, is given in the following:

INTRANSITIVE PROXIMATE PAST		**TRANSITIVE PROXIMATE PAST**	
*iš war-ik	'he slept'	**iš-ru-muq-u*	'he buried it'
*iš-at war-ik	'you slept'	**iš-a-muq-u*	'you buried it'
*iš-in war-ik	'I slept'	**iš-nu-muq-u*	'I buried it'
*iš-ebʔ war-ik	'they slept'	**iš-ki-muq-u*	'they buried it'
*iš-eš war-ik	'you-guys slept'	**iš-e-muq-u*	'you-guys buried it'
*iš-oʔŋ war-ik	'we slept'	**iš-qa-muq-u*	'we buried it'

In conclusion, the COMPLETIVE can be thought of either as the COMPLETIVE or as a more distant past, because it is opposed both to the INCOMPLETIVE and the PROXIMATE PAST.

OPTATIVE

In general, MOOD—here identified as IMPERATIVE and OPTATIVE—is directly opposite from the INCOMPLETIVE in two ways. First, like the COMPLETIVE, it is anti-general, deictically instructing the interpreter to use information from the speech act to arrive at the appropriate interpretational results. The IN-COMPLETIVE, by contrast, is not deictic, but general. Specifically, the information in question is the desire or will of the speaker taken into interpretational account, as, for example, in K'iche' the OPTATIVE *či-war-oq* 'would that he sleep!' means that it is the speaker's desire that someone sleep, whereas, on the other hand, the INCOMPLETIVE *ka-war-ik* 'he sleeps' is a flat statement of fact, asserting simply that his sleeping occurs in general. The second dis-similarity between the INCOMPLETIVE and the OPTATIVE is that of reality. On the one hand, both the COMPLETIVE and the INCOMPLETIVE are allied with reality (REALIS); one reality is specific (completed, perfected action), and the other is

---

[1] It probably worked like the PROXIMATE PAST of Choltí or Tzeltal.

general (potential instantiation into existential reality, as is characteristic of all habits). On the other hand, the OPTATIVE (and, as will be seen, the FUTURE) is quite the opposite. The OPTATIVE, which so often translates 'would that…!' describes, by the arguments of the predication, an action or behavior which never has partaken of reality, nor does it currently, for the speaker is hoping, wishing, or in some way commanding, that an action be realized. Therefore, the OPTATIVE is like the COMPLETIVE in its specificity, and opposite to the INCOMPLETIVE, both in its specificity and its orientation to the speech act.

The reconstruction of the OPTATIVE is given below. Note that the suffixes *-oq* for single-argument predications and *-A?* for double-argument predications accompany the OPTATIVE prefixes, which are *t^yi- preceding ABS3SG, *q-* preceding ABS1PL, and *k-* elsewhere. The proposed reconstruction of OPTATIVE in Common Mayan is shown in the following:

INTRANSITIVE
OPTATIVE

*t^yi war-oq	OPT sleep-SAPO	'would that he sleep'
*k-at war-oq	OPT-ABS2SG sleep-SAPO	'would that you sleep'
*k-in war-oq	OPT-ABS1SG sleep-SAPO	'would that I sleep'
*k-eb? war-oq	OPT-ABS3PL sleep-SAPO	'would that they sleep'
*k-eš war-oq	OPT-ABS2PL sleep-SAPO	'would that you-guys sleep'
*q-o?ŋ war-oq	OPT-ABS1PL sleep-SAPO	'would that we sleep'

TRANSITIVE
OPTATIVE

*t^yi ru-muq-u?	OPT-ERG3SG bury-DAPO	'would that he bury it'
*t^y a-muq-u?	OPT-ERG2SG bury-DAPO	'would that you bury it'
*t^yi nu-muq-u?	OPT-ERG1SG bury-DAPO	'would that I bury it'
*t^yi ki-muq-u?	OPT-ERG3PL bury-DAPO	'would that they bury it'
*t^y e-muq-u?	OPT-ERG2PL bury-DAPO	'would that you-guys bury it'
*t^yi qa-muq-u?	OPT-ERG1PL bury-DAPO	'would that we bury it'

FUTURE

Up to this point the discussion has included the COMPLETIVE (with PROXIMATE PAST), the INCOMPLETIVE, and the OPTATIVE, with these observations: (1) the COMPLETIVE is particular and not general, and is unmarked with respect to the speech act; (2) the INCOMPLETIVE is general and not particular, and is also unmarked with respect to the speech act; and (3) the OPTATIVE is particular and not general, but is marked for taking the speech act into account. The remaining prefixal category of cardinal significance to Common Mayan TAMV—the structural combination of the INCOMPLETIVE and the OPTATIVE—is the FUTURE.

The FUTURE, like the OPTATIVE, is IRREALIS, since the predicate is neither factual nor attestable, taking the speaker's judgment into interpretational account regarding expected events. On the other hand, the FUTURE is like the INCOMPLETIVE, but unlike the OPTATIVE, in that its interpretation is always general. Prediction always involves paying attention not to a specific, singular detail from the past, but to a class or even classes of details out of which future expectations are born, and about which propositions can be made.

Thus, the difference between the OPTATIVE and the FUTURE is that for the OPTATIVE the wish or desire of a specific person is taken into account ('would that he die!') whereas the FUTURE is more closely allied to a general law—it is a propositional statement less tied to the wishes of a particular person and more apt to be the reflection of a perceived law outside the individual ('he will die'). The difference between the INCOMPLETIVE and the FUTURE is that the INCOMPLETIVE is deictically unmarked with respect to the speech act, since the interpreter of the proposition expects the general statement to be found in reality—if not now, then, and if not then, sometime ('people die'). The FUTURE on the other hand, even though it is general and allied with law, that law is still tied to speaker perception ('people will die'). The FUTURE is totally unlike the COMPLETIVE on two counts: it is marked for reference to the speech act, and it is general and not particular.

Figure 3.16 shows the structure of COMPLETIVE, INCOMPLETIVE, OPTATIVE, and FUTURE for intransitives and Figure 3.17 for transitives. This is part of the hypothesis by which the facts of the particular modern Mayan languages are analogically predicted, and inductively checked against the attested data. There is also reason to believe that there was a PROXIMATE FUTURE, just as there was a PROXIMATE PAST, at least for the Q'anjob'alan, Mamean, and K'iche'an languages.

Of the above categories, the FUTURE is the most subject to change, since it is the most marked, and therefore structurally the most primed for change. It is the FUTURE that is most varied in the several languages, but it is always affected in at least one of three ways: it comes to resemble the OPTATIVE—which is the most pervasive change—or it comes to resemble the INCOMPLETIVE, or it is influenced by the directional verb 'to go' (or it changes in any combination of the above three ways). Modern K'iche', for example, has no formal marking for the FUTURE, which, though attested in Colonial times, has been totally taken over by the INCOMPLETIVE (p. 128).

Furthermore, Choltí also has a FUTURE based on the INCOMPLETIVE (p. 171), as does Tzeltalan (p. 186), generally speaking. In any case, given the FUTURE's constant bombardment from its three contiguous neighbors (the directional verb *go* will be discussed on pp. 206, 215), it seems to be a fairly good hypothesis that the FUTURE is a semantically structured subset of both the OPTATIVE and the INCOMPLETIVE.[1]

Single Argument Predications

COMPLETIVE nongeneral non speech act		OPTATIVE nongeneral speech act	
*war-ik	'he slept'	*tʸi war-oq	'would that he sleep'
*war at	'you slept'	*k-at war-oq	'would that you sleep'
*war in	'I slept'	*k-in war-oq	'would that I sleep'
*war eb⁷	'they slept'	*k-eb⁷ war-oq	'would that they sleep'
*war eš	'you-guys slept'	*k-eš war-oq	'would that y-guys sleep'
*war o⁷ŋ	'we slept'	*q-o⁷ŋ war-oq	'would that we sleep'
PROXIMATE PAST			
*iš war-ik	'he just slept'		
*iš-at war-ik	'you just slept'		
*iš-in war-oq	'I just slept'		
*iš-eb⁷ war-oq	'they just slept'		
*iš-eš war-oq	'y-guys just slept'		
*iš-o⁷ŋ war-oq	'we just slept'		
INCOMPLETIVE general non speech act		**FUTURE** general speech act	
*ki war-ik	'he sleeps'	*la war-ik	'he will sleep'
*k-at war-ik	'you sleep'	*l-at war-ik	'you will sleep'
*k-in war-ik	'I sleep'	*l-in war-ik	'I will sleep'
*k-eb⁷ war-ik	'they sleep'	*l-eb⁷ war-ik	'they will sleep'
*k-eš war-ik	'you-guys sleep'	*l-eš war-ik	'you-guys will sleep'
*q-o⁷ŋ war-ik	'we sleep'	*l-o⁷ŋ war-ik	'we will sleep'
		PROXIMATE FUTURE	
		*iš-la war-ik	'he will soon sleep'
		*iš-l-at war-ik	'you will soon sleep'
		*iš-l-in war-ik	'I will soon sleep'
		*iš-l-eb⁷ war-ik	'they will soon sleep'
		*iš-l-eš war-ik	'y-guys will soon sleep'
		*iš-l-o⁷ŋ war-ik	'we will soon sleep'

Figure 3.16. Reconstruction of Common Mayan ASPECT for intransitives.

---

[1]As well as the NOMINATIVE MOOD, as shown below.

Mayan is not the only language among languages of the world whose FUTURE is so influenced. For example, Russell Ultan (1978:118), in an extensive cross-linguistic study of the FUTURE, says that "future tenses evolve chiefly from modals, especially those expressing obligation, volition, uncertainty or unreality, and to a lesser extent from aspectuals or markers of goal-oriented categories." Witness English *will,* for example. The instances of the OPTATIVE MOOD's influencing the Mayan FUTURE are almost universal.

Double Argument Predications

COMPLETIVE nongeneral non speech act		OPTATIVE nongeneral speech act	
*ru-b²an-o	'he did it'	*tⁱ-ru-b²an-a²	'may he do it'
*a-b²an-o	'you did it'	*tʸ-a-b²an-a²	'may you do it'
*nu-b²an-o	'I did it'	*tʸi-nu-b²an-a²	'may I do it'
*ki-b²an-o	'they did it'	*tʸi-ki-b²an-a²	'may they do it'
*e-b²an-o	'you-guys did it'	*tʸ-e-b²an-a²	'may y-guys do it'
*qa-b²an-o	'we did it'	*tʸi-qa-b²an-a²	'may we do it'
PROXIMATE PAST			
*iš ru-b²an-o	'he just did it'		
*iš a-b²an-o	'you just did it'		
*iš nu-b²an-o	'I just did it'		
*iš ki-b²an-o	'they just did it'		
*iš e-b²an-o	'y-guys just did it'		
*iš qa-b²an-o	'we just did it'		
INCOMPLETIVE general non speech act		FUTURE general speech act	
*ki ru-b²an-o	'he does it'	*la ru-b²an-o	'he will do it'
*k-a-b²an-o	'you do it'	*l-a-b²an-o	'you will do it'
*ki nu-b²an-o	'do it'	*la nu-b²an-o	'I will do it'
*ki ki-b²an-o	'they do it'	*la ki-b²an-o	'they will do it'
*k-e-b²an-o	'y-guys do it'	*l-e-b²an-o	'y-guys will do it'
*qi qa-b²an-o	'we do it'	*la q-b²an-a	'we will do it'
		PROXIMATE FUTURE	
		*iš-la ru-b²an-o	'he will soon do it'
		*iš-l-a-b²an-o	'you will soon do it'
		*iš-la nu-b²an-o	'I will soon do it'
		*iš-la ki-b²an-o	'they will soon do it'
		*iš-l-e-b²an-o	'y-guys will soon do it'
		*iš-la q-b²an-o	'we will soon do it'

Figure 3.17. Reconstruction of Common Mayan ASPECT for transitives.

It is further interesting to observe that in many instances the FUTURE was derived from an INCOMPLETIVE, as for example in Tagalog, where "the future stem contains a marker of incompleteness or continuous action," or in Hausa, where "future verbs always take the INCOMPLETIVE suffix" (Ultan 1978:118).

Furthermore, there is "an apparently widespread source of futures or intensives [which] is a basic verb of motion meaning 'go' which functions as an auxiliary" (Ultan 1978:110). Note the periphrastic future in English and Romance languages based on directional verbs, such as *go, ir,* and *aller,* which, as has been shown in Mayan, are closely related to MOOD because of their shared deictic character. They are often used to signal IRREALIS, as in *I'm gonna do it tomorrow, voy a hacerlo mañana,* or *je vais le faire demain.* Both Yukatek (p. 206) and Huastec (p. 215) recruited a FUTURE based on such directionals.

It is significant that the hypothesized FUTURE is the logical combination of the IMPERFECTIVE and the OPTATIVE, and (a) that in the languages of the world, the etymological source of the FUTURE is most often a modal of some sort, or on occasion an imperfective, and (b) that in most cases, the attested futures of the daughter languages are closely related to the OPTATIVE mood, or the INCOMPLETIVE aspect.

TAMV in the Context of More than One Predication

Up to this point the focus has been on the TAMV of simple predications—single verbs. But there is another capital consideration which figures prominently in the overall grammatical system of the common language, and which is vital to the explanation of how the modern languages evolved to their Colonial and modern states. The reference here is to certain special effects on the TAMV which occur when two predications, consisting of a *primary* and a *secondary predication,* come together to form a unitary concept.

More specifically, just as there is a structure of TAMV with respect to inflectional, verbal morphology, as shown in Figure 3.18, so there is an analogous structure for syntactic structure for verbal syntax, as shown in Figure 3.19, where 3.18 is a paradigmatic system, and 3.19 a syntagmatic system (as discussed on page 33). As explained earlier, it is the syntagmatic that is unmarked as compared with the paradigmatic, and this is precisely the description of Mayan history. The more syntagmatic NOMINATIVE VOICE and MOOD influenced the more paradigmatic INCOMPLETIVE and FUTURE. This influence, as will be seen in the course of this book, is the most telling and significant in the history of Mayan grammatical change. Taken together, these two form a system which, as suggested by the arrows in Figure 3.20, indicates the direction of the flow of change throughout the millennia of Mayan language use, as will be shown in succeeding chapters.

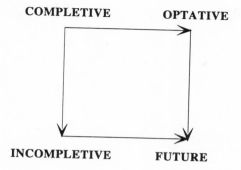

COMPLETIVE   **OPTATIVE**

INCOMPLETIVE   **FUTURE**

Figure 3.18. Paradigmatic structure of verbal morphology.

ABSOLUTIVE   **ABSOLUTIVE**
VOICE   **MOOD**

NOMINATIVE   **NOMINATIVE**
VOICE   **MOOD**

Figure 3.19. The syntagmatic portion of the Common Mayan paradigm.

Exactly the same categorical parameters are at work in the syntagm as in the paradigm. ABSOLUTIVE VOICE and NOMINATIVE VOICE are, like the COMPLETIVE and INCOMPLETIVE, unmarked for involvement in the speech act (they are nondeictic). ABSOLUTIVE MOOD, NOMINATIVE MOOD, OPTATIVE, and FUTURE always take the speech act into account in their interpretation (they are deictic). Furthermore, the ABSOLUTIVE VOICE and the ABSOLUTIVE MOOD are much more particular than their NOMINATIVE VOICE and MOOD counterparts, as will be shown below.

The importance of the above 2^m system in explaining historical change should not be underestimated, for it is the means by which the direction of change can be interpreted in all Mayan subgroupings. Without this visual scaffolding, which represents the logical system of the common language, the understanding—even the recognition—of the changes that have occurred on the grand scale attested for the Mayan language would be ignored. It therefore has significant explanatory bearing on all Mayan language families, particularly on how the NOMINATIVE VOICE affects the INCOMPLETIVE. The effect of the ABSOLUTIVE VOICE on the NOMINATIVE VOICE was far-ranging in Q'anjob'al (p. 83) and Yukatekan (p. 205). And from these consequences there seem to have resulted further important innovations in the Lowland Languages affecting ASPECT, which in turn had further developmental bearing on the innovative formation of split ergativity.

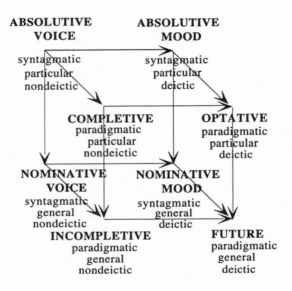

Figure 3.20. Paradigmatic structure of verbal morphology and syntax, as a system.

The four categories of the above syntagmatic system (Figure 3.19), each of which is constituted of two predicates, are amplified in the following discussion. For ease of reference, the categories will be called ABS-VOICE, NOM-VOICE, ABS-MOOD, and NOM-MOOD.

The Category ABS-VOICE

It will be recalled that VOICE was defined in terms of the interdiction of arguments on the transitive verb (with the interdiction of the active argument when the verb is in PASSIVE VOICE, and with the interdiction of the passive argument when the verb is in the ANTIPASSIVE VOICE).

Yet another kind of interdiction exists in the syntagmatic context, where the interdiction occurs in the secondary predicate, and a mandatory recovery of the proscribed argument occurs outside the core of that predicate. Specifically, the proscription of the argument occurs in certain kinds of relative clauses: if the *active* argument of the transitive verb is relativized, either the active or the passive argument is proscribed from the core of that predication. The kind of relativization referred to would always translate into English as *the boy [who hit John]*, or *the man [who stole the money]*, or even *who [is it that] hit me*, where the active (ERGATIVE) argument is relativized, and the ABSOLUTIVE remains untouched. Because it works on the ERGATIVE/ABSOLUTIVE dichotomy, this is called ABS-VOICE. Sentences such as *the boy [who John hit]*, or *the boys [who went to town]*, where the absolutive argument is relativized, do not take the ABS-VOICE.

With active-argument relativization, Mayan languages have two different forms of reduction—one where the active argument is absent from the core of the predication, but recoverable from the head noun, and the other where the passive argument is absent from the core, but recoverable as the object of a preposition in that same sentence. The following is an example of an active argument that is recoverable from the head noun:

> **a šwaˑn š-in-čˀay-ow-ik**
> it John PROX.PAST-ABS1SG-hit-VOICE(REL)-SAPD
> 'it's John who hit me' (Modern K'iche')
> **šam ri š-e-tiˀ-ow-ik**[1]
> mosquito the PROX.PAST-ABS3PL-bite-VOICE(REL)-SAPD
> 'it was the mosquito that bit them' (*Popol Wuj*)

> **Dios š-i-bˀan-o**[2]
> God PROX.PAST-ABS1SG-made-VOICE(REL)
> 'It was God who made me' (Old Kaqchikel)

On the other hand, the active noun may be there in the predication of the relative clause, but with the object separated by a preposition, and thus not in the core of the predication:

> **a šwaˑn š-čˀay-en č-w-eč**
> it John PROX.PAST-hit-VOICE PREP-ERG1SG-to
> 'it's John who hit me' (Modern K'iche')

In both cases—either where the active argument is recoverable from the head noun, or where the passive argument is realized as the object of a

---

[1]The original form, from Villacorta (1927:262), was *xam ri ix e tioqüic*.

[2]The original form, from Brinton (1884:60), was *Dios xi bano*. Notice that Kaqchikel, unlike K'iche', changes the Common K'iche'an RELATIVE VOICE *ow to a simple o.

preposition—there is only one argument present in the core of the predication. As a consequence, the ABSOLUTIVE marks that single argument, and where applicable (not at the end of a breath group), reflexes of Common Mayan *-ik* are suffixed. Some languages such as K'iche', have both ways of relativization, while others have one or the other.

A summary contrasting VOICE of one predication with VOICE of two predications can be found in Figure 3.21. [1]

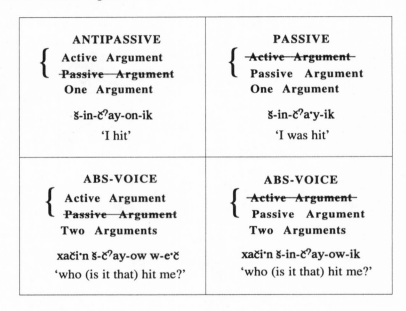

Figure 3.21. Paradigmatic structure of ANTIPASSIVE, PASSIVE, and ABS-VOICE in Cunén K'iche'.

Note that in both types of relativization, the translation is the same. The difference between this kind of VOICE and the PASSIVE and ANTIPASSIVE is the difference between recoverability and nonrecoverability. With relativization, the suppressed argument must be contextually present and recoverable, whereas no such recoverability of the elided argument is guaranteed for the PASSIVE and the ANTIPASSIVE. It seems most reasonable to reconstruct, based on K'iche' and Kaqchikel, *-ow* as the marker for ABS-VOICE, and *-Vn* for all other kinds of voice.

---

[1]The actual reconstruction of the PASSIVE, ANTIPASSIVE, OBJECT INCORPORATION, and ACTIVE RELATIVE is not the purpose here. This will be left for later investigation.

The Category Nom-Voice

The relationship between ABS-VOICE and NOM-VOICE is striking. First, as will be shown below, ABS-VOICE historically influences NOM-VOICE (pp. 83, 205). Second, just as ABS-VOICE entails a suppression of arguments, as with other instances of VOICE in Mayan, so NOM-VOICE entails a suppression of arguments, as shown below. Third, just as those suppressed arguments are recoverable for ABS-VOICE, so they are recoverable in NOM-VOICE. Fourth, just as the transitive is reduced to a single argument, as with other instances of VOICE, so the transitive is reduced with NOM-VOICE.

The difference between ABS-VOICE and NOM-VOICE is the difference between specificity (where relativization narrows the range of reference) and generality (where nominalization widens the referential range). Another difference, as implied by the two names, is the fact that relativization works within the context of the ABSOLUTIVE/ERGATIVE paradigm, whereas nominalization occurs within the context of the NOMINATIVE/ACCUSATIVE paradigm. It is precisely this paradigm that gives the impetus for the innovative split ergativity that characterizes the languages of the Yukatekan and Cholan subgroups.

The exact nature of NOM-VOICE may be described as follows. In the Mayan languages, given a primary and secondary predication, two *syntactic* phenomena are found. First, the primary predicate calls up an argument which is the nominative argument (subject) of the secondary, transitive predication. Second, the secondary predication is the object of a preposition. This kind of removal of the nominative argument from the secondary clause is here called NOMINATIVE VOICE in keeping with the already established paradigm, but is traditionally called *raising*.[1] The following are examples:

Awakatek:
na-ȼaˑn Waʔn taʔn čʔiˑw-aʔn
INC-CONT John PREP wait-NOMLZR
'John is waiting'

na-č-in-ȼaˑn taʔn a-mak-l-eʔn
INC-INC-ABS1SG-CONT PREP ERG2SG-touch-PASS-NOMLZR
'I am touching you'

---

[1]The term *raising* is used here for convenience, though it should be made clear that it is not here seen as some kind of mechanistic process implying a deep structure with ancillary rules, but rather as a semantic-analogical phenomenon, along the theoretical lines taken in this book.

Choltí:
xchic et tuilal misa [š-či-k-et t uy-il-al misa]
FUT-go-FUT-ABS2SG prep ERG3SG-see-PASS Mass
'you will see the Mass'

Tojolab'al:
wan-on way-el
PROG-ABS1SG sleep-NOMLZR
'I am sleeping'

wan-on s-mil-h-el
PROG-ABS1SG ERG3SG-kill-PASS-NOMLZR
'I am killing him'

Again, the diversity of the above examples leaves little doubt that this syntactic phenomenon goes back to Common Mayan times. The syntactic structure can be represented as shown in Figure 3.22 (intransitive) and Figure 3.23 (transitive).

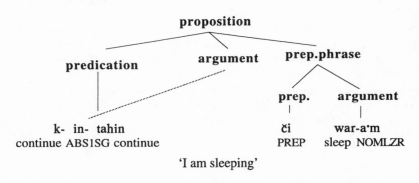

'I am sleeping'

Figure 3.22. Structure of an intransitive proposition in the PROGRESSIVE in Cunén K'iche'.

The relationships pointed out above between ABS-VOICE and NOM-VOICE are readily observable in the syntactic descriptions in Figures 3.26 and 3.27. Note the suppression of arguments where, in this case, the interdicted argument of the secondary predicate shows up as the argument called up by the primary predicate. Note also the conspicuous recoverability of the agent of the secondary predicate, which appears as the primary clause argument (1SG in the example from Figure 3.23). Furthermore, the interdiction of the active argument leaves the transitive verb with the single remaining passive argument; consequently, the transitive verb appears in its PASSIVE VOICE. However, in every case it is the *nominative* (subject of the transitive and intransitive) to which the interdiction applies. The secondary predicate is nominalized since it is the argument of a preposition.

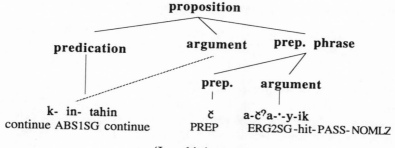

'I am hitting you'

Figure 3.23. Structure of a transitive proposition in the PROGRESSIVE in Cunén K'iche'.

This type of syntactic phenomenon was broadly used in the common language in constructions as varied as the following:

Awakatek:
ha-š-w-il ta?n wa·t-l
PROX.PAST-ABS2SG-ERG1SG-see PREP sleep-NOMLZR
'I saw you sleeping'

ha-š-w-il ta·n s-¢?i·b?-Ø-e?n
PROX.PAST-ABS2SG-ERG1SG-see PREP ERG3SG-write-PASS-NOMLZR
'I saw you writing it'

Ixil:
kat še?t-in ti a-q?os-p-e?
COMPL begin-ABS1SG PREP ERG2SG-hit-PASS-NOMLZR
'I began to hit you'

Tojolab'al:
a-kolt-ay-on y-ahna-h-el
ERG2SG-help-THEME-ABS1SG ERG3SG-cure-PASS-NOMLZR
'you helped me cure him'

The widespread use of NOM-VOICE in the common language as exemplified in the above instances was of great importance, but the prototypical use of NOM-VOICE was the PROGRESSIVE, which had an unrelenting influence on the INCOMPLETIVE.

The PROGRESSIVE aspect is common to all Mayan language subgroups and is therefore assumed to be part of the common language. For the PROGRESSIVE, the primary predication is often recruited from the class of positional verbs, usually having a meanings such as 'to continue,' 'to go on,' or 'to be long.' The Cunén K'iche' examples above amply illustrate the *syntactic* structure which is postulated to have existed in the common language:

intransitive: *primary.verb ABS preposition nominalized.verb

transitive: *primary.verb ABS preposition ERG
                                 +nominalized.passive.verb

There was an innovative change in this system with widely differing results. This change had effects that massively affected the entire grammar of the innovative languages, particularly the Lowland Languages. The change was the loss of raising. This meant, with respect to intransitive verbs, that the primary predicate no longer called up the argument of the secondary predication, but instead called up the entire argument such that the intransitive verb was nominalized and its argument became its possessor:

intransitive: *primary.verb ABS preposition nominalized.verb

The example from Chuj in Figure 3.24 illustrates this.

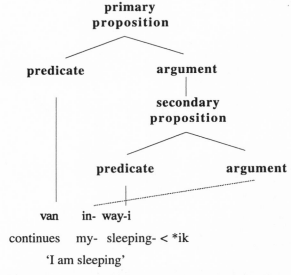

'I am sleeping'

Figure 3.24. Structure of an intransitive proposition in the PROGRESSIVE in Chuj.

Note that both the examples from innovative Chuj and those from conservative Cunén K'iche' conform perfectly to Mayan syntax. The Chuj form, 'continues my sleeping,' is syntactically analogous to a core intransitive sentence of the type 'sleeps my dog,' in the sense that there is a simple predicate with its associated argument. Similarly, the K'iche' form is analogous to the more complex structural type which includes a prepositional phrase, such as 'went I to town,' where there is a predicate with a concomitant argument, and an additional prepositional phrase with its associated argument. Cunén K'iche' preserves the structure that is here postulated to have existed in the common language:

> **k-in-tihn či wr-a·m**
> INC-ABS1SG-continue PREP sleep-NOMLZR
> 'I am sleeping'

Even though the Chuj and K'iche' syntactic structures for the PROGRESSIVE are referentially equivalent—a bilingual speaker of Chuj and K'iche' would hold them so—there is nevertheless an immense consequence for the language that innovates with the Chuj-like structure. The consequence of such a change has to do with *the difficulty of nominalizing any transitive proposition.*

The difficulty emerges from the particular instantiation of a linguistic universal, which is that an argument may be added to a possessive nominal construction, but the addition is always *dyadic.* That is, an argument must consist of a single substantive, as in *John eats,* or a dyadic possessed substantive, as in *John's dog eats,* or even a whole chain of dyadic possession, as in *John's dog's flea's mite eats,* as shown in Figure 3.25[1]

John's dog's flea's mite

Figure 3.25. Structure of binary argument for the possessive.

Possession, therefore, is always built up in terms of the dyadic structure defined above. When an intransitive proposition with its associated argument requires nominalization, it is a simple process because there are two entities—the verb and its argument. When it is nominalized, the verb becomes the nominal, and its argument becomes its possessor, as seen in the above example from Chuj. In fact an English-derived dyad such as *the sleep of John* is perfectly equivalent syntactically to any binary genitive construction, such as *the dog of John.*

---

[1]In Peirce's terms, such a chain has the structure "Secondness of Thirdness" (5.70–5.72).

But a problem arises when the three terms of a transitive proposition—(a) the transitive verb, (b) its active argument, and (c) its passive argument—are analogically scheduled to occupy a slot held by an argument. Unlike the system found in Common Mayan, the three terms simply do not fit into the dyadic order of possession described above.

Several languages have deviated from the Common Mayan system of reduction and raising, including the Q'anjob'alan group, Mam, and Yukatekan. Each innovated in its own particular way, accommodating the impossible three-termed transitive construction in the dyadic slot. This predicament was resolved in the case of Chuj, Q'anjob'al, Akatek, and Jakaltek by recruiting the other marker of dependent clauses—the relative marker, *-Vn*—and extending it to include this kind of dependent clause, as shown in Figure 3.26.

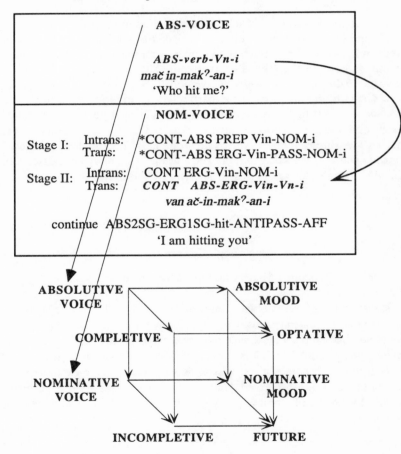

Figure 3.26. Replacement of NOM-VOICE by ABS-VOICE.

This is an excellent example of influence, where the unmarked ABS-VOICE effected change in the more-marked NOM-VOICE. What happened in the Q'an-job'alan languages provides an excellent scenario for explaining what happened to Yukatek Maya, but on a much more far-reaching scale, as explained on page 206.

Mam, another language which lost raising, innovated quite differently. It extended the ERGATIVE marker of the single argument of intransitive verbs (whose original raison d'être was the marker of nominalization), to include the passive argument of the transitive verb. Two examples follow:

> ilti²x tu²n t-ta·n
> necessary PREP ERG3SG-sleep
> 'it is necessary that he sleep'

> ilti²x tu²n t-ok-n-by-o²n-e
> necessary PREP ERG3SG-ABS.DV-ERG1SG-hit-suff-ERG1SG
> 'it is necessary that I hit him'

The loss of raising in Mam is the impetus for the unique pronominal distribution described above.

The Category ABS-MOOD

Up to this point the discussion has included the COMPLETIVE, INCOMPLETIVE, OPTATIVE, FUTURE, ABS-VOICE, and NOM-VOICE. The final two categories are ABS-MOOD and NOM-MOOD, as shown in Figure 3.27.

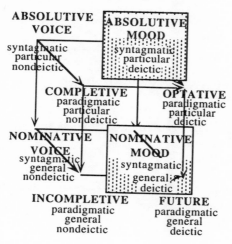

Figure 3.27. Paradigmatic diagram emphasizing ABS-MOOD and NOM-MOOD.

Like the OPTATIVE and FUTURE, both ABS-DV and NOM-DV are deictic—subject to involvement in the speech act, as shown on page 86. And, like ABS-VOICE and NOM-VOICE, these two modal categories each involve the syntactic inclusion of two predicates. The two predicates of the categories of ABS-MOOD are, first, a secondary directional verb, with a meaning such as 'come,' 'go,' 'ascend,' 'descend,' 'enter,' 'exit,' 'cross,' 'stay,' and so forth, and second, a primary, main verb. Examples are as follows, with the secondary verb italicized:

Tzotzil:[1]
i-ʔoč *kom*-el COMP-enter *remain*-NOMLZR
'he entered (and stayed)'

la-s-kuč mu-el *bʔat*-el COMP-ERG3SG-carry.up-AFF *go*-NOMLZR
'he carried it up (going)'

Tojolab'al:
bʔahti-ta-ʔ*oč*-e jump-just-*enter*-NOMLZR
'he just jumped in'

h-ȼaʔ-a-*oč* ton ERG1SG-throw-THEME-*enter* rock
'I threw the rock in'

Chuj:
iš-*kʔe*-čen-nah-ok PROX.PAST-*ascend*-jump-SAPO
'he just jumped in'

iš-in-huˑl-*uč* kʔen PROX.PAST-ERG1SG-throw-*enter* rock
'I threw the rock in'

Q'anjob'al:
(ma)š-ʔ*el*-bʔi-nah-oq COMP-*exit*-stretch-AFF-SAPO
'he stretched (out)'

š-in-maqʔ-*ok*-to-q COMP-ERG1SG-hit-*enter*-go-SAPO
'I nailed it (going) in'

Awakatek:
ha-n-*oʔk*-ȼa-*ȼʔ*it-pu PROX.PAST-ABS1SG-*enter*-*come*-jump-AFF
'I jumped (coming) in'

---

[1]See Robertson (1980:45 ff.)

ha-*ʔok*-in-kʔoʔš-i-ˑl PROX.PAST-*enter*-ERG1SG-throw-THEME-AFF
'I threw it in'

Ixil:
yuh-p-ikʔ-*ok*-in jump-AFF-AFF-*enter*-ABS1SG
'I jumped in'

kat un-suti-*heʔ* COMP ERG1SG-throw-*ascend*
'I threw it up'

K'iche':
š-in-xililobʔ-*kan*-oq COMP-ABS1SG-slip-*remain*-SAPO
'I kept slipping'

š-in-qʔam-*apon*-oq COMP-ERG1SG-move-*arrive.there*-SAPO
'I got it over there'

The comprehensive distribution of the above data requires its postulation in Common Mayan. In all the instances given above, regardless of whether the verb is transitive or intransitive, the directional verb modifies the *absolutive* argument—the argument called up by the intransitive verb, or the passive argument of the transitive verb. Because of this modificational focus on the ABSOLUTIVE, I will call it the ABSOLUTIVE DIRECTIONAL VERB, or the ABS-DV.

Interestingly, the Mayan ABS-DV is semantically very close to the English particles, such as *in, out, up, down,* and so on, in their uncanny resemblance to each other, at least in their modificational capacity. They both modify the absolutive arguments of transitive and intransitive verbs. Consider, for example, *I fell down,* and *he pushed me down.* In both instances, it is the *absolutive* argument that is modified—FIRST PERSON *I,* as the intransitive argument, *am down* in the first sentence, and FIRST PERSON *I (me),* as the transitive passive argument, *am again down* in the second sentence. My investigations have shown that the particles in English, like the ABS-DV in Mayan, always modify the absolutive argument. In explaining the ABS-DV I earlier said that

> ...the ABS-DV appears with those verbs which imply movement of the absolutive noun. Verbs such as *jump, swim, hop, crawl, roll* are good examples of intransitive verbs with which the ABS-DV is likely to co-occur, while *throw, send, bring, take, push* exemplify transitive verbs with which the ABS-DV's commonly appear. The semantic content of both sets of verbs implies motion (physical displacement) of the absolutive noun (subject of the intransitive/object of the transitive). This implied movement is given greater precision by the

ABS-DV, which assigns a specific directional type to the absolutive noun (Robertson 1980:47).

It will be noted that in much of the above ABS-DV data, what is attached is a reflex of Common Mayan *-oq*—the same morpheme that marks the Common Mayan OPTATIVE. At first glance it might seem curious that a marker for MOOD would also appear with this particular construction, the ABS-DV. A superficial analysis might lead one to the simple-minded conclusion that mood and verbs are entirely different from each other and that the reflex of Common Mayan *-oq* appearing in both contexts is really not the same marker, but two distinct homonyms.

The fact that such postulation of homonymy never really explains anything, but on the contrary blocks the road to inquiry, requires its abandonment in favor of a theory that can reasonably explain why *-oq* is used to mark both the OPTATIVE and the ABS-DV. Simply put, the theory is that the Interpretant instructs the interpreter to take the participants of the speech act into account. In other words, both the OPTATIVE and the ABS-DV are indexical.

Consider, for example, the difference between *Heaven help him!* and *Heaven helps him!* The first, which is an instance of the so-called subjunctive MOOD, requires an interpretation that takes the speaker's mood or feeling into account. The second, a declarative, is to be interpreted as a flat statement of fact, totally independent of the speaker's mood or feelings. In Mayan, for example, the interpretation of the K'iche' OPTATIVE *či-war-oq* 'May he sleep!' takes the speaker's mood or feelings into account, whereas the sentence *ka-war-ik* 'He sleeps' is a flat, declarative statement of fact without regard to the speaker.

If MOOD instructs the interpreter to take the speaker's point of view into account, directional verbs similarly require an interpretation that includes the speaker's point of view. Consider the following Q'anjob'al sentences,

(ma-)š-in-ʔah-tʔuq-nah-oq
COMPL-ABS1SG-ascend-jump-AFF-SAPO
'I jumped up'

(ma-)š-in-ay-woq-an-oq
COMPL-ABS1SG-descend-sit-AFF-SAPO
'I sat down'

š-in-maqʔ-ok-to-q
COMPL-ABS1SG-hit-enter-go-SAPO
'I nailed it in'

š-w-ok-il-te-q
COMPL-ABS1SG-take-exit-come-SAPO
'I took it out'

The third sentence, for example, includes the verbs of motion *ok* 'enter' and *to* 'go,' meaning 'I nailed it in (to the wall),' where the nail *goes* into the wall, thus taking the point of view of the speaker into account. (If the speaker were somehow *in* the wall, then the verb *te* 'come' would be used.) This sentence can be contrasted with the fourth sentence, 'I took it out of (the wall),' which contains the verbs of motion *el* 'go/come off/out of' and *te* 'come.' In this instance, since the passive argument is coming toward the speaker, the verb *te,* which modifies the *coming* object, must be used. Both are instances of indices, since the point of view of the speaker must be considered. If a disembodied voice, coming from all directions, instructed an interpreter to *come here,* obedience would be impossible, since part of the actual meaning of *come* and *here* is 'location of speaker.'

Hence, putting aside the homonymic theory of *-oq* in favor of the deictic theory presented above, we learn that in the attested languages, reflexes of the Common Mayan modal *-oq* are used to signal both MOOD and directionals, because both are highly deictic, requiring that the here-and-now of the speaker be taken into interpretational account. It is for this reason that the category under discussion is called ABS-MOOD.

Finally, it is crucial to note here for later consideration that the relationship between the primary and secondary verbs is morphological. It is not a syntactic relationship, since the secondary directional verb is a simple affix in the verbal complex.

The Category Nom-Mood

Just as Common Mayan had a category for the ABS-DV, there is a related category that I have termed NOMINATIVE DIRECTIONAL VERB (NOM-DV), where the directional verb modifies the nominative noun—the subject of the transitive as well as the intransitive—defined here as the argument of the intransitive, and the active argument of the transitive. This is again a wide-spread phenomenon in the Mayan languages, making it logically prudent to presume its existence in Common Mayan antiquity. Instances are given below:

Tzotzil:[1]
xul ak?-b?-at-uk-un
arrive.here give-IND.OBJ-PASS-OPT-ABS1SG
'I *arrived (here)* to be given it.'

la pas-o
come do-OPT

---

[1]These Tzotzil data are from Cowan (1969).

'*come* do it'

Tojolab'al:
wah way-k-on
go sleep-OPT-ABS1SG
'I *went* (in order to) sleep'

wah h-mak^ʔ-e^ʔ
go ERG1SG-hit-DAPO
'I *went* (in order to) hit him'

Chuj:
iš-*kan*-viŋ vay-aŋ
PROX.PAST-*remain*-MALE sleep-IMPER
'he *kept on* sleeping'

iš-*kan*-viŋ in-s-mak^ʔ-a^ʔ
PROX.PAST-*remain*-MALE ABS1SG-ERG3SG-hit-DAPO
'he *kept on* hitting me'

Q'anjob'al:
š-in-*ul*-way-oq
COMP-ABS1SG-*arrive.here*-sleep-SAPO
'I *came here* to sleep'

š-ač-*ʔul*-in-maq^ʔ-a^ʔ
COMP-ERG2SG-*arrive.here*-ERG1SG-hit-DAPO
'I *came here* to hit you'

Ixil:
kat *ʔul*-in-wat-oh
COMP *arrive.here*-ABS1SG-sleep-SAPO
'I *came here* (in order) sleep'

kat *ʔul* un-q^ʔos-aš
COMP *arrive.here* ERG1SG-hit-ABS2SG
'I *came here* to hit you'

K'iche':
š-in-*el*-war-oq
COMPL-ABS1SG-*enter*-sleep-SAPO
'I *came* (in order to) sleep'

š- *ul*-ox-č̓ay-aʔ
COMPL-*come*-ERG1PL-hit-DAPO
'We *came* to hit him'

In every instance of the above examples, the directional verb modifies the subject of both the intransitive and the transitive. And , like the ABS-DV, the NOM-DV also uses the directional verbs which are deictic, and as a consequence the verbs are in the optative mood— *-oq* if the subject of an intransitive is used, and *-Aʔ* if the subject of a transitive is used. The difference is that with the ABS-DV, the ABSOLUTIVE is modified, and so only the reflex of *-oq* is used, whereas with the NOM-DV, the subjects of both transitives and intransitives are modified, as shown in Figure 3.28.

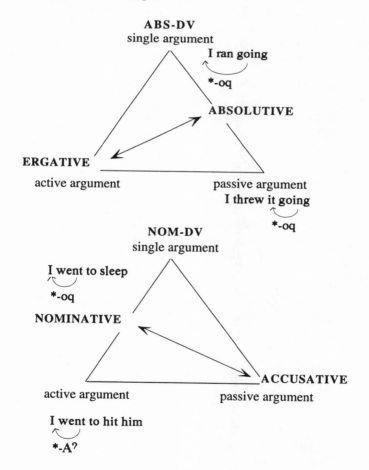

Figure 3.28. The distribution of *-oq* and *-Aʔ* in Common Mayan.

Finally, note again that, as with the ABS-DV, the tendency is for the NOM-DV to become a morphological part of the verbal complex, with the difference that the NOM-DV tends to take on the character of an auxiliary. In some languages, like K'iche' or Kaqchikel, however, it is a strictly morphological incorporation into the verbal complex.

The Relationship between NOM-VOICE and NOM-MOOD

NOM-VOICE and NOM-MOOD, as shown in the above discussion, stand in a markedness relationship, and therefore NOM-VOICE, which is unmarked, has a more comprehensive range of reference, since it includes many other kinds of syntactic structures including directionals. NOM-MOOD is more marked in that it includes only directionals. For example, the Tojolab'al NOM-VOICE and NOM-MOOD are equivalent. Note, however, that unlike Cunén K'iche', there is no preposition between the main and the dependent verb:

Tojolab'al:
NOM-MOOD: **oč-way-k-on**
enter-sleep-SAPO < *oq-ABS1SG
'I began to sleep'

NOM-VOICE: **oč-on way-el**
enter-ABS1SG sleep-AFF
'I began to sleep'

A comparison of Tojolab'al, Cunén K'iche', and Q'anjob'al reveals this phenomenon to be present in languages that are so distantly related as to leave little doubt that both these forms existed in the common language.

Cunén K'iche':
NOM-MOOD: **š-k²u·n-wr-aq**
COMP-arrive.here-sleep-SAPO
'he came to sleep'

š-k²u·n-u-b²n-a²
COMP-arrive.here-ERG3SG-do-DAPO
'he came to do it'

NOM-VOICE: **š-k²u·n či war-a·m**
COMP-arrive.here PREP sleep-NOMLZR
'he came to sleep'

š-k²u·n č-u-b²a-·-n-i·k

COMP-arrive.here PREP-ERG3SG-do-PASS-do-SAPD
'he came to do it'
Q'anjob'al:
NOM-MOOD: **ṣ-ač-ʔul-in-maqʔ-aʔ**
    COMP-ABS2SG-arrive.here-ABS1SG-hit-dapo
    'I arrived here to hit you'

NOM-VOICE: **maṣ-hay in-s-maqʔ-on-i**
    COMP-come ABS1SG-ERG3SG-hit-DEPEND.CLAUSE-AFF
    'he arrived here to hit me'

Although in the Choltí grammar I could not find evidence for the phenomenon NOM-DV, there are many instances of nominalization:
Choltí:
    ṣ-či-k-et t uy-il-al misa
    FUT-go-FUT-ABS2SG PREP ERG3SG-see-PASS Mass
    'you arrive to see Mass'

All these data taken together make it entirely reasonable that these two forms are of Common Mayan antiquity.

Another Kind of Nominalization

Another kind of nominalization existed in the common language that significantly influenced some of the categories just discussed. The forms were *-V·y* (polysyllabic transitives) *-V·l*. Their original function was a complement to directional verbs, as can be seen in its Colonial K'iche' reflexes (Martínez n.d.):

> Los participios de presente como *amans* se forman en los verbos activos acabado in *h:* en *i* vg. de *loƐoh: loƐoi.* Ussase del con los pronombres posesivos: Uech: auech: rech &a. *in loƐoi auech* 'yo te amo.' A los monosilabas añadeseles una *l* y asi hacen sus participios vg *colo* salvar *colol uech* 'mi salvador.'

> [The present participles like *amans* are formed in transitive verbs ending in -*h*, using -*y*, as from *loqʔo-h: loqʔo-y.* Possessive pronouns are used: *w-ech, aw-eč, r-eč* etc. *in loqʔo-y aw-eč* 'I love you.' With monosyllabic verbs an *l* is suffixed, thereby forming the participial: *colo* 'to save,' *col-o-l w-eč* 'my savior.'[1]]

---

[1]This also means 'he saves me.'

Notice that these nominalizations have manifestations of VOICE as well.
"active": *in loɛoi auech* [in loqʔ-o-y aw-eˑč]
ABS1SG love-THEME-NOMLZR ERG2SG-PREP
'yo te amo' [I love you]

"antipassive": *loɛonel* [loqʔ-o-ˑn-el]
love-theme-ANTIPASS-NOMLZR
'él que ama' [he who loves]
"passive": *loɛoxel* [loqʔ-o-ˑš-el]
love-THEME-PASS-NOMLZR '
él que está amado' [he who is loved]

Notice here that this overlaps with the category NOM-VOICE/NOM-MOOD:

K'iche' (Anleo n.d.):
NOM-VOICE
xbe chutihoxic [š-bʔe č-u-tixo-š-ik][1]
COMP-go PREP-ERG3SG-teach-PASS-SAPD
'he went to teach it'

xbetihonok [š-bʔe-tixo-ˑn-αɋ]
COMP-ABS3SG-go-teach-ANTIPASS-SAPO
'he went in order to teach'

xbetihonel [š-bʔe-tixo-ˑn-*el*]
COMP-ABS3SG-go-teach-ANTIPASS-*NOMLZR*
'he went in order to teach'

It is also important to point out that the Lowland Languages, including Tzeltalan, Huastec, Cholan, and Yukatekan, innovated by using -*Vˑl* as the marker for NOM-VOICE:

K'iche': k-in-taˑxin či wr-aˑm
Kaqchikel: ni-taxin či war-an
Poqomchi: či-k-in či wir-ik
Awakatek: na-ȼaˑn Waʔn t-aʔn čʔiˑw-aʔn
Chuj: van in-vay-i
Tojolab'al: van-on vay-el
Tzeltal: yak-on ta weʔ-el

---

[1]I made this form up, based on similar examples from Colonial K'iche'. This is a transitive use, since I'm not sure what the intransitive (ANTIPASSIVE) would be.

Choltí: yual in-wen-el[1]
Huastec: ešom t-in čem-el
Yukatek: táan in-wen-el

With the exception of Huastec, all of the intransitive forms above take either the conservative, raised form, *main.verb* + ABSPREP INTRANS-NOMLZR or the innovative, nonraised form *main.verb* ERGINTRANS-NOMLZR (see page 77). Huastec takes the innovative, nonraised form *main.verb* PREP ABS-INTRANS-NOMLZR. It is noteworthy, however, that the Lowland Languages all have *-el* to mark the CONTINUATIVE. This corresponds nicely with other linguistic and cultural facts. The Lowland Languages have reconstructed forms for siblings-in-law distinct from the forms for the Mamo-K'iche'an languages: the lowland forms were **bal* 'male speaker to male hearer,' **mu?* 'male to female and female to male,' and *hawan* 'female to male'; the Mamo-K'iche'an forms were *baluq* 'male to male,' **et^yam* 'male to female,' **išnam* 'female to male,' and **alib?* 'female to female.'[2] Furthermore, the term for 8,000 for the Lowland Languages was **pik* and for Mamo-K'iche'an was **chuy*; for 200 was **laxuŋwinaq* for the Lowland Languages, but **o-tuk* for Mamo-K'iche'an.[3] It is quite clear that the nominalized form, *-el*, was a shared, lowland innovation, the etymology of which comes from the Common Mayan **-V·l*.

The Relationship between NOM-VOICE (Progressive) and the INCOMPLETIVE

An important fact of Mayan grammar is that the PROGRESSIVE is strongly affected by the INCOMPLETIVE. As will be seen in the discussion of the several languages below, it is very common for the syntax which constitutes the structure of the PROGRESSIVE to become a morphological part of the INCOMPLETIVE aspect. This typically happens in one of several ways. In Modern Tzeltal, for example, the independent predication of the PROGRESSIVE *yak* simply augments the INCOMPLETIVE. Here, the line between syntax and morphology is thin indeed. Notice that the *k* is lost from *yak* in the tighter morphological setting.

PROGRESSIVE
yak-on ta we?-el

---

[1]This means 'I am doing it,' or 'I do it.' There is also a form for transitives, which is *jual en ti caz te* 'aora corta este palo.'

[2]Note that Q'anjob'alan has *baš* (Akatek) or *baluč* (Chuj). Here and in other regards, Q'anjob'alan is separate from both the highland and lowland languages.

[3]For a complete discussion of these highly significant cultural and linguistic distinctions, see Robertson (1984c). Huastec was a decimal system.

PRED-ABS1SG PREP eat-NOMLZR
'I am eating'

INCOMPLETIVE
ya-š-tal-on
< yak-INC-come-ABS1SG
'I come'

Besides augmentation, it sometimes happens that the PROGRESSIVE simply displaces the INCOMPLETIVE, as, for example, in Huastec (p. 212), Cholan (p. 145), and Yukatekan (p. 202). In Choltí (Morán 1695), for instance, the old INCOMPLETIVE, *š*- (from Common Mayan INCOMPLETIVE **ki*-), was displaced to the FUTURE by the PROGRESSIVE *wal* as in, for example, *yual inpaɛxiel* [wal in-pakš-i-el] PROG ERG1-come.back-AFF-NOMLZR 'I come back,' and *yual inɛubu* [wal in-kub-u] PROG ERG1-believe-DAPD 'I believe it.'[1] Notice that the *subjects* of both the intransitive and transitive sentences are marked by the same ERGATIVE pronouns, and this is an innovation in the INCOMPLETIVE. The source of this newly derived nominative/accusative typology is the subject/object opposition which includes the categories NOM-DV and NOMINALIZATION (discussed on p. 107).

The discussion of the relationship between the PROGRESSIVE and the IN-COMPLETIVE leads to a more general observation regarding the relationship between NOM-VOICE and the INCOMPLETIVE aspect. First, the process of nominalization extends far beyond the PROGRESSIVE as described above. In many cases the verb which acts as the main verb qualifies the verbal action of the dependent verb. For instance, it is common in Mayan to use reflexes of the Common Mayan term **ok* 'to enter' to give an inceptive meaning 'to begin.'

oč-on way-el
enter-ABS1SG sleep-NOMLZR
'I began to sleep' (Tojolab'al)

š-n-ok č-u-ȼʔiba-š-íˑk
COMP-ABS1SG-enter PREP-ERG3SG-write-PASS-SAPD
'I began to write it' (Cunén K'iche')

kat ṣeʔt-in t-i v-oqʔ-eʔ
COMP begin-ABS1SG ERG3SG-PREP ERG1SG-cry-AFF
'I began to cry' (Ixil)

---

[1]For a more complete discussion of the relationship between the PROGRESSIVE and split-ergative, see the discussion below of poqomchi' and of Choltí.

kat §e²t-in t-i oq²-el
COMP begin-ABS1SG ERG3SG-PREP cry-NOMLZR
'I began to cry' (Ixil)[1]

Another common main verb which has an aspectual value comes from the verb *lah, 'to finish,' as also with other verbs with a similar meaning:

§-lah-w-i in-way-i
COMP finish-ANTIPASS-SAPD ERG1SG-sleep-AFF
'I finished sleeping' (Q'anjob'al)

§-lah-w-i in-s-maq²-on-i
COMP-finish-ANTIPASS-SAPD ABS1SG-ERG3SG-hit-DEPEND.CLAUSE-AFF
'he finished hitting me' (Q'anjob'al)

š-in-totax či nu-wa·²-im
COMP-ABS1SG-finish PREP ERG1SG-eat-NOMLZR
'I finished eating' (Totonicapan K'iche')

š-in-totax č-u-ȼ²ib²a-š-ik
COMP-ABS1SG-finish PREP ERG3SG-write-PASS-SAPD
'I finished writing it' (Totonicapan K'iche')

The point is that although these are syntactic instances of the ways two verbs are combined, they are also semantic instances of descriptions of verbal action—verbal action that continues, that begins, that ends, and so forth—for syntax is a kind of semantics. Such aspectual considerations come to play an especially important role in Yukatekan grammar, both diachronically and synchronically. As was shown (p. 33), and as has often happened, these formerly syntactic constructions move toward morphological integration.

The Influence of Nom-Mood on the Future

On page 69 it was shown that the FUTURE has been influenced by the INCOMPLETIVE and the OPTATIVE as well as by the directional verb *go*, not only in Mayan, but generally in the history of the languages of the world. The reason for this influence in Mayan becomes clearer in consideration of the structure of the Common Mayan TAMV, as shown in Figure 3.29.

---

[1]Note that in one case there is no deletion (the ERG1SG pronoun is on the dependent verb 'cry'), and in the other case the subject is absent, and there is subsequent nominalization.

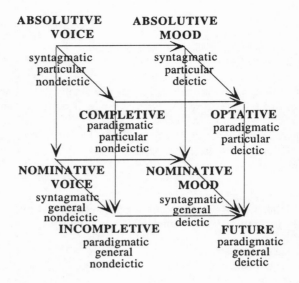

Figure 3.29. Summary of TAMV in the common language.

The FUTURE is the structural culmination of the OPTATIVE, NOMINATIVE MOOD, and the INCOMPLETIVE ASPECT. It should not be surprising to see, therefore, what will be shown throughout the rest of this book: each of the three constitutive categories generally influences the Common Mayan FUTURE.

Chapter 4. Mamean

Mam

The previous chapters have given (a) certain principles by which language change might occur, and (b) the reconstruction of the Common Mayan TAMV from which those principles can predict deductive results. It remains now to compare inductively the results of those potentially occurring results with the actual facts of the attested languages, both Colonial and modern. This and the remaining chapters are written to that end.

The most interesting characteristic of Mam in the comparative process is its propensity to complicate the antecedent system of the common language both phonologically and morphologically.[1] The differences between the phonological systems of Common Mayan and modern Mam have already been outlined (see Campbell 1977), and it turns out that the modern system is significantly more complex than the common language. The reasons for such complication remain obscure, but at least the facts are known. On the other hand, there has been no such systematic outlining of the morphological differences between the common language and attested Mam, and thus the historical explanation has only begun.[2] The appreciation of such developmental elaborations requires first an outline of such complications from the earlier system, and then their explanation.

First, modern Mam distinguishes between dependent and independent clauses in the COMPLETIVE, whereas only one form of the COMPLETIVE existed in its antecedent system:

pre-Mam:
*winaq iš-wataˀn nu-xah iš-waˑˀn w-uˑkˀil
man *PROX. PAST*-sleep ERG1SG-house *PROX. PAST*-eat ERG1SG-with
'the man who slept in my house ate with me'

Mam:
xu ši·naq š-ta·n n-xay-e *ma*-waˑˀn w-uˑkˀil-e
the man *PROX. PAST*-sleep ERG1SG-house-ERG1SG *PROX. PAST*-eat ERG1SG-

---

[1]Nora England (1983:4), for example, said that "Mam has the (undeserved) reputation of being the most difficult of all the Mayan languages." With respect to the shift, even from Common Mamo-K'iche'an, the representation seems accurate.

[2]See Robertson (1975, 1980) for some references.

with-ERG1SG
'the man who slept in my house ate with me'

In Mam, in the PROXIMATE PAST, *ma*- marks independent clauses and *ş*-marks dependent clauses; in pre-Mam **iš*- marked both dependent and independent clauses. How this happened will be explained below.

Another complication is the augmentation of the INCOMPLETIVE from NOM-VOICE which had the effect of causing a change from the simpler Common Mayan ABSOLUTIVE pronouns, which were **Ø* '3SG,' **at* '2SG,' **in* '1SG,' **eb²* '3PL,' **eš* '2PL,' **o²ŋ* '1PL.' These changed to the more complicated, modern Mam pronouns, **Ø* '3SG,' **Ø...e* '2SG,' **čin/in...e* '1SG,' **či/e* '2PL,' **o/qo* '1INCLUSIVE,' **o/qo...e* '1EXCLUSIVE.' Furthermore, in Common Mayan the morpheme for the INCOMPLETIVE was **k(i)-*, in contrast to Mam's *n-* < *ȼun-/ȼin-*.

A third complication is related to the discussion of directional verbs on page 115. In the common language, the ABS-DV's were used only with verbs that implied some motion of the object, such as *throw, push,* and the like. However, in the modern language the use of directionals extends to virtually all transitives:[1]

ma·²-ku²-ş-n-mq-u-²n-e t-pwa·q
COMP-descend-go-ABS1SG-bury-THEME-Vt-AFF ERG3SG-money
'I buried his money'

This change was highly significant in complicating the grammar, since it changed the whole face of the language. By peeling off this outer layer, however, the original system became more obvious, as will be shown below. Further related to the change in the directionals is the fact that the morpheme signaling deictic modification of the ABSOLUTIVE, **-oq*, has universally been lost or replaced.[2]

Many of the above-mentioned changes are summarized in Figures 4.1 and 4.2.

COMPLETIVE

As already noted in the above discussion and schema, the COMPLETIVE and

---

[1] The only exceptions are verbs such as *receive, hear, accept, buy, gather in,* and *grab*, where motion toward the speaker is implied.

[2] Another change occurred in the pronoun system both when the original second person markers (ERG *a*- and ABS *a t*) were replaced by a third-person marker and a suffix (today, *t...e* and *Ø...e*); also, the distinction between the inclusive and exclusive first-person plural pronouns emerged. Although the explanation for these changes will not be given here because they are out of the purview of this work, the explanations can be found in Robertson (1980:69ff; 1987a).

PROXIMATE PAST originally had one form apiece (**Ø-* and **iš-*) in the common language, but Mam complicated the system by developing two additional forms (*o-* and **ma·ʔ-*), totaling four. Two of the forms (**iš-* > *š, *Ø-* > *Ø-*), which today occur in dependent clauses, are direct reflexes of the common language, while the remaining two are innovations taken from temporal adverbs (**miy/*may* > *ma*) 'past time of today,' and (**ox* > *o*) 'past time before today,' which occur in independent clauses.

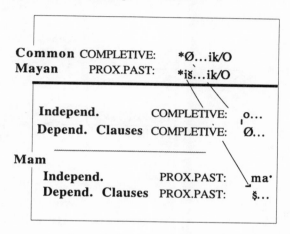

Figure 4.1. Summary of changes in Mam for the COMPLETIVE and the PROXIMATE PAST.

An explanation of this modern state of affairs in Mam appeals to the earlier discussed principle of *displacement,* where a newly introduced sign will result in a division of the unmarked category of the grammatical system into two categories, one unmarked and the other marked. In this system, the newly introduced sign occupies the least marked category, and the old, original sign occupies the more-marked category, as explained on page 41. In this specific case, the introduction of the innovative signs *o-* and *ma-* resulted in a division of the unmarked category (COMPLETIVE) into two categories, where the new signs came to occupy the newly formed unmarked categories (independent clauses), and the original signs, *Ø-* and *š-,* came to occupy the newly formed marked categories (dependent clauses).[1]

The innovative morphemes *o-* and *ma(·ʔ)-* have their origin in the Common

---

[1]For a more thorough discussion of this phenomenon, see Robertson (1975). Nora England (1983:161 ff.) reports that the same relationship exists between *o-* and *Ø-* as exists between *ma-* and *š -*. The *o-/Ø-* relationship was not reported in my original paper.

Mayan forms *oŋ- (DISTANT PAST), and *mVy- (PROXIMATE PAST), as evidenced by Choltí *on-i,* Mam *ox-či?,* and K'iche' *ox-er,* all of which mean DISTANT PAST and all of which are reconstructible to *oŋ.[1] Furthermore, *mayal* (Q'anjob'al), *mayk^y?* (Mam), and *miy-er* (K'iche'an) mean PROXIMATE PAST. Apparently, the innovative aspectual inflection for PROXIMATE PAST *ma* has its proximate origin in the morpheme *mayk^y?* (originally from *ma-), and its distant origin in the morpheme *o* in the morpheme *oxči?* (originally from *oŋ).

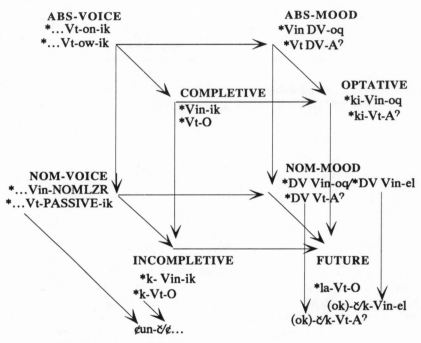

Figure 4.2. Summary of change in TAMV for Mam.

This hypothesis is the more reasonable because prefixed adverbials of time require the unmarked pronominal set, with no tense/aspect markers, whereas suffixed adverbs result in normal aspectual marking:

in-ta-ˑn-e eˑw
ABS1SG-sleep-SUFF-ABS1SG yesterday
'I slept yesterday'
eˑw čin-ta-ˑn-e

---

[1]The reflex of Common Mayan *ŋ is *n* in Cholan, and *x* in K'iche'an.

yesterday ABS1SG-sleep-AFF-ABS1SG
'I slept yesterday'

čin-ta-ˀl-e nčiˀx
ABS1SG-sleep-FUT-ABS1SG tomorrow
'I will sleep tomorrow'

nčiˀx čin-ta-ˀn-e
tomorrow ABS1SG-sleep-SUFF-ABS1SG
'I will sleep tomorrow'

Notice that the unmarked ABS1SG pronoun (see page 176 below), *čin-*, is used when the temporal adverbs *nčiˀx* and *eˑw* are prefixed, and that no other distinction between the two sentences exists (even the *aˑl* marker of the future is lost); the entire aspectual difference is carried by the temporal adverbs themselves. This then permits an analogical projection backwards in time, where *maˑkyˀ* was preposed sententially, thus:

*maˑkyˀ čin-ta-aˑn-e
today ABS1SG-sleep-SUFF-ABS1SG
'I just slept'

There came an oppositional relationship with the aspectual marker *ṣ-*, resulting in the displacement described earlier. Figure 4.3 summarizes the displacement.

Pre-Mam

ABS3SG	ABS2SG	ABS1SG	ABS1SG
Ø	Ø…e	in…e	in…e
ABS3PL	ABS2PL	ABS1EX	ABS1N
i	i…e	qo…e	qo

Mam

unmarked	Ø	Ø…e	čin…e	čin…e
marked	Ø	Ø	in…e	in…e
unmarked	i	či…e	qo…e	qo
marked	i	i…e	o…e	o

Figure 4.3. Summary of changes in Mam for the INCOMPLETIVE and the PROGRESSIVE.

Influence of the PROGRESSIVE on the INCOMPLETIVE

The second innovation noted above involves two related but different changes: *augmentation by influence* and *displacement*. First, the Common Mayan INCOMPLETIVE, **k(i)-,* was augmented by what was apparently the independent verb of the PROGRESSIVE (NOM-VOICE), *¢un-/¢in-,* reduced to *n-* in many modern Mam dialects. It is quite likely that the etymology of this form is found in the PROGRESSIVE of Awakatek *¢a·n.*[1] Many such instances of augmentation by the PROGRESSIVE can be found, as described on page 203, for example. In Mam of San Ildefonso Ixtahuacan, a full form does exist (though rarely used) alongside the reduced form:

> (¢i)n-qo-ʔoqʔ-e t-iʔx > n-qo-ʔoqʔ-e t-iʔx
> INC-ABS1PL-cry-ABS1EXC ERG3SG-about
> 'we cry about him'

Furthermore, in the Ixchiguan dialect of Mam, there is apparently not even a reduced form:

> ¢un-Ø-ta-·n t-e Juan
> INC-ABS3SG-sleep-AFF ERG3SG-PREP Juan
> 'Juan is crying/cries'

This, then, is another instance of the PROGRESSIVE influencing the INCOMPLETIVE, which is almost *de rigueur* in the Mayan languages.

The effects of this augmentation by influence were far-reaching. In the pre-Mam II stage shown in the figure below, the **k(i)-* before front vowels was palatalized, according to a general phonological process that took place in Mam, as in, for example, **ke·x > če·x* 'deer/horse' and **kikʔ > čikʔ* 'blood.' Then, sometime before modern times, Mam had reanalyzed the morphemes, forcing the former marker of the INCOMPLETIVE, *č-/q-,* to become the first sound of the contiguous following pronoun:[2]

Common:

*ki-Verb	**k-e-Verb*	3SG	3PL

---

[1] It should be noted that in Colonial times (Reynoso 1644), the morpheme is *¢u m -.*

[2] The chronological sequence may have varied from what is presented in the figure. The order, however, does not affect the explanation. Note that there was a complication in the second-person pronoun which was here literally glossed over, since there was a time when there was a distinction between polite and familiar, until the polite took over the familiar. This is represented but not explained in the passage from pre-Mam II to Mam in the chart below. For an explanation, see Robertson (1987a).

*k-at-Verb	*k-eš-Verb	2SG	2PL
*k-in-Verb	*q-oʔŋ-Verb	1SG	1PL

pre-Mam I:

*¢Vn-ki-Verb	*¢Vn-k-e-Verb	3SG	3PL
*¢Vn-k-at-Verb	*¢Vn-k-eš-Verb	2SG	2PL
*¢Vn-k-in-Verb	*¢Vn-q-o-Verb	1SG	1PL

pre-Mam II:

*(¢V)n-či-Verb	*(¢V)n-č-i-Verb	3SG	3PL
*(¢V)n-k-at-Verb	*(¢V)n-k-eš-Verb	2SG	2PL
*(¢V)n-č-in-Verb	*(¢V)n-q-o-Verb	1SG	1PL

Mam:

n-Verb	n-či-Verb	3SG	3PL
n-Verb-e	n-či-Verb-e	2SG	2PL
n-čin-Verb	n-qo-Verb	1SG	1PLINC
	n-qo-Verb-e		1PLEXC

The reanalysis of the INCOMPLETIVE *k- > č- and ABS resulted in a new pronominal series. This new series came to occupy the new category, leaving the old, original marker in the marked category, as shown in 4.3. Thus, the reflex of *k- + ABS generalized to all non-zero morpheme markers, so that, for example, *š-in... is today š-čin.[1] Only the marked, dependent clauses of the COMPLETIVE contain the reflex of the original, plain ABSOLUTIVE. It is important to note, however, that prevocalically, in 3SG, the form is ¢: n-¢-ʔaqʔnaˑn 'he is working.'

The most probable source for the ¢- is the OPTATIVE 3SG *tʸ-, since Common Mayan *tʸ goes to ¢ in Mamean and č in K'iche'an. The means by which it was transferred from the more-marked OPTATIVE to the less-marked INCOMPLETIVE is not clear, although it is possible that with the reanalysis of the aspectual prefixes, which would have included the OPTATIVE ¢-, it became a part of the unmarked series, and spread to all aspects and moods (except the dependent clause of the COMPLETIVE) once its strict morphemic value was lost and it became a part of the pronominal system.[2]

It should not escape notice that there is another, similar pronominal change, based on resegmentation, which surely goes hand-in-hand with the

---

[1] Actually, š-čin is reduced to šin.

[2] It would be possible, of course, to postulate the *tʸ as a part of the INCOMPLETIVE of the common language, but that would be inadvisable, since č- marks the OPTATIVE in K'iche'an, and the FUTURE in Awakatek. Mam is the only language where its reflex appears in the INCOMPLETIVE, and it seems reasonable that it has to do with the process of fusion described above.

one described above. Here, however, the innovation of a new pronominal series occurs in the nonaspectual conjugation:

§xa·l	person	'he is a person'
§xa·l-e	person-CLITIC	'you are a person'
§xa·l-qi·n-e	person-1SG-CLITIC	'I am a person'
§xa·l-qe	person-3PL	'they are persons'
§xa·l-qe-ye	person-3PL-CLITIC	'you-guys are persons'
§xa·l-qo?-ye	person-1PL-CLITIC	'we (exclusive) are persons'
§xa·l-qo?	person-1PL	'we (inclusive) are persons'

The etymology of this set, like that of the innovative set discussed above, is due to a reanalysis of morpheme boundaries, but unlike the above, which was a fusion of independent morphemes, this was a fission, where the *q* was appropriated from the reflex of the Common Mayan form *-inaq,* which is the marker of single-argument, nonaspectual predicates. A comparison of Mam, Awakatek, and Kaqchikel puts the whole shift into relief:

Mam	Awakatek	Kaqchikel	
sikt-ni-qi·n-e	sikt-naq-in	in-kos-inaq	'I am tired'
sikt-ni	sikt-naq	kos-inaq	he is tired'

Just as the loss of the morpheme boundary between INCOMPLETIVE **k-* > *č-* and ABS resulted in a new pronominal series in the aspectual set of pronouns, so the addition of a new morpheme boundary resulted in a new pronominal series in the nonaspectual set. This new series came to occupy the new category, leaving the old, original marker in the marked category, as shown in Figure 4.4. In this case, the new pronominal series, which appropriated to itself the **q* of **-inaq,* came to occupy the newly formed, unmarked category, while the original pronominal series was restricted to the marked category, signaling existential location:

(a)t(-a?)	'he is (somewhere)'
(a)t(-a?-y)e	'you are (somewhere)'
(a)t-i·n-e	'I am (somewhere)'
(a)t-e?	'they are (somewhere)'
(a)t-e?-ye	'you-guys are (somewhere)'
(a)t-o?	'we (INC) are (somewhere)'
(a)t-o?-ye	'we (EXC) are (somewhere)'

One is struck with the strength of analogy in these two examples from Mam. The exact order in which the morpheme reanalysis occurred is not entirely clear, although it is highly probable that the influence of the PROGRESSIVE (NOM-VOICE) on the INCOMPLETIVE started the process. On the other hand, it is almost certain that one shift provoked the other, and that in both cases, displacement was manifest. In the aspectual system of pronominal inflection, the restricted category was the dependent clauses of the COMPLETIVE, whereas in the nonaspectual system of inflection, it was the inflection of the important, but marked existential 'be' verb *at,* the reflex of Common Mayan **ar.*

Pre-Mam

ABS3SG	ABS2SG	ABS1SG	ABS1SG
Ø	Ø-e	-i·n-e	-i·n-e
ABS3PL	ABS2PL	ABS1EXC	ABS1INC
e?	e?-ye	-o?-ye	-o

Mam

unmarked	Ø	Ø...e	qi·n...e	qi·n...e
marked	Ø	Ø...e	i·n...e	i·n...e
unmarked	qe	qe...ye	qo?...ye	qo?
marked	e?	e?...ye	o?...ye	o?

Figure 4.4. Summary of changes in Mam of the non aspectual pronominal series.

The third complication—that the ABS-DV must be incorporated prefixally into the transitive verbal complex—is actually part of a more extensive change involving NOM-MOOD, the OPTATIVE, and the FUTURE since, as seen above, the FUTURE was heavily influenced by both NOM-MOOD and the OPTATIVE. It should not be surprising to see such a relationship, given the structure defined earlier.

It is proposed that the change took the following course. First, the **la-*FUTURE of Common Mayan was augmented by the OPTATIVE **-oq,* replacing the preexisting **-ik.*[1] In the meantime, the primary markers of the NOM-MOOD, **-oq* and **-A?,* were replaced by *-el.* Then **-oq* (which is no longer attestable in Mam) was subsequently replaced by *-V·l.* The conservative K'iche' grammars

---

[1] The possibilty of **-oq* coming from the OPTATIVE is evidenced by the similar influence in Awakatek and in many other languages.

of Colonial times provide the clue to understanding the provenance of -*V·l*.

It will be recalled (p. 85) that in Common Mayan, the OPTATIVE/FUTURE **-oq* co-occurs with the ABS-DV. There was apparently an alternative to **-oq* in the form of an agentive suffix, -*V·l*, as attested in Colonial K'iche' (Anleo n.d.). Compare also Q'anjob'al, which only has -*oq*, and Modern Poqomchi' with -*V·l*.

Q'anjob'al:
hay way-oq
come sleep-SAPO
'he came in order to sleep'

K'iche' (Anleo):
xbetihonok [š-b⁷e-tixo-·n-*oq*]
COMP-go-teach-ANTIPASS-SAPO
'he went in order to teach'

xbetihonel [š-b⁷e-tixo-·n-*el*]
COMP-go-teach-ANTIPASS-NOMLZR
'he went in order to teach'

Poqomchi':
k⁷ul-loq⁷-*o·l*
COME-buy-NOMLZR
'he came in order to buy'

Mam:
ma·⁷-Ø-po·n Ta·t Li·š by-o·l t-e· ta·t če·p
PROX.PAST-ABS3SG-arrive. there Mr. Andrés hit-NOMLZR ERG3SG-
PREP Mr. Joseph
'Andrés got there in order to hit Joseph'

Notice that in Poqomchi' and K'iche' both -*oq* and -*o·l* are suffixed in the context of directional verbs; -*oq* is morphological, and -*o·l* syntactic.

Furthermore, in addition to its use in directionals, -*V·l* is used as a kind of FUTURE (Martínez n.d.):

En los bervos neutros se forma este futuro de la simplicidad y mudando, el *ic* en *el*, Vg. de *camic* que significa morir *camel* moriturur: de *petic* que significa, venid *petel*, venturus: la case el verbo *beic*, que hace *beenal:* iturus ussase de ello ante poniendo los pronombres primitivos *in, at* etc *inbeenal, incamel. In tihonel* yo he de enseñar.

[With the intransitive verbs this future is formed with the simple stem by changing *ik* to *el*, as for example, with *kamik*, which means 'die,' to *kamel* 'has to die'; with *petik*, which means 'come,' to *petel*, 'has to come.' The verb *beik* changes to *be?enal*. These are all used by preposing the primitive pronouns *in, at*, etc., *in-be?en-al, in-kam-el, in-tijon-el* 'I have to teach.']

Therefore, the distribution of *-V·l* as a marker of directionals and as an influencer of the FUTURE, on the level of syntax, is precisely the distribution of **-oq*, on the level of morphology.

The etymology of Mam's *-V·l* is now clear. Because the OPTATIVE/FUTURE **-oq* as well as the agentive **-V·l* had the role of marking the incorporation of the directional verbs of motion into the verbal complex, ultimately **-V·l* came to replace **-oq* in its role of marking auxiliary directionals. Furthermore, the newly instantiated primary marker of NOM-DV, *-el*, came to influence the FUTURE, as in the structure on page 176. Therefore, the *-V·l* FUTURE marker in Mam is the reflex of the old AGENTIVE marker widely seen in other Mayan languages.

The replacement of the morphological **-oq* with the syntactic **-o·l* had an effect not only on the FUTURE, but on the ABS-MOOD as well, where the more-marked NOM-MOOD influenced the less-marked ABS-MOOD. This is an instance of markedness reversal.

An explanation for this shift emerges from consideration of the fact that in the common language the ABS-DV followed the main verb, as exemplified by K'iche' (Totonicapan):

> *š-in-q?am-apon-oq*
> COMPL-ERG1SG-move-*arrive.there*-SAPO
> 'I dragged it over there.'

In contrast, in Cunén K'iche', the NOM-DV precedes:

> *š-k?u·n-wr-aq*
> COMPL-arrive.here-sleep-SAPO < **-oq*
> 'he came to sleep.'

In Mam, the ABS-DV precedes:

> ok-š-n-šo·?n-n-e xu·n šaq t-u·xa
> enter-go-ERG1SG-throw-DAPD-ERG1SG one rock ERG3SG-inside
> 'I threw the rock inside' (speaker outside the house)

> ok-¢-n-šo·?n-n-e xu·n šaq t-u·xa
> enter-come-ERG1SG-throw-DAPD-ERG1SG one rock ERG3SG-inside

'I threw the rock inside' (speaker inside the house).

The scenario for the change can be shown in terms of the schema for markedness reversal given in Figure 4.5. Similarly, the Mam ABS-MOOD and NOM-MOOD underwent markedness reversal as shown in Figure 4.6.

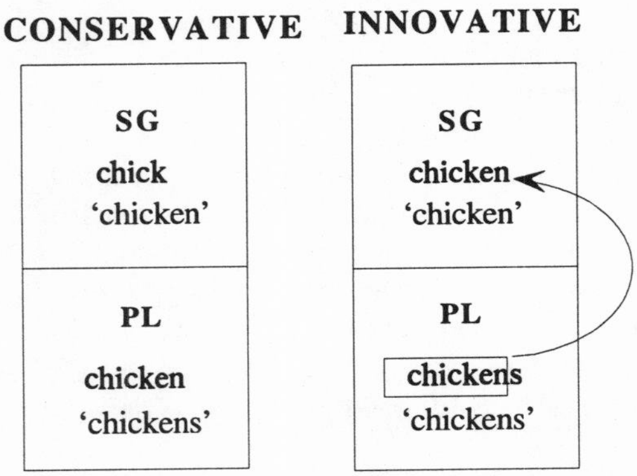

CONSERVATIVE   INNOVATIVE

Figure 4.5. Markedness reversal schema.

Several observations are in order. First, the condition of 'degrees of the same kind' (p. 30) is met by virtue of the obvious fact that both NOM-DV and ABS-DV use deictic directional verbs. Second, notice that Mam brought up the forms directly from the more-marked NOM-MOOD, and that for both the transitive and intransitive, something was added to the more-marked NOM-MOOD—in the case of the intransitive it was the -*V·l* spoken of earlier, and for the transitive it was the -*kx*, whose etymology is uncertain. Third, another synonymous form exists for the transitive NOM-DV which was obviously created on analogy with the intransitive NOM-DV, as shown below:

ma-čin-§-e ta-·l
PROX.PAST-ABS1SG-go-ABS1SG sleep-NOMLZR
'I went (in order to) sleep'
(a) **ma-čin-§-e mq-u·l-e t-e·**
PROX.PAST-ABS1SG-go-ABS1SG bury-NOMLZR-ERG1SG ERG3SG-PREP
'I went (in order to) bury it.'

(b) **ma-§i²-n-mq-u²-kx-e**
PROX.PAST-go-ERG1SG bury-DAPO-AFF-ERG1SG
'I went (in order to) bury it'

Notice that displacement has occurred, where the newly formed (a) above, which treats the transitive verb like an intransitive, has displaced (b), where the -*u?*- is derived from the original Common Mayan **-A?*.

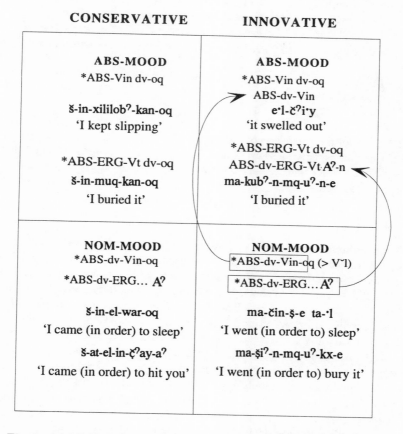

Figure 4.6. Markedness reversal of ABS-MOOD and NOM-MOOD in Mam.

Additionally, it is important to note that transitive verbs in modern Mam can occur either with or without directionals, but with few exceptions the appearance of the ABS-DV is compulsory. While in most Mayan languages the transitive verb simply requires two arguments, in Mam it requires not only two arguments but also a directional whose function is to modify the ABSOLUTIVE pronoun. This constitutes possibly the most significant change in Mam grammar.

The older form of transitive—without the directional—is very rare, in contrast to the newly acquired form with the directional. The forms for the directionals not occurring on the transitive are listed below:

Directional Not in Verbal Complex

ma'ʔ-t-múq	PROX.PAST-ERG3SG-bury	'He buried it'
ok-t-mq-úʔ	FUT-ERG3SG-bury-DAPO	'He will bury it'
ma'ʔ-t-kʔam	PROX.PAST-ERG3SG-receive	'He received it'
ok-t-kʔm-áʔ	FUT-ERG3SG-receive-DAPO	'He will receive it'

Directional Present in Verbal Complex

ma'ʔ-kuʔ-ş-t-mq-uʔ-n   PROX.PAST-descend-go-ERG3SG-bury-SUFF
            'He buried it'

The reason for the expansion of the ABS-DV, for the transitive verb, to include all tenses and aspects of Mam is not clear, although it might be noted that Q'anjob'alan, which shares other borrowed traits with Mam (p. 57), similarly expanded the use of ABS-DV.

Summary of Mam

Mam, although quite different from the common language, is nonetheless a logical postcedent of that language. The aspectual system, which distinguishes independent from dependent clauses, still preserves the antecedent system in its dependent clauses, and shows the innovative, adverbially derived tense/aspectual markers in the independent clauses. This is a perfect example of the principle of displacement, as explained earlier.

Furthermore, it was observed that of the system *-ik, *-O, *-oq, *-Aʔ, the only one to remain was *-Aʔ, which spread by markedness reversal from the NOM-DV to the ABS-DV. The *-oq, on the other hand, as marker of the FUTURE and the directionals was totally lost, being replaced by the -V·l, which was shown to have existed at least in Common Mamo-K'iche'an times, and possibly earlier, as a syntactic marker of both directionals and as a kind of future. Possibly the most significant change in Mam grammar was the displacement of the simple transitive with the ABS-DV, which is today the most commonly used form of the transitive verb. Finally, the ABSOLUTIVE pronouns čin- and či- are shown to have come from the Common Mayan *k-in and *k-ebʔ, where the *k- is the aspect marker of the INCOMPLETIVE.

Awakatek

Awakatek underwent many of the same changes as Mam. Like Mam it innovated by distinguishing the dependent from the independent clause in the PROXIMATE PAST, but unlike Mam it underwent even more extensive changes in the system of the directionals. And as in Mam the OPTATIVE deeply influenced the FUTURE, although unlike Mam there is still a trace, though highly marked, of the original FUTURE.

The INCOMPLETIVE

Awakatek, like almost all other of the Mayan languages, augmented the INCOMPLETIVE *ki-, in this case with the morpheme na-. Furthermore, as in Mam, the original *k- of the INCOMPLETIVE palatalized before front vowels (as in Common Mayan *kiʔ > čiʔ 'sweet'), but remains k otherwise, as for example before ABS2SG, š.[1]

Dependent and Independent Clauses in the PROXIMATE PAST

Like Mam, Awakatek aspectually distinguishes between dependent and independent clauses in the PROXIMATE PAST, with the difference that in Mam the dependent clauses are marked with š- and the independent with ma-, while in Awakatek m- marks the dependent and ha- the independent, as shown in Figures 4.7, 4.8 and 4.9.

INCOMPLETIVE

	Common	Awakatek
3SG	*ki...ik	na...
2SG	*k-at...ik	na-k-š...
1SG	*k-in...ik	na-č-in...
3PL	*k-ebʔ...ik	n-č-i...
2PL	*k-eš...ik	??
1PL	*q-oŋ...ik	n-q-a...

Figure 4.7. Summary of changes in Awakatek for the INCOMPLETIVE.

Here are some examples of m- and ha- in dependent and independent clauses.[2]

    na· m-o·qʔ eʔt
where PROX.PAST-cry LOC
'where is it that he cried?'

    ye ya·h ye-n-s-ȼʔax-o-n

---

[1]The ABS3SG is a reflex of *at, going through the stages *ač > *aš > s. The shift from *t to č is a regular, unconditioned Mamean shift (Common Mayan *tu·x 'steam bath' > ču·x in Mamean), while the Awakatekan shift from č to š is conditioned: č → š /___C, as in, e.g., čičʔ 'blood,' in-ščʔ-el ERG1SG-blood-AFF, 'my blood.'

[2]Note that m assimilates to the following consonant.

the man the-PROX.PAST-ERG3SG-wash-THEME-AFF
'the man who washed you'

ha-čin-oˑqˀ
'I cried (today)'

Single-Argument Predication

	COMPLETIVE		PROXIMATE PAST		
	Common	**Awakatek**	**Common**	**Awakatek**	
				Dependent	Independent
3SG	*...ik	...	*iš...ik	m-...	ha-...
2SG	*at...ik	ač...	*iš-at...ik	m-k-ač...	ha-k-š...
1SG	*in...ik	in...	*iš-in...ik	m-č-in...	ha-č-in...
3PL	*ebˀ...ik	i...	*iš-ebˀ...ik	m-č-i...	ha-č-i...
2PL	*eš...ik	iš...	*iš-eš...ik	m-č-iš...	ha-č-iš...
1PL	*oˀŋ...ik	oˀ...	*iš-oˀŋ...ik	m-q-a...	ha-q-a...

Figure 4.8. Summary of changes in Awakatek for the COMPLETIVE and PROXIMATE PAST in single-argument predications.

Double-Argument Predication[1]

	COMPLETIVE		PROXIMATE PAST		
	Common	**Awakatek**	**Common**	**Awakatek**	
				Dependent	Independent
3SG	*ru...O	S...	*iš-ru...O		ha-S...
2SG	*a...O	a...	*iš-a...O	m-a...	ha-a...
1SG	*nu...O	in...	*iš-nu...O	m-in...	ha-in...
3PL	*ki...O	?	*iš-ki...O	m-či...	ha-či...
2PL	*e...O	?	*iš-e...O	m-i...woq	ha-i...woq
1PL	*qa...O	?	*iš-qa...O	m-qa...	ha-qa...

Figure 4.9. Summary of changes in Awakatek for the COMPLETIVE and PROXIMATE PAST in double-argument predications.

---

[1]The *S* below stands for the ERG3SG pronoun, which is null except when it occurs before sibilants, where it assumes the point and manner of articulation of the following sibilant. For an explanation of its provenance from *ru-* see Robertson (1977b, 1984d).

Figure 4.10 summarizes the stages of change in the Awakatek RECENT PAST.

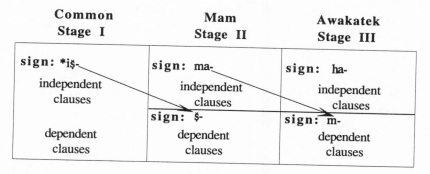

Common Stage I	Mam Stage II	Awakatek Stage III
sign: *iš- independent clauses	**sign: ma-** independent clauses	**sign: ha-** independent clauses
dependent clauses	**sign: š-** dependent clauses	**sign: m-** dependent clauses

Figure 4.10. Summary of changes in Awakatek for dependent and independent clauses in PROXIMATE PAST.

Influence of the INCOMPLETIVE by NOM-VOICE

It has already been demonstrated that among the Mayan languages an overwhelming tendency exists for the NOM-VOICE to influence the INCOMPLETIVE (p. 93). This apparently happened in Awakatek, where the old INCOMPLETIVE *k-* was augmented by *na,* whose etymology is likely related to a *na(k)-* INCOMPLETIVE found in Colonial Poqomchi' (which historically came from the NOM-VOICE PROGRESSIVE [p. 144.), and an INCOMPLETIVE *nak-* in Q'eqchi' (p. 149). Furthermore, Ixil, which is a split-ergative language, has an INCOMPLETIVE which is apparently based on an old **na(k)-*ERG-vin CONTINUATIVE. A final piece of evidence that *na(k)-* was historically the marker of an original continuative is the fact that in Mam a negative PRESENT PERFECT exists which is conjugated like the CONTINUATIVE: *na?-n w-o·q?-e* PRESENT.PERFECT-AFF ERG1SG-cry-CLITIC 'I haven't cried yet.'

Displacement of FUTURE by OPTATIVE

One of the most interesting characteristics of Awakatek is the supplanting of the FUTURE by the OPTATIVE as seen in Figure 4.11, which involves two of the principles described above, *influence* and *displacement.* Here, the original FUTURE, **la-* was displaced by the OPTATIVE, **ki/ȼ...oq/A?,*[1] and the original FUTURE **la-* was consequently displaced to mark certain embeddings:

---

[1]Because the data are wanting, I am not sure if the **-a?* is preserved.

ta·hweʔn (kuʔn) *l*-č-in-wit
necessary (that) FUT < *k- ABS1SG sleep
'It's necessary that I sleep'

ki-*l*-š-wit
not-FUT-ABS2SG-sleep
'Don't sleep!'

leʔoʔ minu·t *l*-č-in-wit
five minutes FUT-<*k-ABS1SG-sleep
'In five minutes I'll sleep'

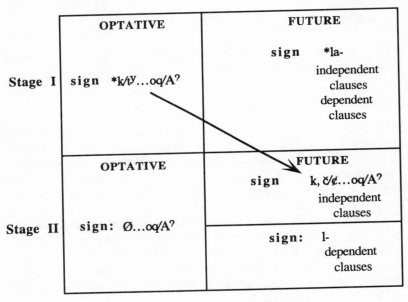

Figure 4.11. Displacement of FUTURE by OPTATIVE in Awakatek.

The unmarked FUTURE in Awakatek is based on the old OPTATIVE, while the prefixes **ki/tʸ-* for the OPTATIVE were replaced by Ø-. Such replacement of an unmarked morpheme in a system by Ø-, with the original sign moving to a marked category, is another instance of the process of displacement. The shift from the 3SG marker **tʸ* to ȼ is a normal sound shift (e.g., Common Mayan **tʸaʔŋ* > ȼaʔx 'ashes' in Mamean).

A summary of changes in Awakatek for the COMPLETIVE, INCOMPLETIVE, OPTATIVE, and FUTURE can be seen in figure 4.12.

COMPLETIVE	OPTATIVE
Completive: *Ø...ik/O Prox. Past: *iš...ik/O	*ki/t^y...oq/A?
Completive: Ø... **Independent Clauses** Proximate Past: **ha...** **Dependent Clauses** Proximate Past: **m...**	Ø...oq?

INCOMPLETIVE	FUTURE
*ki...ik/O č,k/Ø... 3. na-Ø... 3p. na-č-i... 2. na-k-š... 2p. ? 1. na-č-in... 1p. na-qa...	Future: *la...ik/O Prox. Future: *iš-la...ik/O Future: č,k/¢...oq/A? Future (Dependent) 1-č?/k...

Figure 4.12. Summary of changes in Awakatek for the COMPLETIVE, INCOMPLETIVE, OPTATIVE, and FUTURE.

The Directional Verbs: ABS-MOOD and NOM-MOOD

It will be recalled that the original system of directionals looked like the following K'iche' examples, which essentially conserve the structure of the original system, as illustrated in Figure 4.13.

My research shows remarkable but related changes from this original system. First, the ABS-MOOD took over the NOM-MOOD *semantically*, so that the NOM-DV, which historically modified the subjects of intransitives and transitives, became equivalent to an ABS-DV, modifying the absolutive pronouns, the subjects of intransitives, and objects of the transitives. This shift is made possible by the structure of the system, since ABS-MOOD is less marked than NOM-MOOD. The second change—a consequence of and concomitant with the above change—had the effect of associating the postposed directionals of the old ABS-DV with the INCOMPLETIVE aspect, and the old preposed NOM-DV with the COMPLETIVE. Each of these changes will be discussed below.

ABS-DV INTRANSITIVE	NOM-DV INTRANSITIVE
*ABS...dv-oq	*ABS-dv...oq
š-in-xililib⁷-kan-oq COMP-ABS1SG-slip-stay-SAPO 'I kept slipping'	š-in-el-war-oq COMP-ABS1SG-get.here-sleep-SAPO 'I came (in order to) sleep'
ABS-DV TRANSITIVE	NOM-DV TRANSITIVE
*ABS-ERG...dv-oq	*ABS-dv-ERG...A⁷
š-in-muq-kan-oq COMP-ABS1SG-bury-stay-SAPO 'I kept burying it'	š-at-el-in-č⁷ey-a⁷ COMP-ABS2SG-get.here-ABS1SG-hit-DAPO 'I came (in order to) hit you'

Figure 4.13. Directional verbs in K'iche'.

It is likely that *before* NOM-MOOD became ABS-MOOD, a change very similar to what happened in Mam occurred in Awakatek. That is, *-Vl* took over the old *-oq*, resulting in a pre-Awakatekan system that looked much like Mam's system today:

> *in-ši⁷ wata-·l
> (ASP-)ABS-DV VIN-V·l
> 'I went (in order to) sleep'

> *in-ši⁷ muq-u·l aw-e·¢
> (ASP-)ABS-DV VT-V·l ERG2SG-PREP
> 'I went (in order to) bury you'

> *ač-ši⁷-in-muq-u·l
> (ASP-)ABS1-DV ERG1-VT-V·l
> 'I went (in order) to bury you'

The only difference between the Awakatek and the Mam forms (p. 107) of the NOM-DV was simply that instead of the old *-V⁷*, the *-V·l* came to replace it, just as it had done earlier with the *-oq*.

The next stage was the association of the COMPLETIVE with NOM-MOOD and the INCOMPLETIVE with ABS-MOOD, as shown in Figure 4.14.

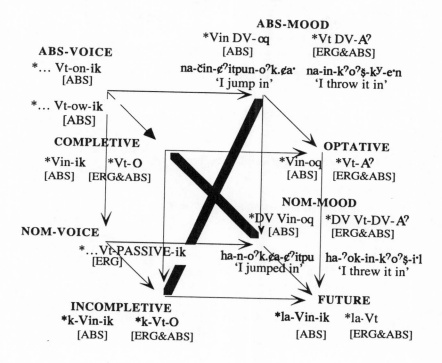

Figure 4.14. Association of the INCOMPLETIVE with ABS-MOOD and the COMPLETIVE with NOM-MOOD in Awakatek.

Just as in Mam, where a markedness reversal had moved the form of the old NOM-MOOD to ABS-MOOD (see page 108), so in Awakatek there was a similar reversal of NOM-MOOD to be associated with the COMPLETIVE, and the ABS-MOOD with the INCOMPLETIVE. The reason for this double markedness reversal is this: NOM-MOOD (with suffixation of the directional) became ABS-MOOD (with prefixation of the directional), making a potential synonymy. The reversal by association with aspect gave reason for the existence of the prefixation/suffixation distinction.

Examples of the new, aspectual meaning associated with the old NOM-MOOD and ABS-MOOD follow. Notice that in the INCOMPLETIVE (<*ABS-MOOD) the directional is suffixed, and in the COMPLETIVE (<*NOM-MOOD) the directional is prefixed:

Single-Argument Predications

Incompletive (directional suffixed)

na-čin-ȼʔit-p-un-oʔk
INC-ABS1SG-jump-AFF-AFF-enter.come
'I jump in'

č-in-kʔol-e-q-kuʔ-n
INC-ABS1SG-sit-AFF-SAPO-descend-AFF
'I will sit down'

Completive (directional prefixed)

.ȼaˑha-n-oʔk-ȼa-ȼʔit-p-u
COMPL-ABS1SG-enter-come-jump-AFF-AFF
'I jumped in'

ha-čin-kuʔ-tiˑm-p-i
PROX.PAST-ABS1SG-descend-fall-AFF-SAPD
'I fell down'

Double-Argument Predications
Incompletive (directional suffixed)

na-in-kʔoʔṣ-eʔ-n
INC-ERG1SG-throw-ascend-AFF
'I throw it up'

na-in-kʔoʔṣ-l-eˑn
INC-ERG1SG-throw-descend-AFF
'I throw it down'

Completive (directional prefixed)

ha-heˑʔ-in-kʔoʔṣ-o-ˑl
COMP-ascend-ERG1SG-throw-THEME-AGNT
'I threw it up'

ha-kuˑʔ-in-kʔoʔṣ-o-ˑl
COMP-descend-ERG1SG-throw-THEME-AGNT

'I threw it down'

The probability that this is close to an accurate explanation of the historical development of the Awakatek directional verbs seems quite high in light of the following considerations. First, in my work with Awakatek I discovered no NOM-DV, which is, so far as I know, unique in the Mamo-K'iche'an language subgroup. This gives credence to the hypothesis that the opposition COMPLETIVE/INCOMPLETIVE displaced the opposition NOMINATIVE/ABSOLUTIVE modification in the directionals. Second, the directionals stay as prefixes in the unmarked COMPLETIVE and as suffixes in the marked INCOMPLETIVE. Such a tight parallel makes it likely that the parameters of the paradigm itself (and not the structural relationships) were changed. Third, the first stage is essentially the same as that of Mam, which could be expected, given the genetic and geographic proximity of the two languages. Finally, the suffix -*V·l* seems to have its etymological source in the same syntactic construction as explained above for Mam.

Summary of Awakatek

In many ways Awakatek conserves much of the system of the common language, as witnessed by (1) the conservation of the original OPTATIVE morphology, but as markers of the FUTURE; (2) the conservation of the original FUTURE, **la-*, but in a more-marked form, as a result of having been displaced by the OPTATIVE; (3) the conservation of the original COMPLETIVE, **k-*, but with palatalization before front vowels, as in Mam. In other ways, however, the innovations are so extensive that it would have been impossible for the reconstruction to have been completed without consideration of certain changes in Mam: (1) the postulation of Mam as pre-Awakatek in the COMPLETIVE, with *ṣ-* and *ma-;* (2) the shift in the directionals, where -*V·l* replaces Common Mayan **-oq*.

Furthermore, despite the importance of Colonial documents—they simply cannot be ignored—it is nonetheless possible to begin to make up for their want by taking into account the reconstructions of closely related neighboring languages. With respect to the COMPLETIVE, for example, it would be impossible to get from Common Mayan to Awakatek without consideration first of how Common Mayan changed to Mam. It turns out that the Mam COMPLETIVE is the intermediary link without which the Awakatek forms would have to remain forever unexplained (all other things remaining the same).[1] It is also important to consider Mam with respect to the rather dramatic change in the Awakatek directionals.

---

[1] To a lesser extent the same is true of the Mam and Awakatek directionals.

Finally, one of the most significant changes in Awakatek is the collapsing of ABS-MOOD with the INCOMPLETIVE and NOM-MOOD with the COMPLETIVE.

Ixil

Several observations emerge as one compares Ixil to the common language, as demonstrated in Figure 4.15. Perhaps most obvious is the fact that unlike the rest of Mamo-K'iche'an, Ixil is a split-ergative language much like the Lowland Languages. In the INCOMPLETIVE the ergative marks the subject of both transitives and intransitives, while in the COMPLETIVE the ergative-absolutive system prevails. The reason for such split ergativity surely results from the fact that Ixil was deeply influenced by the Cholan language family, where split ergativity is grammatically central.[1]

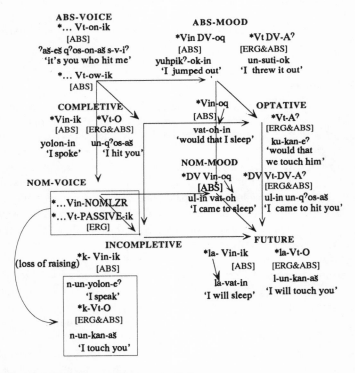

Figure 4.15. Summary of TAMV in Ixil.

---

[1]For a more extensive discussion of Cholan influence on Ixil see Robertson (1977a:208–209).

The source of the split ergativity is, as suggested elsewhere, the PROGRESSIVE of the NOM-VOICE, which can be reconstructed to be something like the following:

Common Mayan:
*na-ABS PREP VIN-NOMLZR
*na-ABS PREP ERG-VT+PASS-NOMLZR

Ixil (loss of raising):
n-un-yolon-e?
*na ERG1sg-VIN-AFF
'I speak'

n-un-kan-aš
*na ERG1SG-VT-ABS2SG
'I touch you'

In other ways, however, Ixil is quite conservative. It preserves the original FUTURE marker, *la-;* it conserves the original *Ø-* for the COMPLETIVE; and it conserves the original system of ABS-VOICE and NOM-VOICE, as seen in Figure 4.16.

INCOMPLETIVE, COMPLETIVE, OPTATIVE, and FUTURE

	COMPLETIVE	**OPTATIVE**
Common Mayan	Completive: *Ø...ik/O Prox. Past: *iš...ik/O	*ki/tʸi...oq/A?
Ixil	Ø/kan...	...oh/V?
	INCOMPLETIVE	**FUTURE**
Common Mayan	*ki...ik/O	Future:　　*la...ik/O Prox. Future: *iš-la...ik/O
Ixil	n-ERG...O	la-...A?

Figure 4.16. Summary of changes in the COMPLETIVE, INCOMPLETIVE, OPTATIVE, and FUTURE from Common Mayan to Ixil.

From the above schema several changes are immediately apparent. First, the categories PROXIMATE PAST and PROXIMATE FUTURE were lost. Second, the FUTURE was influenced by the OPTATIVE, since *-Aˀ* took over *-ik/-O*. Third, OPTATIVE prefixes were lost. The most far-reaching change, however, took place in the INCOMPLETIVE, where (as mentioned above) the ERGATIVE came to mark single-argument predications.

The FUTURE, *la-*, is preserved from Common Mayan times. Note that there is no apparent influence from the OPTATIVE **-oq* on the FUTURE, which is otherwise often present in the FUTURE in other languages. The FUTURE, *la-*, is also seen in Awakatek, but only in its displaced state, as a marker of certain embedded clauses. Other instances of the same FUTURE can be seen in Chuj, Choltí, and Yukatek Maya.

Note that, except for *la-*, the original prefixes of Common Mayan TAMV have all been lost. The only remaining vestige of the OPTATIVE is the *-oh* < **-oq*.

Directional Verbs

The directional verbs are essentially like those of K'iche', which preserves the original Common Mayan system, as seen in Figure 4.17.

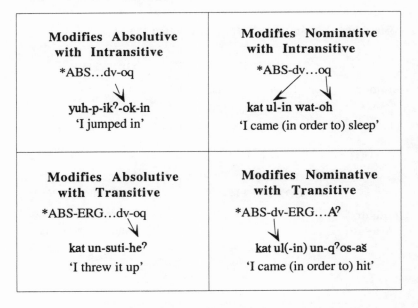

Figure 4.17. Summary of changes in directional verbs from Common Mayan to Ixil.

The chief difference between the common language and Ixil is that Ixil lost the reflex of *-oq* from the ABS-DV for the intransitive, and apparently the reflex of the *-A?* for the NOM-DV transitives. The fact that the systems of directionals in both Ixil and K'iche' (see below) resemble each other so closely is striking.

Conclusion

Ixil is in many ways closely related to the other two Mamean languages, Mam and Awakatek, but—contrary to Kaufman's (1974) claim that Ixil and Awakatek are more closely related than Mam and Awakatek—the truth seems to be that Mam and Awakatek are the more closely related in consideration of these facts: (a) both Mam and Awakatek both keep the Common Mayan INCOMPLETIVE *ki-* (b) they both share a PROXIMATE PAST, with Awakatek having gone one stage beyond Mam, after sharing an identical development of the reflex of *ma·y,* 'past time of today,' which to replace an earlier *š-* (c) they apparently shared a similar system of directionals before Awakatek's drastic revision described above. Therefore it seems more reasonable to place Awakatek with Mam and not with Ixil. The revision suggested in Figure 4.18 seems reasonable.

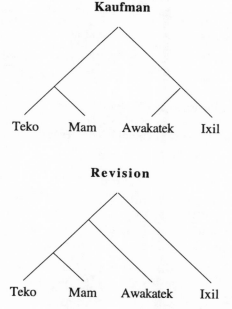

Kaufman

Teko   Mam   Awakatek   Ixil

Revision

Teko   Mam   Awakatek   Ixil

Figure 4.18. Revision of Kaufman's subgrouping in Mamean.

Chapter 5. K'iche'an

K'iche'

This chapter will deal first with Colonial, and then Modern K'iche'.

Colonial K'iche': INCOMPLETIVE, OPTATIVE, and COMPLETIVE

In many ways Colonial K'iche' is the most conservative of all the Mayan languages. It conserves the suffixes of VOICE (*-ik > -ik, *-O > -O*) and of MOOD (*-oq > -oq, *-A? > -A?*), as well as the OPTATIVE prefixes with the regular sound change of *t^{y}i-* to *či-*. The INCOMPLETIVE *ki- > ka-* is also preserved, without the usual augmentation that is found in all other Mayan languages, as demonstrated in Figure 5.1.

INCOMPLETIVE

	SINGLE-ARGUMENT PREDICATION		DOUBLE-ARGUMENT PREDICATION	
	Common	Col.K'iche'	Common	Col.K'iche'
3SG	*ki...ik	ka-...ik	*ki-ru...O	k-u...O
2SG	*k-at...ik	k-at...ik	*k-a...O	k-a...O
1SG	*k-in...ik	k-in...ik	*ki-nu...O	ka-nu...O
3PL	*ki...eb?	k-e·...ik	*ki-ki...O	ka-ki...O
2PL	*k-eš...ik	k-iš...ik	*k-e...O	k-i...O
1PL	*k-o?ŋ...ik	q-ox...ik	*ki-qa...O	ka-qa...O

Figure 5.1. The INCOMPLETIVE in Colonial K'iche'.

Figure 5.2 demonstrates the extremely conservative nature of the OPTATIVE in both single and double argument predications.

OPTATIVE

	SINGLE-ARGUMENT PREDICATION		DOUBLE-ARGUMENT PREDICATION	
	Common	Col.K'iche'	Common	Col.K'iche'
3SG	*t^{y}i...oq	či...oq	*t^{y}i-ru...A?	č-u...A?
2SG	*k-at...oq	k-at...oq	*t^y-a...A?	č-a...A?
1SG	*k-in...oq	k-in...oq	*t^{y}i-nu...A?	či-nu...A?
3PL	*ki...eb?	k-e·...oq	*t^{y}i-ki...A?	či-ki...A?
2PL	*k-eš...oq	k-iš...oq	*t^y-i...A?	č-i...A?
1PL	*q-o?ŋ...oq	q-ox...oq	*t^{y}i-qa...A?	či-qa...A?

Figure 5.2. OPTATIVE in Colonial K'iche'.

The least-conservative portion of the paradigm of Colonial K'iche' is found in the COMPLETIVE and in the FUTURE (Figures 5.3-5.6), as discussed on page 69.

COMPLETIVE
Single-Argument Predication

	COMPLETIVE		PROXIMATE PAST	
	Common	**K'iche'**	**Common**	**K'iche'**
3SG	*...ik	š-Ø...ik	*iš...ik	mi-š...ik
2SG	*...at	š-at...ik	*iš-at...ik	mi-š-at...ik
1SG	*...in	š-in...ik	*iš-in...ik	mi-š-in...ik
3PL	*...eb?	š-e·...ik	*iš...eb?	mi-š-e·...ik
2PL	*...eš	š-iš...ik	*iš-eš...ik	mi-š-iš...ik
1PL	*...o?ŋ	š-ox...ik	*iš-o?ŋ...ik	mi-š-ox...ik

Figure 5.3. The single-argument COMPLETIVE and PROXIMATE PAST in Colonial K'iche'.

Double-Argument Predications

	COMPLETIVE		PROXIMATE PAST	
	Common	**K'iche'**	**Common**	**K'iche'**
3SG	*ru...O	š-u...O	*š-u...O	mi-š-u...O
2SG	*a...O	š-a...O	*š-a...O	mi-š-a...O
1SG	*nu...O	š-nu...O	*š-nu...O	mi-š-nu...O
3PL	*ki...O	š-ki...O	*š-ki...O	mi-š-ki...O
2PL	*e...O	š-i...O	*š-e...O	mi-š-i...O
1PL	*qa...O	š-qa...O	*š-qa...O	mi-š-qa...O

Figure 5.4. The double-argument COMPLETIVE and PROXIMATE PAST in Colonial K'iche'.

In K'iche', both prefixal TENSE/ASPECT and suffixal VOICE/MOOD were affected by change. In the prefixal COMPLETIVE, the adverbial *mi,* which means 'past time of today,' augmented the already-existing *š-* (which also refers to past time of today), resulting in the form *miš-*.

Common Completive/Past	Colonial K'iche' Completive/Past	
*war-ik	š-war-ik	'he slept'
*at-war-ik	š-at-war-ik	'I slept'
*in-war-ik	š-in-war-ik	'you slept'
*war-eb?	š-e?-war-ik	'they slept'

*eš-war-ik	š-iš-war-ik	'you-guys slept'
*oʔŋ-war-ik	š-ox-war-ik	'we slept'

Recent Past	**Recent Past**	
*iš-war-ik	mi-š-war-ik	'he slept'
*iš-at-war-ik	mi-š-at-war-ik	'you slept'
*iš-in-war-ik	mi-š-in-war-ik	'I slept'
*is-ebʔ-war-ik	mi-š-e-war-ik	'they slept'
*iš-eš-war-ik	mi-š-iš-war-ik	'you-guys slept'
*iš-oʔŋ-war-ik	mi-š-ox-war-ik	'we slept'

Single-Argument Predication

	FUTURE		PROXIMATE FUTURE	
	Common	**Col.K'iche'**	**Common**	**Col.K'iche'**
3SG	*la...ik	či...ik	*iš-la...ik	š-či...ik
2SG	*l-at...ik	k-at...ik	*iš-l-at...ik	š-k-at...ik
1SG	*l-in...ik	k-in...ik	*iš-l-in...ik	š-k-in...ik
3PL	*la...ebʔ	k-eˑ...ik	*iš-la...ebʔ	š-k-eˑ...ik
2PL	*l-eš...ik	k-eš...ik	*iš-l-eš...ik	š-k-eš...ik
1PL	*l-oʔŋ...ik	q-ox...ik	*iš-l-oʔŋ...ik	š-q-ox...ik

Figure 5.5. Innovation of the Colonial K'iche' single-argument predication
FUTURE.

Double-Argument Predication

	FUTURE		PROXIMATE FUTURE	
	Common	**Col.K'iche'**	**Common**	**Col.K'iche'**
3SG	*la-ru...O	či-ru...O	*iš-la-ru...O	š-či-ru...O
2SG	*l-a...O	č-a...O	*iš-l-a...O	š-č-a...O
1SG	*la-nu...O	či-nu...O	*iš-la-nu...O	š-či-nu...O
3PL	*la-ki...O	či-ki...O	*iš-la-ki...O	š-či-ki...O
2PL	*l-e...O	č-e...O	*iš-l-e...O	š-č-e...O
1PL	*la-qa...O	či-qa...O	*iš-la-qa...O	š-či-qa...O

Figure 5.6. Innovation of the Colonial K'iche' double-argument predication
FUTURE.

In this case, the FUTURE prefix *la-* was replaced by *či-/k-* from the OPTATIVE
paradigm, although the suffixal portion of the paradigm, *-oq,* remained.[1]

---

[1]In other cases, as for example in Q'anjob'al, the suffix *-oq* itself is used as
the prefix signaling future time.

This is a perfect example of markedness reversal, motivated by augmentation, as explained on page 23. Recall the example from English (p. 26), which is now compared with what happened in the move from Common Mayan to Colonial K'iche', as shown in Figure 5.7.

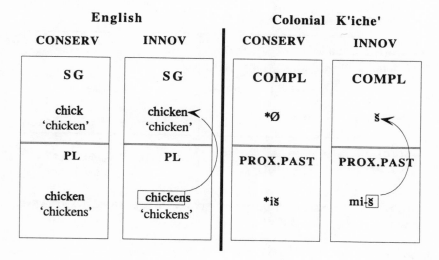

Figure 5.7. Comparison of markedness reversal in English and Colonial K'iche'.

Colonial K'iche' FUTURE

While the INCOMPLETIVE is the conserving part of the paradigm, and while the COMPLETIVE innovated as described above, the FUTURE innovated with influence from the OPTATIVE, as summarized in Figure 5.8.

Modern speakers of K'iche' might wonder whether the PROXIMATE PAST and PROXIMATE FUTURE, or even the FUTURE itself, really did exist in earlier K'iche'. Such forms are readily attested in the grammars, as for example in *Arte de Lengua Guiché* (n.d.), where the anonymous author says,

> y notese que quando el preterito perfecto fuere proximo se la a de anteponer a la particula del verbo un *mi* vg. ...*mixinnimah a tzih* obedicí luego tu palabra. Tambien para el futuro proximo se le añade a la particula al verbo una *x* vg. aora te asotaré *xcatnurapah.*

> [and note that when the perfect preterite would be next, it is necessary to prefix the particle *mi*, e.g., *mixinnimah a tzih* [mi-š-in-nima·-x a-¢i·x] 'I just obeyed your word.' Also for the proximate future the

particle *x* is added to the verb, e.g., 'now I'm going to whip you'
xcatnurapah [š-k-at-nu-rapa·x].]

	COMPLETIVE	OPTATIVE
Common Mayan	Completive: **Ø...ik/O* Prox. Past: **iš...ik/O*	**ki/t^yi...oq/A?*
Colonial K'iche'	Completive: š...ik/O Prox. Past: mi-š...ik/O	ka/či...oq/A?

	INCOMPLETIVE	FUTURE
Common Mayan	**ki...ik/O*	Future: **la...ik/O* Prox. Future: **iš-la...ik/O*
Colonial K'iche'	ka...ik/O	Future: ka/či...ik/O Prox. Future: š-ka/či...ik/O

Figure 5.8. Summary of changes in the COMPLETIVE, INCOMPLETIVE, OPTATIVE, and FUTURE in Colonial K'iche'.

Modern K'iche'

COMPLETIVE, INCOMPLETIVE, OPTATIVE, and FUTURE

As noted, the grammar of Colonial K'iche' closely resembles the grammar of the common language, with only a few changes. On the other hand, as suggested above, Modern K'iche' is more different from the Colonial language than the Colonial language is from the common language. The differences are these: (a) the PROXIMATE PAST and PROXIMATE FUTURE have both been lost, and (b) the FUTURE no longer exists in the modern language. The simple INCOMPLETIVE is used today where the future would have been used in Colonial and pre-K'iche'. These differences are diagrammed in Figure 5.9. Note that here it is the INCOMPLETIVE and not the OPTATIVE that takes over the FUTURE. The preceding discussions of Mam and Awakatek, as well as Colonial K'iche', have shown a strong influence of the OPTATIVE on the FUTURE. Modern K'iche', however, replaced the FUTURE with the INCOMPLETIVE. Note that this same influence occurred in Tzotzil (p. 186) and Choltí (p. 171). The reason for the influence on the FUTURE in both languages is due, of course, to the location of the FUTURE in the paradigm, since it is a logical combination of the OPTATIVE (irrealis) and the INCOMPLETIVE (general): the FUTURE is both irrealis and general. This kind of influence is, to quote Watkins (1970:59), "motivated, indeed virtually predetermined, by the position of the forms of the morphological structure."

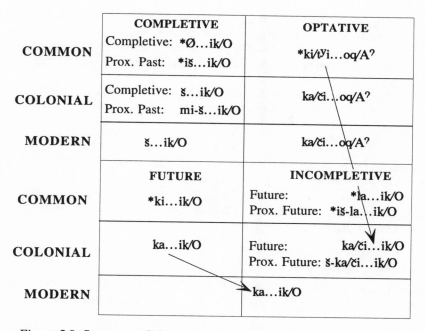

	COMPLETIVE	OPTATIVE
COMMON	Completive: *Ø…ik/O Prox. Past: *iš…ik/O	*ki/tʸi…oq/Aʔ
COLONIAL	Completive: š…ik/O Prox. Past: mi-š…ik/O	ka/či…oq/Aʔ
MODERN	š…ik/O	ka/či…oq/Aʔ
	FUTURE	**INCOMPLETIVE**
COMMON	*ki…ik/O	Future: *la…ik/O Prox. Future: *iš-la…ik/O
COLONIAL	ka…ik/O	Future: ka/či…ik/O Prox. Future: š-ka/či…ik/O
MODERN		ka…ik/O

Figure 5.9. Summary of changes in the COMPLETIVE, INCOMPLETIVE, OPTATIVE, and FUTURE from the common language to Colonial K'iche' to Modern K'iche'.

Other changes have been effected in the OPTATIVE in some K'iche' dialects. In the modern Nahualá dialect, for example, the following contrast with the paradigm from Colonial times is noted:

Colonial	**Modern (Nahualá)**		
	Paradigm I	**Paradigm II**	
či-war-oq	–	**war-oq**	'would that he sleep'
k-at-war-oq	**k-at-war-oq**	č-at-war-oq	'would that he sleep'
k-in-war-oq	k-in-war-oq	**č-in-war-oq**	'would that I sleep'
k-eˑ-war-oq	–	č-eˑ-war-oq	'would that they sleep'
k-iš-war-oq	**k-iš-war-oq**	k-iš-war-oq	'would that you-guys sleep'
q-ox-war-oq	k-ux-war-oq	**k-ux-war-oq**	'would that we sleep'

Apparently, the aspect marker *či-*, originally restricted to 3SG, is in the process of imposing its form on the rest of the paradigm. According to Mondloch (1978:35), there are two paradigms, where *ka-* is preferred over *či-* anywhere SECOND PERSON is involved (2SG, 2PL, 1PL—i.e., the IMPERATIVES), while *či-* is preferred elsewhere (NONIMPERATIVES). The forms in bold are the preferred forms. The taking over of *ka-* by *či-* is an example of Watkins' Law

(1962:90), where 3sg "will tend to impose its form on the rest of the paradigm, irrespective of the form of the 2sg or any other PERSON, owing to the peculiar functional position of the 3sg as 'la personne zéro,' 'la non-personne....' " In his original formulation, Watkins (1962:91) explains that the

> replacement of the Sanskrit precative is to be envisaged as a reinterpretation of the 3sg form with ending, here *bhuya-s,* as containing a zero ending, i.e., *bhuyas-Ø,* with the -*s* part of the stem, to which the productive endings for other persons can be added: *bhuyas-am* etc.

Similarly, the replacement of the K'iche' *k-* consists of the reinterpretation of the marker occurring uniquely with 3sg, *či-*, as a zero prefix, i.e., as *Ø-war-oq,* with the *či-* progressing upward through the system, replacing *ka-*. Watkins' Law is an instance of influence as defined earlier, since 3sg, NONPERSON, is unmarked as compared with PERSON.

The Directional Verbs

As pointed out earlier, K'iche' preserves intact the system of NOM-DV and ABS-DV which existed in Common Mayan times, as shown in Figure 5.10.

Modifies Nominative with Intransitives	Modifies Nominative with Transitives
*ABS-DV.. oq	*ABS-DV-ERG...A?
š-in-el-war-oq	š-at-el-in-č?ay-A?
'I came (in order to) sleep'	'I came (in order to) hit you'
Modifies Absolutive with Intransitives	Modifies Absolutive with Transitives
*ABS...DV-oq	*ABS-ERG...DV-oq
š-in-xilixob?-kan- oq	š-in-xu·r-ul-oq
'I kept slipping'	'I dragged it here'

Figure 5.10. Directional verbs in Modern K'iche'.

Summary of Colonial K'iche'

The summary of the shift from the common language to Colonial K'iche' is represented in Figure 5.11,[1] which does not included the PROXIMATE PAST nor the PROXIMATE FUTURE because of limitations of space. Observe that the paired opposites INCOMPLETIVE and OPTATIVE were relatively less affected by change than their opposites, the COMPLETIVE and FUTURE. It is particularly interesting to compare the Mamean change in the COMPLETIVE with the change already reported in K'iche'. Mam and Awakatek perfectly illustrate *displacement*, where the original form took on a more restricted object (**iš- > š-* marks dependent clauses), and the new innovative form (*ma·-*) takes on the primary object of marking independent clauses. On the other hand, in the example from K'iche'—the cognate form *mi-er* 'past time of today'—did not displace the original **iš-*, but augmented it, thus causing a markedness reversal, where the signs in the new system, *mi-š* (RECENT PAST) and *š-* (COMPLETIVE), have exactly the same relationship to each other as those in the original system, *š-* (RECENT PAST) and *Ø-* (COMPLETIVE). These two changes demonstrate nicely the *possibilities* of change, based on the structure of the original system, where on the one hand displacement is at work, but on the other hand markedness reversal (by augmentation) occurs. Both are possibilities based on the original system, instances of which have already been reported for Mam and K'iche'. I know of no other way to explain these two changes.

Colonial Kaqchikel

Colonial Kaqchikel and K'iche' are very closely related, and therefore many of the changes already discussed in K'iche' can be found in Kaqchikel, with some obvious differences. For example, Kaqchikel has entirely lost all reflexes of the VOICE/MOOD suffixes (**-ik, *-O, *-oq*) in the independent clauses, with the exception of the double argument OPTATIVE predicate marker, **-A?*, the only remainder of the original four:[2]

š-i-war	COMP-ABS1sg-sleep	'I slept'
š-in-a-č⁷ey	COMP-ABS1sg-ERG2sg-hit	'you hit me'
ti-war	INC-sleep	'would that he sleep!'
k-in-a-č⁷ay-a?	INC-ABS1-ERG2-hit-DAPO	'hit me!'

---

[1]For brevity I have made up the forms, based on Colonial grammar. The actual forms with different verbs are readily seen in Colonial grammars of K'iche'.

[2]Note that the *-ik* remains in NOM-VOICE, where it has been reanalyzed as a transitive nominalizer: *y-i-taxin č-u-b⁷an-ik* INC-ABS1SG-continue PREP-ERG3SG-do(PASSIVE)-NOMLZR.

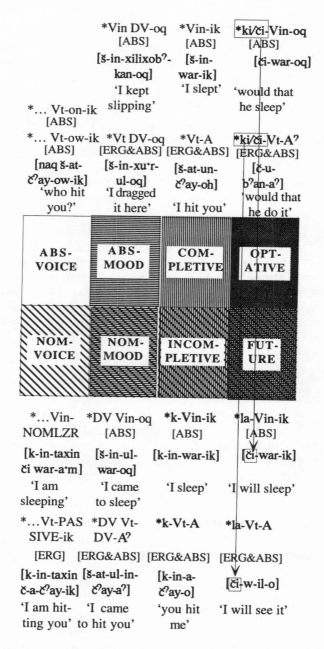

Figure 5.11. Summary of changes in the TAMV from the Common language to Colonial K'iche'.

COMPLETIVE, INCOMPLETIVE, OPTATIVE, and FUTURE

Another difference is that the OPTATIVE prefix occurring in 3 SG position, the reflex of *t^yi-, which became *ȼ(i)*- in K'iche' and other K'iche'an languages (*ȼ*- in Mamean), was replaced by *ti*-. Its etymology is uncertain.

In the COMPLETIVE, Colonial Kaqchikel underwent structural changes identical to those of Colonial K'iche', but by using the same analogical system Kaqchikel extended the shift to the FUTURE and to the INCOMPLETIVE as shown in Figure 5.12

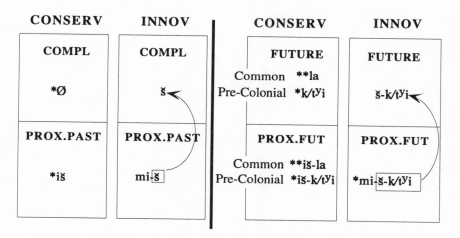

Figure 5.12. Shift in the COMPLETIVE and FUTURE in Colonial Kaqchikel.

Like Colonial K'iche', Colonial Kaqchikel innovated by replacing the FUTURE *la*- with the prefixes for the OPTATIVE, *k-/t^yi-, and as in K'iche', *iš- > š*- replaced *Ø*-, and *mi-š*- replaced *š*-, following the pattern of markedness reversal. Unlike K'iche', but logically carrying the process one step further by analogy with the COMPLETIVE, Kaqchikel innovated in the FUTURE by replacing *ti-/k*- with *š-ti/k*, and PROXIMATE FUTURE *š-ti/k* with *mi-š-ti/k*, although by Colonial times the newly unmarked form *š-ti/k* (FUTURE) had taken over entirely the PROXIMATE FUTURE. This is not surprising for two reasons. First, except for morphological differences, an almost identical change took place in Poqom (p. 139). Second, Utlan (1978:88–89) points out that so-called retrospective languages (languages whose present can refer to time-gone-by) have more distinctions in the past than in the future. Furthermore, the replacing of *ti-/k*- with *š-ti/k* caused the *ti-/k*- to replace the reflex of the old *ki*- INCOMPLETIVE. Schematically, Figure 5.13 shows the entire system of changes (note that the dark arrows show the structural changes Kaqchikel has in common with K'iche').

According to figure 3.13, the PROXIMATE FUTURE had been lost by Colonial times; by modern times the PROXIMATE PAST had similarly been lost.[1]

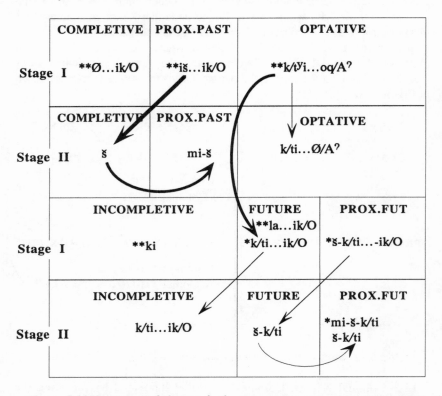

Figure 5.13. Summary of changes in the COMPLETIVE, INCOMPLETIVE, OPTATIVE, and FUTURE for Colonial Kaqchikel.

As mentioned earlier, Kaqchikel lost all the markers for VOICE and MOOD (the *-ik, *-oq,* and *-O*) except the *-A⁷* morpheme, which marks the OPTATIVE in double-argument predications (transitives). Because the OPTATIVE prefixal markers had taken over the INCOMPLETIVE, the only thing that could distinguish the INCOMPLETIVE from the OPTATIVE was the suffixes *-oq* and *A⁷*, and with the loss of *-oq,* the language no longer formally marked the distinction between the INCOMPLETIVE and the OPTATIVE for all single-argument predications, although the forms continued to be distinguished in the transitive:

---

[1]Note that identical structural changes took place in Poqom.

	Incompletive	Optative
Intransitive	k-i(n)-war	k-i(n)-war
	'I sleep'	'would that I sleep'
Transitive	k-i(n)-ru-č'ey	k-i(n)-ru-č'ay-aʔ
	'he hits me'	'would that he hit me'

Furthermore, both Kaqchikel and K'iche' had lost the markers for the IMPERATIVE, and as a consequence of these two losses, Colonial Kaqchikel made no distinction between, say, 'you sleep' and 'sleep!': *ta-war.* To remedy this homophony, Kaqchikel augmented the INCOMPLETIVE as shown on page 135, as was done almost universally in the Mayan languages.

Between the attested Colonial data and the modern data, however, an innovative development occurred which renewed the earlier distinction between the INCOMPLETIVE and the OPTATIVE, not only for double-argument, but especially for single-argument predications as well.[1] The process by which the distinction was made was augmentation on the INCOMPLETIVE, already seen in all the languages heretofore discussed, save K'iche'. In the case of Kaqchikel, *tan,* an "auxiliary verb which denotes that the action is occurring at the present moment" (Saenz 1940:357, my translation), was added to the INCOMPLETIVE.

Common Stage I	16th Cent Stage II	19th Cent Stage III	20th Cent Stage IV	20th Cent Stage V	
*tʸi-war-ik	ti-war	tan-ti-war	n.di-war	ni-war	'he sleeps'
*k-at-war-ik	k-at-war	tan-k-at-war	n.g-at-war	y-at-war	'you sleep'
*k-in-war-ik	k-in-war	tan-k-in-war	n.g-in-war	y-in-war	'I sleep'
*tʸi-war-ebʔ	k-e-war	tan-k-e-war	n.g-e-war	y-e-war	'they sleep'
*k-eš-war-ik	k-iš-war	tan-k-iš-war	n.g-iš-war	y-iš-war	'you-guys sleep'
*q-ox-war-ik	q-ox-war	tan-q-ox-war	n.g-ox-war	y-ox-war	'we sleep'
*tʸ-war-oq	ti-war	ti-war	ti-war	ti-war	'would that he sleep'
*k-at-war-oq	k-at-war	k-at-war	k-at-war	k-at-war	'would that you sleep'
*k-in-war-oq	k-in-war	k-in-war	k-in-war	k-in-war	'would that I sleep'
*tʸi-war-ebʔ	k-e-war	k-e-war	k-e-war	k-e-war	'would that they sleep'
*k-eš-war-oq	k-iš-war	k-iš-war	k-iš-war	k-iš-war	'would that you-guys sleep'
*q-ox-war-oq	q-ox-war	q-ox-war	q-ox-war	q-ox-war	'would that we sleep'

As seen above in Stages IV and V, there was a wearing away of the morpheme *tan,* such that when I did field work in Patzicía in the late 1960s with a man in his sixties,[2] he gave the paradigm *ndi- (< tanti-), (n)gi- (<t*

---

[1]We are particularly fortunate to have the Colonial record because without it, we would have lost the thread of the process of change, not only from Colonial to modern times, but also from Common to Colonial times. The picture would have been quite murky.

[2]Daniel Mich.

ank-), whereas younger speakers gave a paradigm even further removed, *ni-*
(< tanti), y- (< (n)gi- < tank- (n)gi-). With these newly formed distinctions
the OPTATIVE was now distinct from the COMPLETIVE.

Summary of Kaqchikel

One of the most interesting changes in Kaqchikel is the analogical extension
that took place from the COMPLETIVE, paralleling the change earlier described
in K'iche'. Since the FUTURE was similarly affected, the structure of changes—which otherwise must remain obscure and only partially accounted
for—emerges. It is by *system* that such extensive explanations are possible.
Note that even though Colonial Kaqchikel has no PROXIMATE FUTURE, it
seems almost certain that for a time in its prehistory such a FUTURE existed.

Tz'utujil

COMPLETIVE, INCOMPLETIVE, OPTATIVE, and FUTURE

The changes occurring in Tz'utujil from the common language to Colonial
times are virtually identical to those changes discussed for Colonial Kaqchikel.
For example, apparently the *i-š* came to mark the PROXIMATE PAST, while *š-*
came to mark the COMPLETIVE/PAST, while the *-ki/š-ti,* originally the form for
PROXIMATE FUTURE, came to mark the FUTURE, and the original FUTURE, **ki-/ti-,*
came to mark the simple INCOMPLETIVE, displacing the original **ki-.* Unlike
Kaqchikel, however, not all the markers for VOICE/MOOD were lost: *-ik,* the
marker of a single argument became *i,* while the single-argument modal **-oq*
became *-o.*

On the other hand, the marker of double argument (transitives), **-O > -O,*
as with Kaqchikel, was lost, whereas the original modal marker, *-A?,* was
maintained. A comparison is given in Figure 5.14.

The shift from Colonial Tz'utujil to the modern language was also much
like the Kaqchikel shift. Like Kaqchikel, Tz'utujil augmented the INCOMPLETIVE
*ki-/ti- during the eighteenth century, but with a morpheme *tan-* (not *an-* as
in Kaqchikel):

Common	Colonial	18th Cent	19th Cent	20th Cent	
Mamo-K'iche'an stage I	Tz'utujil stage II	Tz'utujil stage III	Tz'utujil stage IV	Tz'utujil stage V	
*tʸi-war-ik	ti-war-i	kanti-war-i	n-war-i	n-war-i	'he sleeps'
*k-at-war-ik	k-at-war-i	kank-at-war-i	nk-at-war-i	n-at-war-i	'you sleep'
*k-in-war-ik	k-in-war-i	kank-in-war-i	nk-in-war-i	n-in-war-i	'I sleep'
*k-eb⁷-war-ik	k-e-war-i	kank-e-war-i	nk-e-war-i	n-e-war-i	'they sleep'
*k-eš-war-ik	k-iš-war-i	kank-iš-war-i	nk-iš-war-i	n-iš-war-i	'you-guys sleep'
*q-ox-war-ik	q-ox-war-i	kanq-ox-war-i	nq-o-war-i	n-oq-war-i	'we sleep'

*tʸi-war-oq	ti-war-o	ti-war-i	ti-war-i	ti-war-i	'may he sleep'
*k-at-war-oq	k-at-war-o	k-at-war-i	k-at-war-i	k-at-war-i	'may you sleep'
*k-in-war-oq	k-in-war-o	k-in-war-i	k-in-war-i	k-in-war-i	'may I sleep'
*k-eb'-war-oq	k-e·-war-o	k-e·-war-i	k-e·-war-i	k-e·-war-i	'may they sleep'
*k-eš-war-oq	k-iš-war-o	k-iš-war-i	k-iš-war-i	k-iš-war-i	'may you-guys sleep'
*q-ox-war-oq	q-ox-war-o	q-ox-war-i	q-o·-war-i	q-o·-war-i	'may we sleep'

Several changes obviously occurred between the common language and the later stages. First, as pointed out earlier, *-ik* became *-i*, just as *-oq* became *-o*, after which the unmarked *-i* took over the more-marked *-o*. Second, in accordance with Watkins' Law, the unmarked 3 SG *n-* (< *kan-ti*) took over the other TENSE/ASPECT markers originally derived from *kan-k-*. In general, both the replacement of *-o* by *-i* and the replacement of the reflexes of *kan-k-* by *ni-* are instances of influence, where an unmarked member of a paradigm comes to stand in the place of its more-marked counterpart(s).

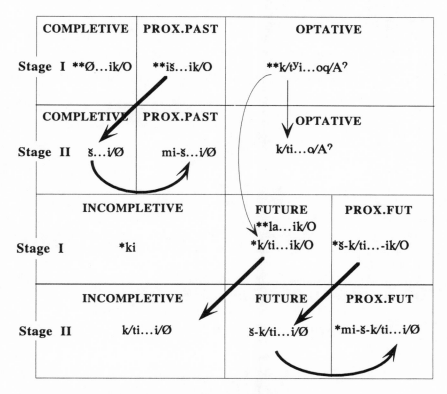

Figure 5.14. Summary of changes in the COMPLETIVE, INCOMPLETIVE, OPTATIVE, and FUTURE for Colonial Tz'utujil; heavy lines indicate changes similar to Kaqchikel.

In Dayley's grammar (1985:87), the ABS1PL is *oq*, whereas the original, pre-Tz'utujil form was **ox*, from Common Mayan **o?ŋ*. This innovation is explainable by the fact that Shumway (1985:9) has both *noq* and *nqo* for the INCOMPLETIVE/PRESENT aspect. Apparently, *nqo* comes from *kan + q-ox*. The **n-q-ox- > n-q-o˙* was reanalyzed as *n-qo-*, so that the original aspect marker *q* became a part of the PERSON marker. Then, *qo-* was metathesized to *oq*, by analogy with the rest of the VC absolutive markers, such as 1SG *in*, 2SG *at*, and 2PL *iš*. Good evidence for this analysis is given by contrasting the pre-Tz'utujil paradigm with the present Tz'utujil paradigm, where **qox* becomes *qo˙*:

pre-Tz'utujil	Tz'utujil	
*ti-	ti-	3SG
*k-at	k-at	2SG
*k-in	k-in	1SG
*k-eb?	k-e˙	3PL
*k-iš	k-iš	2PL
*q-ox	q-o˙	1PL

Another change occurred in the dialect represented in Shumway (1985), as can be seen in the following paradigm:

t-	3SG
k-at	2SG
t-in	1SG
tk-e	3PL
k-iš	2PL
t-oq	1PL

What seems to be happening here is that the 3SG *t* spread upward through the paradigm to every form but the SECOND PERSON, as again suggested by Watkins' Law.

The future also shows a similar leveling. As seen in the pre-Tz'utujil form, 3SG *t* imposed itself on the rest of the paradigm:

pre-Tz'utujil	Tz'utujil
*š-ti-	š-t-
*š-k-at	š-t-at
*š-k-in	š-t-in
*š-k-e	š-t-e
*š-k-iš	š-t-iš
*š-q-ox	š-t-oq

In this case, 3sg *š* + *t* overtook the TENSE/ASPECT markers of the original, pre-Tz'utujil paradigm.

Summary of Tz'utujil

Tz'utujil is somewhere between K'iche' and Kaqchikel in its divergence from the common language in partially preserving the suffixes. It is like Kaqchikel in the shift from the Common Mayan OPTATIVE, 3sg **tʸi-*, to *ti-*, which is an irregular sound change. One is struck by the degree to which 3sg is taking over the rest of the paradigm.

Poqom

The materials listed below as "Colonial Poqom" are extracted from both Zúñiga (n.d.) and Morán (1720) because neither grammar is complete by itself. The two grammars correspond very closely; the chief difference is that the final consonants of the morphemes that mark voice and mood are lost in the dialect represented by Morán. That is, Common Mayan **-ik* and **-oq* remained *-ik* and *-ok* in Zúñiga (Poqomchi'), but become *-i* and *-o* in Morán (Poqomam). For convenience I will refer to both of these as Poqom, unless there is a need to distinguish between them.

COMPLETIVE

What happened in Colonial Poqom is in many ways like what happened in K'iche' and Kaqchikel. First, there was a markedness reversal in the COMPLETIVE, just as in K'iche' and Kaqchikel. But in Poqom, the marker of PROXIMITY is *a-* and not *mi-* as illustrated in Figure 5.15.

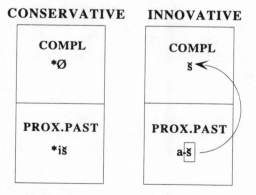

Figure 5.15. Markedness reversal in the COMPLETIVE of pre-Poqom.

FUTURE

Furthermore, like Kaqchikel (but unlike K'iche'), Poqom underwent a shift of markedness reversal in the FUTURE, as seen in Figure 5.16.

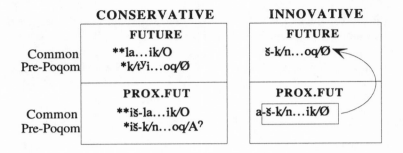

Figure 5.16. Markedness reversal in the FUTURE of pre-Poqom.

Notice from the above illustration that, as with all K'iche'an languages, the *-la-* FUTURE was lost to the *-ki-* prefix, and as with many languages, *-oq* took over the FUTURE. Of substantial interest here is the fact that the PROXIMATE FUTURE was in a state of flux (as attested in Morán's grammar), where either of the suffixes *-i* < *-ik* or *-o* < *-oq* were used. Given the reconstruction of the FUTURE in the common language, this is certainly what would be expected—that the more-marked PROXIMATE FUTURE would undergo the shift from *-ik* to *-oq* later than the less-marked simple FUTURE. In other words, the OPTATIVE suffix *-oq* influenced the simple FUTURE, but it did not totally take over its more-marked counterpart PROXIMATE FUTURE, as attested by Morán's grammar in Colonial times. This observation is in accordance with the principle which states that change is introduced in the less-marked categories of a grammatical system, and then, by influence, spreads to the more-marked categories. This influence on the FUTURE by the OPTATIVE and the INCOMPLETIVE can be summarized in Figure 5.17.[1]

Figure 5.18 shows the process of change from Common Mayan times to Colonial Poqom.

As for the etymology of the proximate marker, *a-*, it is not unreasonable to speculate that the *a-* FUTURE was borrowed from a Cholan language, since *a-* similarly marks the FUTURE in Colonial Choltí:

Nota que el presente de los verbos neutros se haçe futuro en *ruz*,

---

[1]Recall, however, that we are only giving the unmarked COMPLETIVE and the unmarked FUTURE. The marked PROXIMATE FUTURE, it will be recalled, was in the throes of being influenced by the OPTATIVE.

anteponiendole una *a* vg. *apaℇxielen* 'tengo de uolberme', *azatpael ox* 'aueis os de perder.'[1]

[Note that the present of the intransitive verbs become a *ruz* future by preposing an *a;* for example *apaℇxielen* 'I have to come back,' *atzatpael ox* 'you guys have to lose.']

	COMPLETIVE	OPTATIVE
Stage I	*Ø...ik/O	*ka/t^yi...oq/A?
Stage II	š...ik,Ø	ka/či...oq/Ø

	INCOMPLETIVE	FUTURE
Stage I	*ka...ik/O	*la...ik/O
Stage II	k/n...ik/Ø	š-k/n...oq/Ø

Figure 5.17. Influence of the INCOMPLETIVE and the OPTATIVE on the FUTURE in Colonial Poqom.

Furthermore, in Smailus' (1973) analysis of Chontal of 1610, *a-* marks the PROXIMATE PAST, and there are at least two instances I found where it is also used to mark the PROXIMATE FUTURE. Note also that in Morales' *Arte de lengua Cacchí (Q'eqchi')* there are two equivalent temporal adverbial particles, *acaℇ* and *ixcaℇ*. It is significant that *mix* [miš] is the K'iche'/Kaqchikel marker for RECENT PAST, while *a-* is used in Poqomchi'. It is also true that both Poqomchi' and Q'eqchi' had extensive influence from Cholan.

So far as I can determine, there is not enough information to say where the INCOMPLETIVE 3SG *n-* comes from, but it is not uncommon for Mayan to develop such a distinction.[2]

Another INCOMPLETIVE

Up to this point, another kind of INCOMPLETIVE for Colonial Poqomchi' has gone unmentioned which is reminiscent of the so-called split-ergative commonly found in Yukatekan and neighboring Lowland Languages. In Colonial

---

[1]It should be noted that the normal future in Choltí is made with *š-* and *-k* < *-oq: š-pakš-ik en* 'volvereme (I will come back)'

[2]See Robertson (1980:62-65).

Poqom—unlike in Yukatek Maya, where split ergativity is more expansive—split ergativity is found only in a single part of the INCOMPLETIVE aspect:

Single Argument

na rilari	[na-r-il-ar-i]	'he is seen (right now)'
na avilari	[na-aw-il-ar-i]	'you are seen (right now)'
na vilari	[na-w-il-ar-i]	'I am seen (right now)'
na quilari taque	[na-k-il-ar-i take]	'they are seen (right now)'
na avilari ta	[na-aw-il-ar-i ta]	'you-guys are seen (right now)'
na quilari	[na-q-il-ar-i]	'we are seen (right now)'

Double Argument

naru vanom	[na-ru-bʔan-oˑm]	'he does it (right now)'
naa vanom	[na-a-bʔan-oˑm]	'you do it (right now)'
nanu vanom	[na-nu-bʔan-oˑm]	'I do it (right now)'
naqui vanom	[na-ki-bʔan-oˑm]	'they do it (right now)'
naa vanom ta	[na-a-bʔan-oˑm ta]	'you-guys do it (right now)'
naka vanom	[na-qa-bʔan-oˑm]	'we do it (right now)'

This is called the "first present" in the Colonial Grammars and is said to have the meaning 'to do something currently/now.' This is contrasted to the unmarked "second present," which has the meaning of generality or habituality:

Single Argument

nilari	[n-il-ar-i]	'he is seen'
tilari	[t-il-ar-i]	'you are seen'
quinilari	[kin-il-ar-i]	'I am seen'
quilari taque	[k-il-ar-i take]	'they are seen'
tilari ta	[t-il-ar-i ta]	'you-guys are seen'
cohilari	[q-ox-il-ar-i]	'we are seen'

Double Argument

nruvan	[n-ru-bʔan]	'he does it'
navan	[n-a-bʔan]	'you do it'
nuvan	[n-nu-bʔan]	'I do it'
nquivan	[n-ki-bʔan]	'they do it'
navan ta	[n-a-bʔan] ta	'you-guys do it'
nacavan	[n-qa-bʔan]	'we do it'

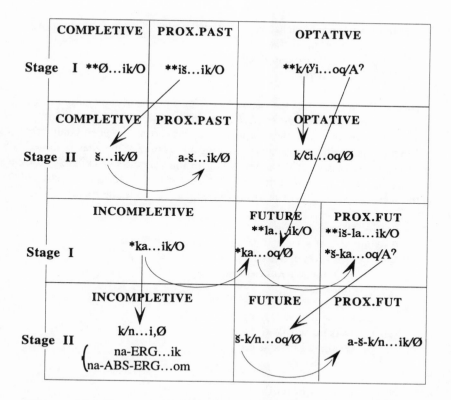

Figure 5.18. Summary of changes of TAMV from Common Mayan to Colonial Poqom.

The morphology of the so-called first present is likely incipient split ergativity, almost certainly from the pressures of Cholan—probably from Choltí, given the many other kinds of borrowings, both lexical and grammatical, that are readily apparent in Poqomchi' and Q'eqchi'. The etymological source can surely be found in the PROGRESSIVE, which is pan-Mayan, as discussed above. Note that Modern Poqomchi' has both patterns, with and without raising, in the PROGRESSIVE, but these are not synonymous. Raising is unmarked and typical, whereas nonraising is exceptional:

Raising: predicate + ABSOLUTIVE PREPOSITION verbal.noun
k[?]ahči[?]-k-in či wir-ik

PROG-AFF-ABS1SG PREP sleep-PROG
'I am sleeping'

Nonraising: predicate ERGATIVE + verbal.noun
k²ahči² nu-wir-ik
continue ERG1SG-sleep-AFF
'I am sleepy'

This brief exposition of the facts allows for a possible explanation of the innovative "first present," *na*-ERG...*i(k)* in Colonial Poqom. It seems entirely reasonable to propose that the morpheme *na*- came from the positional/verbal *nak*, which according to Zúñiga (n.d.) meant 'actuality in what is done,'[1] and meant PROGRESSIVE. Then a new form for the PROGRESSIVE (*k²ahči²*) took over the primary function of the PROGRESSIVE, and the old form was restricted to the secondary function of marking ongoing actuality in the IMPERFECTIVE.

Stage I: pre-Poqomchi':
Raising: verbal + ABSOLUTIVE PREPOSITION verbal.noun
*nak-k-in či wir-ik
continue-AFF-ABS1SG PREP sleep-SAPD
'I am sleeping'

Nonraising: verbal ERGATIVE + verbal.noun
*nak nu-wir-ik
continue ERG1SG-sleep-SAPD
'I am sleepy'

Stage II: Poqomchi':
I. verbal + ABSOLUTIVE PREPOSITION verbal.noun
či²-k-in či wir-ik
continue-AFF-ABS1SG PREP sleep-SAPD
'I am going to sleep'

II. verbal + ERGATIVE + verbal.noun
či² nu-wir-ik
continue ERG1SG-sleep-SAPD
'I am sleepy'

At this point, the form *na-nu-wir-ik* (PROG-ERG1SG-sleep-SAPD) 'I sleep right now'[2] became the so-called first present of Colonial grammar.

---

[1]This is actually Gate's excerpt from Zúñiga, where he has the nasty habit of mixing English and Spanish. "Actuality" is undoubtedly from the Spanish *actualmente* 'now'.

[2]For comparative purposes I made up this form based on the documented forms given above.

Furthermore, one must consider the possibility that the Lowland Languages followed a similar pattern, but in fact expanded the pattern by replacing the original INCOMPLETIVE with a newly recruited PROGRESSIVE. This, then, would be the foothold for the spread of the ERGATIVE to mark all uncompleted actions, thus creating the split-ergative system as described above.

A quick piece of supporting evidence for this developmental theory of split ergatives suggests itself on reading the Colonial *Arte en Lengua Ɛholtí* (Morán 1695) Here the equivalent of Colonial Poqomam's PROGRESSIVE can be found to cover the semantic territory of both the INCOMPLETIVE and the PROGRESSIVE of most Mayan languages:

> yual u uixnel
> [iwal-u-wiš-n-el]
> CONT-ERG3SG-go-AFF-NOMLZR
> 'he is going, he goes'

> yual a uixnel
> [iwal-a-wiš-n-el]
> CONT-ERG2SG-go-AFF-NOMLZR
> 'you are going, you go'

> yual in uixnel
> [iwal-in-wiš-n-el]
> CONT-ERG1SG-go-AFF-NOMLZR
> 'I am going, I go'

> yual u uixnelob
> [iwal-u-wiš-n-el-ob?]
> CONT-ERG3PL-go-AFF-NOMLZR-ABS3PL
> 'they are going, they go'

> yual i uixnel
> [iwal-i-wiš-n-el]
> CONT-ERG2PL-go-AFF-NOMLZR
> 'you-guys are going, you-guys go'

> yual Ɛa uixnel
> [iwal-ka-wiš-n-el]
> CONT-ERG1PL-go-AFF-NOMLZR
> 'we are going, we go'

The FUTURE, on the other hand has ABSOLUTIVE pronouns. This is highly significant, suggesting that Choltí was historically a straight- (and not split-) ergative language:

xɛhiɛ Pedro
[š-či-k Pedro]
FUT-go-SAPO
'Pedro will go'

xɛhic et
[š-či-k-et]
FUT-go-SAPO-ABS2SG
'you will go'

xɛhic en
[š-či-k-en]
FUT-go-SAPO-ABS1SG
'you will go'

xɛhic ob
[š-či-k-ob?][1]
FUT-go-SAPO-ABS3PL
'they will go'

xɛhic ox
[š-či-k-oš]
FUT-go-SAPO-ABS2PL
'you-guys will go'

xɛhic on
[š-či-k-on]
FUT-go-SAPO-ABS1PL
'we will go'

In fact, page 172 shows in detail that in Choltí this FUTURE was originally an INCOMPLETIVE—the descendant form from the proposed Common Mayan INCOMPLETIVE *ki-, and that its use as a FUTURE was likely the result of displacement by the newly formed split-ergative INCOMPLETIVE.

Thus, the only difference between Colonial Poqom, whose so-called present uses the ERGATIVE to mark intransitive constructions, and Choltí, whose INCOMPLETIVE similarly uses the ERGATIVE to mark intransitive constructions, is the fact that Colonial Poqomchi' also has another "present," which is a reflex of the Common Mayan INCOMPLETIVE. If the "first present" had taken over the "second present," Poqomchi' would, like Choltí, have been well on

---

[1] I complete the paradigm, since the grammar only contains information up to first person singular.

its way to becoming a full-blown split-ergative language. Such was the case Choltí (as suggested on page 145), which represents the least-developed stage of split ergativity to be found in the Lowland Languages.

Modern Poqomchi'

Figure 5.19 summarizes the changes from Colonial times to modern Poqomchi'.[1]

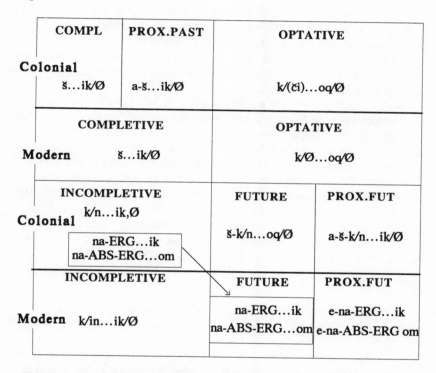

Figure 5.19. Summary of changes from Colonial to Modern Poqomchi'.

With respect to Figure 5.19, several observations are in order. First, the distinction in the COMPLETIVE between the unmarked and the PROXIMATE PAST was lost, as happened in K'iche' and Kaqchikel, so that in Modern Poqomchi' only the simple COMPLETIVE remains. Second, the OPTATIVE is virtually the same as in Colonial times. Third, the INCOMPLETIVE—which is a reflex of Common Mayan—remained intact, but the split-ergative INCOMPLETIVE became

---

[1]The data for Modern Poqomchi' are from *Gramatica Pokonchi',* by Padre Ricardo Terga, Virgilio Lem Pop, and Esteban Stewart.

a NONPROXIMATE FUTURE, as seen below, displacing the Colonial PROXIMATE FUTURE. Furthermore, the Colonial PROXIMATE FUTURE was displaced by an *a* FUTURE built on the *e na* +PRESENT. It is not improbable that the *e* comes from the Colonial *a* of the same function.

Summary of Poqom

Poqom is a particularly interesting language in the way it underwent change from the common language for several reasons. First, when compared to K'iche' and Kaqchikel, Poqom truly developed a system virtually identical to that postulated for Kaqchikel, with markedness reversal not only in the COMPLETIVE but in the FUTURE as well. The extent of the analogical development of the system shows again the importance of looking at paradigmatic analogy in explaining historical change.

Another point of interest is the incipient split ergativity, especially in Colonial times. Like so many of the other languages, Poqom innovated by the influence of the progressive of NOM-VOICE on the INCOMPLETIVE. The investigation of the probable source of the split ergativity in this language provides the scenario for a generalization typically found in the Lowland Languages. In this case the syntagmatic PROGRESSIVE apparently became morphologized by coming into competition with the INCOMPLETIVE. This hypothesis is certainly strengthened by looking carefully at Choltí. Finally, modern Poqomchi' provides another instance where the INCOMPLETIVE took over the FUTURE, with unequivocally attested evidence that the Colonial INCOMPLETIVE (from the PROGRESSIVE) displaced the Colonial FUTURE.

Q'eqchi'

The changes that occurred in Q'eqchi' diverge from what has been observed heretofore. Up to this point, the Mam and pre-Awakatek COMPLETIVE changed via the process of displacement, where the new sign *ma·-* took over the primary object of the *š-* < *iš-*—namely, independent clauses—while *š-* was restricted to a secondary object—namely, dependent clauses. The second kind of change observed in the other K'iche'an languages, was a kind of markedness reversal, where *mi-* was added to *š-* < *iš-*, reinforcing the PROXIMATE PAST, while the original PROXIMATE PAST became the COMPLETIVE. There is yet a third way in which the COMPLETIVE was affected. In Sipakapa K'iche', for example, *mi-* was added to the INCOMPLETIVE, and the resultant combination has the meaning PROXIMATE PAST:

mi-k-in-k'at-ik	'I just got burned'
š-in-wr-ik	'I slept'
k-in-wr-ik	'I sleep'

INCOMPLETIVE and COMPLETIVE

Q'eqchi' apparently changed along these same lines, only more extensively. Here, the INCOMPLETIVE was augmented with both a form *na-* and a form *ta-*. This augmentation caused a markedness reversal, so that the original IN-COMPLETIVE **ka-* > *k-* moved up into the unmarked COMPLETIVE, yielding *o-* DISTANT PAST, *k-* MEDIATE PAST and *š-k-* RECENT PAST.[1] The phenomenon can be visualized in Figure 5.20. This is another markedness reversal, where the two prefixes, *na-* and *ta-*, likely from the PROGRESSIVE, were added to the reflex of Common Mayan INCOMPLETIVE **k-*, yielding *nak-* and *tak-* respectively, thus moving the old reflex of the INCOMPLETIVE **ki* into the COMPLETIVE. Note that in the PROXIMATE PAST, *š-k*, can take the form *š-*, as pointed out by Morales (n.d.).

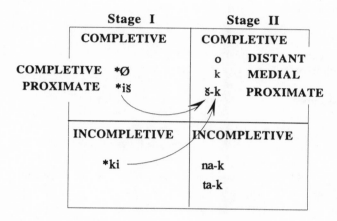

Figure 5.20. Summary of changes in the COMPLETIVE of Colonial Q'eqchi'.

Note that *nak-* is said to have the quality "de presencialidad" and *tak-* "de actualidad que expresa mas la precocialidad" (Morales, n.d.). It is possible that the *na-* is related to the *na-* of Awakatek (**na-k-in-...* > *način-*), which also reinforces the INCOMPLETIVE, but it is almost surely cognate with the

---

[1]Morales (n.d.) is clear on the so-called preterit: "Hay tres pretéritos; el primero denota que ha mucho tiempo pasó ó se hizo la cosa...; el segundo pretérito denota que ha pocos días que se hizo la cosa...; el tercer pretérito denota haber poco rato que se hizo la cosa, y este se hace con las mismas partículas del segundo, anteponiendoles una *š*." [There are three preterites; the first denotes that a lot of time has passed since the thing was done...; the second denotes that it has been only a few days since the thing was done...; the third denotes that it was just a short time ago since the thing was done, and this is done with the same particles as the second, prefixing an *š*.]

positional/verbal *nak* of Poqom, which according to Gates (n.d.) meant "actuality in what is done." Furthermore, it is possible that the Q'eqchi' *ta-* is cognate with Kaqchikel *tan*, which was similarly augmentally prefixed to the INCOMPLETIVE in Colonial times. It is noteworthy that Saenz (1940:357) defines *tan* as an "auxiliary that denotes action that takes place at the present moment," which seems to coincide nicely with Colonial Q'eqchi's *ta-*, which denotes "actualidad" (Morales). The *o·-* of the DISTANT PAST is undoubtedly cognate with the morpheme similarly used in Mam to signal the DISTANT PAST, *o-*, coming from **oŋ-*, which means 'distant past.'[1]

OPTATIVE and FUTURE

Finally, as in all other K'iche'an languages, the OPTATIVE influenced the FUTURE, in this case taking it over completely, as explained by Morales (n.d.):

> El imperativo es el mismo Futuro ya dicho y algunas veces le suelen añadir un *aq* á la postre para denotar mas imperio.

> [The imperative is the same as the future already mentioned, and sometimes an *-aq* is added to the end to denote more authority.]

It is noteworthy that the reflex of Common Mayan **-oq (> -aq)* is still optionally present in the OPTATIVE (IMPERATIVE).

It will be noted that in the OPTATIVE, the original **k-* has been lost in favor of the 3 SG *či- < *tʸi-*. This is precisely what happened in the Nahualá dialect of K'iche', with the explanation based on Watkins' Law: the unmarked 3SG influenced the rest of the paradigm. Note also that the original distinction between PROXIMATE and DISTANT FUTURE has been lost. Figure 5.21 summarizes the entire shift.

From Colonial to Modern Q'eqchi'

COMPLETIVE, INCOMPLETIVE, OPTATIVE, and FUTURE

The shift from Colonial to Modern Q'eqchi' involves several rather interesting shifts, again explainable in terms of the paradigmatic structure. First, the Colonial INCOMPLETIVE *tak-* moved into the FUTURE, displacing the Colonial *či-*, which served as both the OPTATIVE and the FUTURE. In discussing the meaning of the modern *či-*, Stewart (1978:96–97) says the following:

---

[1]Choltí has a form *oni*, which is cognate with K'iche'an *ox-er < *oŋ-er*, which Morán (1695) translates as "antiguamente" or "anciently."

The combination of tense, aspect, and mood labeled here OPTATIVE/IM-PERATIVE is the most complex T/A/M inflection. In terms of time this inflection indicates action which is just about to occur or which begins at the moment of speaking, thus dividing future time with the prefix *ta-*. This inflection also may indicate an immediate desire on the part of the speaker mixed with an element of doubt that the desire will be fulfilled, and in this sense may be said to be optative or exhortative. Finally, this inflection may be used to mark imperative, either alone or in conjunction with a special imperative suffix.

	COMPLETIVE	PROX.PAST	OPTATIVE	
Stage I	*Ø...ik/O	*iš...ik/O	*ki/t^{y}i...oq/A?	

	DIST.PAST o...k/Ø	OPTATIVE	
Stage II	MED.PAST k...k/Ø	či...(o)q/Ø	
	PROX.PAST š-k...k/Ø		

	INCOMPLETIVE	FUTURE	PROX.FUT
Stage I	*ki...ik/O	*la...ik/O	*iš-la...ik/O

	INCOMPLETIVE	FUTURE	
Stage II	nak...k/Ø	či...(a)q/Ø	

Figure 5.21. Summary of changes of TAMV from Common Mayan to Colonial Q'eqchi'.

The PAST/COMPLETIVE has lost the DISTANT PAST, except apparently in some dialects (i.e, Carchá and Chamil; see Stewart, 1978:95). Also, the Colonial grammar has two alternating forms for the PROXIMATE PAST, as explained by Morales (n.d.):

Tercer Pretérito antepone la š á las partículas del segundo, y muchas veces sincopan el *ški,* y solo anteponen el verbo á la š v.g. *š-koxlax in čol:* habiendo de decir; *škikoxlah in čol.*

[The third preterite preposes the š to the particles of the second, and very often it syncopates the *ški,* and only puts the š before the verb, for example, *š-koxlax in čol:* instead of saying *škikoxlah in čol.*]

Thus, because there was this variation in Colonial times, the unmarked š- won out over the more-marked *šk-.* The entire scheme from Common Mayan to modern times is given in Figure 5.22.

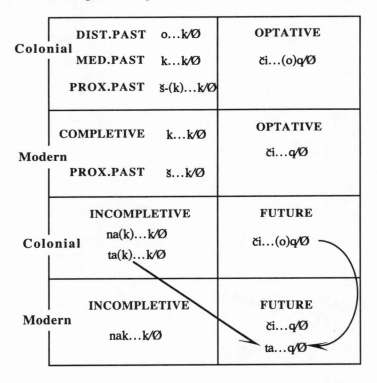

Figure 5.22. Summary of changes of TAMV from Colonial to Modern Q'eqchi'.

Summary of Q'eqchi'

Q'eqchi', unlike the other languages discussed, took its INCOMPLETIVE into the COMPLETIVE by markedness reversal. This phenomenon, as pointed out, happened in Sipakapa K'iche' and, as shown on page 160, in Jakaltek as well. Also, up to this point, markedness reversal has only been attested among the categories of the COMPLETIVE; this is the first instance in which markedness reversal has gone from the COMPLETIVE to the INCOMPLETIVE. Furthermore, as is happening in Nahualá (p. 129), where the 3 SG *či-* of the OPTATIVE is taking over the rest of the paradigm, so in Q'eqchi' the same *či-* took over the rest of the paradigm.

It is particularly interesting to note that in the history of Q'eqchi' the FUTURE was deeply affected first by the OPTATIVE, which completely took over the FUTURE by Colonial times, and then by the INCOMPLETIVE, where the Colonial INCOMPLETIVE *ta-* displaced the OPTATIVE *či-*. This should not be surprising, given this same influence, both from the OPTATIVE and from the INCOMPLETIVE, which was commonly attested in the other languages heretofore discussed.

Chapter 6. Q'anjob'alan

Q'anjob'alan is an interesting language family because as a family it is quite conservative, although each individual language has innovated in its own peculiar way. It is unfortunate that there are no Colonial grammars (so far as I am aware) because they would undoubtedly yield insights similar to those that are so useful in understanding the history of the other Colonially attested branches of the Mayan family.

Q'anjob'al

COMPLETIVE and PROXIMATE PAST

In Q'anjob'al today the distinction between the COMPLETIVE and the PROXIMATE PAST has been lost, even though there are two forms, *ma-š-* and *š-,* as can be seen in Figures 6.1 and 6.2

	COMPLETIVE		PROXIMATE PAST	
	Common	**Q'anjob'al**	**Common**	**Q'anjob'al**
3SG	*...ik	(ma)š...i	*iš...ik	(ma)š...i
2SG	*...at	(ma)š-ač...i	*iš-at...ik	(ma)š-ač...i
1SG	*...in	(ma)š-in...i	*iš-in...ik	(ma)š-in...i
3PL	*...eb⁷	(ma)š...eb⁷	*iš⁷...eb⁷	(ma)š...eb⁷
2PL	*...eš	(ma)š-eš...i	*iš-eš...ik	(ma)š-eš...i
1PL	*...o⁷ŋ	(ma)š-on...i	*iš-o⁷ŋ...ik	(ma)š-on...i

Figure 6.1. The single-argument COMPLETIVE and PROXIMATE PAST in Q'anjob'al.

Despite the fact that there is no distinction between the prefix *ma-š-* and the prefix *š-* (*maš-way-i* and *š-way-i* both translate 'he slept'),[1] it is highly likely that prehistorically they both have the same source as the two Colonial K'iche' forms *mi-š-* (PROXIMATE PAST) and *š-* (COMPLETIVE). Thus it is suggested that in Q'anjob'al prehistory, as is attested in Colonial K'iche', *ma-š-* marked

---

[1]At least so far as can be elicited by giving a minimal pair to an informant, there was no immediate explanation for the difference between the two forms.

the PROXIMATE PAST, and *ş*- the COMPLETIVE. That is, the reflex of the Common Mayan PROXIMATE PAST *iş* was augmented by the morpheme meaning 'past time of today,' *mayal*, yielding *ma-ş-*, and the old morpheme *ş- < *iş-* took over the meaning of the COMPLETIVE, as shown in Figure 6.3.

	COMPLETIVE		PROXIMATE PAST	
	Common	Q'anjob'al	Common	Q'anjob'al
3SG	*...ik	(ma)ş-s...Aʔ	*iş-u...O	(ma)ş-s...Aʔ
2SG	*...at	(ma)ş-a...Aʔ	*iş-a...O	(ma)ş-a...Aʔ
1SG	*...in	(ma)ş-in...Aʔ	*iş-nu...O	(ma)ş-in...Aʔ
3PL	*...ebʔ	(ma)ş-s...ebʔ	*iş-ki...O	(ma)ş-s...ebʔ
2PL	*...eš	(ma)ş-e...Aʔ	*iş-e...O	(ma)ş-e...Aʔ
1PL	*...oʔŋ	(ma)ş-ko...Aʔ	*iş-qa...O	(ma)ş-ko...Aʔ

Figure 6.2. The double-argument COMPLETIVE and PROXIMATE PAST in Q'anjob'al.

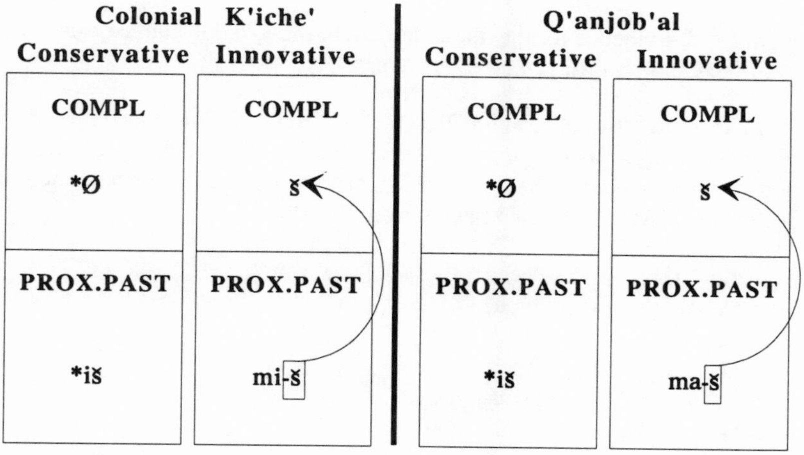

Figure 6.3. Parallel changes of the PROXIMATE PAST and the COMPLETIVE in Colonial K'iche' and Q'anjob'al.

Normally, the expectation would be that *ş-*, which would have been the unmarked COMPLETIVE, would take over the more-marked *maş-*, the marker of the PROXIMATE PAST, as happened in K'iche'. This apparently did not happen. Instead, the kind of augmentation discussed earlier, of the type *thaw/unthaw*, or *bigger/more bigger,* or *s-/sy-* ERG3SG occurred where there are two forms which are interpreted similarly.

INCOMPLETIVE

The INCOMPLETIVE is here proposed to be directly descendent from the Common Mayan INCOMPLETIVE **ki-,* as outlined in Figure 6.4.

	SINGLE-ARGUMENT PREDICATION		DOUBLE-ARGUMENT PREDICATION	
	Common	Q'anjob'al	Common	Q'anjob'al
3SG	*ki...ik	či...i	*ki-ru...O	či-s...Aʔ
2SG	*k-at...ik	č-ač...i	*k-a...O	č-a...Aʔ
1SG	*k-in...ik	č-in...i	*ki-nu...O	č-in...Aʔ
3PL	*ki...ebʔ	či...ebʔ	*ki-ki...O	či-s...Aʔ
2PL	*k-eš...ik	č-eš...i	*k-e...O	č-e...Aʔ
1PL	*k-oʔŋ...ik	č-on...i	*ki-qa...O	či-ko...Aʔ

Figure 6.4. Evidence for the direct descent of the Q'anjob'alan INCOMPLETIVE from the Common Mayan INCOMPLETIVE.

It is likely that for pre-Q'anjob'alan the INCOMPLETIVE **ki-* was replaced by *či-.* The following scenario suggests itself. Q'anjob'al, like Mamean, palatalizes *k* before front vowels, as e.g., **kiʔ > čiʔ* 'sweet.' As a consequence, a pre-Q'anjob'al paradigm would have looked like this:

*ki...ik	'he...'
*k-ač...ik	'you...'
*k-in...ik	'I...'
*ki...ebʔ	'they...'
*k-eš...ik	'you-guys...'
*k-oŋ...ik	'we...'

By palatalization the paradigm would have changed to one very similar to that of Awakatek, as seen in the following comparison:

pre-Q'anjob'al		Awakatek
*či...ik'	'he...'	...
*k-ač...ik	'you...'	k-š...
*č-in...ik	'I ...'	č-in
*či...ebʔ	'they...'	či...

*č-eš...ik	'you-guys...'	k-š
*k-oŋ...ik	'we ...'	q-a

One could further expect, therefore, a leveling based on 3SG, again based on Watkins' Law:

či...ik	'he...'
č-ač...ik	'you...'
č-in...ik	'I...'
či...eb?	'they...'
č-eš...ik	'you-guys...'
č-on...ik	'we...'

OPTATIVE and FUTURE

Furthermore, as happened in Awakatek, the reflex of the OPTATIVE prefix *ki-/tʸi-* was lost, leaving only *-oq,* while a prefix plus *-oq* replaced the old FUTURE. In the case of Q'anjob'al, since the *ki-* was lost, the reflex of *-oq* was used as both a prefix and a suffix for the FUTURE as illustrated in Figure 6.5.

		SINGLE-ARGUMENT PREDICATION		DOUBLE-ARGUMENT PREDICATION	
		Common	Q'anjob'al	Common	Q'anjob'al
OPTATIVE	3SG	*tʸi...oq	...oq-eb?	*tʸi-ru...A?	s...oq-eb?-i
	2SG	*k-at...oq	...an	*tʸ-a...A?	...A?
	1SG	*k-in...oq	...oq-in	*tʸi-nu...A?	in...A?
	3PL	*ki...eb?	...oq-eb? eb?	*tʸi-ki...A?	
	2PL	*k-eš...oq	...an-eq	*tʸ-i...A?	...eq
	1PL	*q-o?ŋ...oq	...oq-on	*tʸi-qa...A?	ko...A?
FUTURE	3SG	*la...ik	oq...oq	*la-ru...O	oq-s...A?
	2SG	*l-at...ik	oq-ač...oq	*l-a...O	oq-a...A?
	1SG		oq-in...oq	*la-nu...O	oq-in...A?
		*la...eb?	oq...oq-eb?	*la-ki...O	oq-s...eb?
	2PL	*l-eš...ik	oq-eš...oq	*l-i...O	oq-e...A?
	1PL	*l-o?ŋ...ik	oq-on...oq	*la-qa...O	oq-ko...A?

Figure 6.5. Comparison of the OPTATIVE and the FUTURE in Common Mayan and Q'anjob'al.

One of the more interesting differences between the original system and modern Q'anjob'al is the loss of the distinction between the MOOD/VOICE suffixes *-O* DECLARATIVE (it is *-o* if stem vowel is **o,* and **-u* if **u*) and **-A?* OPTATIVE. That is, the more-marked *-A?* took over the less-marked *-O* This is once again markedness reversal, which has the required element: degrees of the same kind. In this case, as illustrated in Figure 6.6, both the suffix *-A?* and the prefix *-oq* mean IRREALIS, so that the *-A?* can take the place of the less-marked **-O.*

Q'anjob'al
CONSERVATIVE   INNOVATIVE

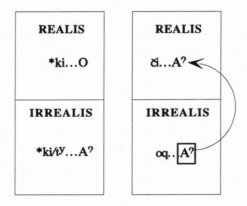

Figure 6.6. Example of markedness reversal in Q'anjob'al.

The Directional Verbs

Q'anjob'al comes very close to preserving the original system of directional verbs with the exception that, like Mam, there was a markedness reversal in the intransitive (but unlike Mam, not in the transitive). The ABS-DV of the intransitive was moved from suffix to prefix, on analogy with the NOM-DV. In this regard, recall that Mam, on analogy with the NOM-DV, came to prefix all directionals to the main verb (p. 109). In accordance with the observation that changes in paradigmatic systems are introduced first in the unmarked categories, it should not be surprising to observe that the change in Q'anjob'al took place first with the intransitives, as shown in Figure 6.7. One might suspect that the marked correlate, the transitives, will also follow suit at some future time.

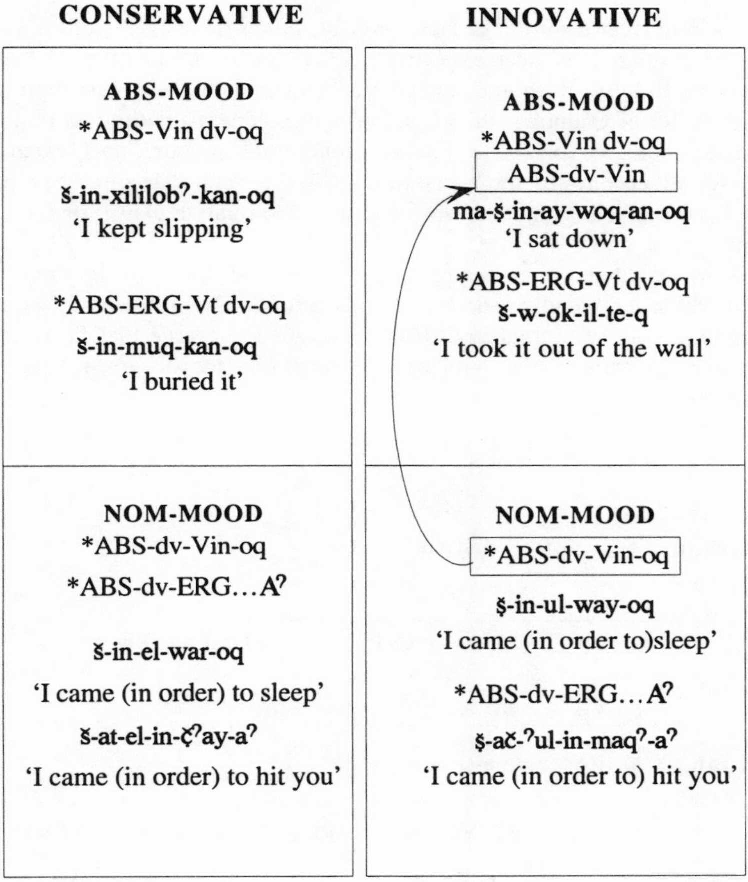

CONSERVATIVE	INNOVATIVE
ABS-MOOD *ABS-Vin dv-oq š-in-xililob⁷-kan-oq 'I kept slipping' *ABS-ERG-Vt dv-oq š-in-muq-kan-oq 'I buried it'	**ABS-MOOD** *ABS-Vin dv-oq ABS-dv-Vin ma-š-in-ay-woq-an-oq 'I sat down' *ABS-ERG-Vt dv-oq š-w-ok-il-te-q 'I took it out of the wall'
NOM-MOOD *ABS-dv-Vin-oq *ABS-dv-ERG...A⁷ š-in-el-war-oq 'I came (in order) to sleep' š-at-el-in-č⁷ay-a⁷ 'I came (in order) to hit you'	**NOM-MOOD** *ABS-dv-Vin-oq š-in-ul-way-oq 'I came (in order to)sleep' *ABS-dv-ERG...A⁷ š-ač-⁷ul-in-maq⁷-a⁷ 'I came (in order to) hit you'

Figure 6.7. Markedness reversal of the directional verbs in Q'anjob'al.

Summary of Q'anjob'al

In its prehistory, Q'anjob'al was probably very nearly like K'iche'an for its markedness reversal in the COMPLETIVE, where *ma-,* meaning 'past time of today,' reinforced the PROXIMATE PAST **iš-* > *š-* of the common language. It was also like Mam and Awakatek in palatalizing the **ki-* INCOMPLETIVE, but different in that the paradigm was regularized, resulting in *či-* as the marker. It was like Awakatek in reducing the OPTATIVE prefix to Ø-, and sending the original OPTATIVE to mark the FUTURE; in addition, in the FUTURE the original suffix **-oq* (which marks single-argument predications as IRREALIS) became prefixed, thus augmenting the suffixal IRREALIS *-oq* and *-A⁷*. This was a perfect circumstance for markedness reversal, given the degrees of the same kind, and as might have been expected the *-A^? took over the original *-O of the REALIS. Finally, it should be recalled that one of the most important characteristics of Q'anjob'al (and Q'anjob'alan in general) is the fact that the old marker for ABS-VOICE (the relative pronominal marker, -on-i) extended itself by influence to the more-marked NOM-VOICE, such that all embeddings came to be marked with what was originally the relative clause marker, as explained on page 75.

This important and revealing change gives a good deal of insight into the way in which the paradigmatic system of Common Q'anjob'alan as well as Common Mayan was organized. It is important to observe that in Yukatek Maya, independently, but in a similarly motivated way, the ABS-VOICE influenced the NOM-VOICE.

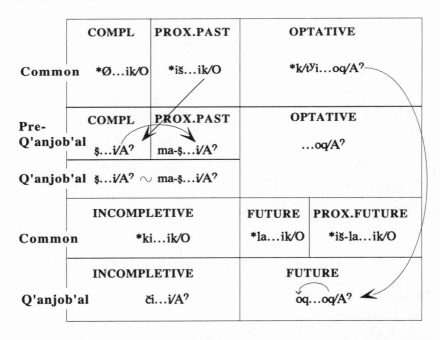

Figure 6.8. Summary of changes in the COMPLETIVE, INCOMPLETIVE, OPTATIVE, and FUTURE from Common Mayan to Q'anjob'al.

Jakaltek

COMPLETIVE and PROXIMATE PAST

Jakaltek is much like Q'anjob'al, except that its COMPLETIVE is like Colonial

Q'eqchi's, where the old **ki-* marker stands after the ʃ- of the COMPLETIVE and before the ABSOLUTIVE pronouns in the COMPLETIVE:

ʃ-way-i	'he slept'
ʃ-k-ač-way-i	'you slept'
ʃ-k-in-way-i	'I slept'
ʃ-way-eb?	'they slept'
ʃ-k-eʃ-way-i	'you-guys slept'
ʃ-k-oŋ-way-i	'we slept'

On the other hand, before the ergative pronouns, only ʃ- is attested:

ʃ-s-č?ax-a	'he washed him'
ʃ-a-č?ax-a	'you washed him'
ʃ-in-č?ax-a	'I washed him'
ʃ-s-č?ax-a	'they washed him'
ʃ-e-č?ax-a	'you-guys washed him'
ʃ-ko-č?ax-a	'we washed him'

The explanation of these results might be as follows, given what is known of the rest of Mayan. First, Jakaltek went through a change like Mamean, K'iche'an, and the rest of the Q'anjob'alan languages in preserving but changing the form of the distinction between the COMPLETIVE and the PROXIMATE PAST. Unlike Mam and K'iche', but like Q'eqchi' (and Sipakapa K'iche'—page 148), Jakaltek took the **ki-* of the INCOMPLETIVE and preposed the ʃ- of the COMPLETIVE. But, as happened in many of the languages since the Conquest, the distinction between COMPLETIVE and PROXIMATE PAST was subsequently lost, resulting in the modern distribution shown above.

This would have meant that the signs from the COMPLETIVE INTRANSITIVE (ʃ) and its opposite, the INCOMPLETIVE TRANSITIVE (ʃk-) would have been lost. The shaded areas in Figure 6.9 are unattested.

Finally, it must be explained why the *k* in ʃ-k-in did not palatalize, as it was proposed to have done in the INCOMPLETIVE with, e.g., **k-in > č-in, ki- > č-i*, etc. The explanation is found in that none of the languages in the portion of Guatemala that roughly comprises the Department of Huehuetenango (Mam and Awakatek, as well as the Q'anjob'alan languages) palatalized if such palatalization would have resulted in two sibilants in the same word. Thus Mam has, for example, **ki? > či?* 'sweet,' but the word *k?i?ʃ* 'thorn' does not palatalize. Similarly, in Q'anjob'al the form is *k?iʃ*. Thus, in the context of the COMPLETIVE ʃ-, *k* was protected from palatalization.

A comparison between Jakaltek and Q'anjob'al in the context of 3sg reveals a conservative Q'anjob'al *či-*, but an innovative Jakaltek ʃ-:

či-way-i 'he slept' (Q'anjob'al)
š-way-i 'he slept' (Jakaltek)

This difference is readily explainable. The *i* of *či-* was elided, resulting in a preconsonantal *č.* It is a common phonological occurrence in Q'anjob'alan (and in Mamean, for that matter) for the sequence C[affricate]+C to become C[fricative]+C, such as in the verb 'to bathe,' *-atin > *-ačin > *-ačn > -ašn. Also, in many of the Q'anjob'alan languages the reflex of the ABS2SG *at* is *ač* or *aš*, depending on whether the morpheme immediately precedes a consonant.

COMPL/INTRANS		COMPL/TRANS	
š-way-i	'he slept'	š-s-č'ax-a	'he washed him'
š-ač-way	'you slept'	š-a-č'ax-a	'you washed him'
š-in-way	'I slept'	š-in-č'ax-a	'I washed him'
š-way-eb	'they slept'	š-s-č'ax-eb'	'they washed him'
š-eš-way	'you-guys slept'	š-e-č'ax-a	'you-guys washed him'
š-oŋ-way	'we slept'	š-ko-č'ax-a	'we washed him'
PROX.PAST/INTRANS		PROX.PAST/TRANS	
š-way-i	'he slept'	šk-s-č'ax-a	'he washed him'
šk-ač-way-i	'you slept'	šk-a-č'ax-a	'you washed him'
šk-in-way-i	'I slept'	šk-in-č'ax-a	'I washed him'
š-way-eb'	'they slept'	šk-s-č'ax-eb'	'they washed him'
šk-eš-way-i	'you-guys slept'	šk-e-č'ax-a	'you-guys washed him'
šk-oŋ-way-i	'we slept'	šk-ko-č'ax-a	'we washed him'

Figure 6.9. I. Paradigm illustrating the system implied by the Immediate Interpretants COMPLETIVE/PROXIMATE PAST and INTRANSITIVE/TRANSITIVE.

FUTURE

Finally, unlike Q'anjob'al, Jakaltek did not prefix the *-oq* as a marker of the FUTURE, but rather the FUTURE was influenced by the INCOMPLETIVE. The Jakaltek system is summarized in Figure 6.10.

A comparison of the suffixes of TAMV between Jakaltek and Q'anjob'al shows that Jakaltek is conservative, while Q'anjob'al is innovative: DECLARATIVE, *-A;* OPTATIVE, *-A².* Day (1967:71, 78), for instance, gives these data on Jakaltek:

č-a-maq²-a 'you hit something'
č-a-maq²-a² 'you will hit something'

č-a-poč̓ʔ-o   'you kill something'
č-a-poč̓ʔ-oʔ 'you kill something'
č-a-č̓ʔun-u   'you plant something'
č-a-č̓ʔun-uʔ 'you will plant something'

Summary of Jakaltek

Jakaltek and Q'anjob'al are obviously very closely related. They are in many ways similar to the most conservative of the K'iche'an languages (e.g., Colonial K'iche'). They show obvious vestiges of the COMPLETIVE, and their INCOMPLETIVE is a reflex of the Common Mayan *ki-. The FUTURE in both languages is derived primarily from the OPTATIVE, although there is also some apparent influence from the INCOMPLETIVE. (Recall that the INCOMPLETIVE completely took over the FUTURE in K'iche' and Q'eqchi'.) The structure of the system of directional verbs is likewise very similar, with the exception that Q'anjob'al innovated by prefixing the ABS-DV in the intransitive.

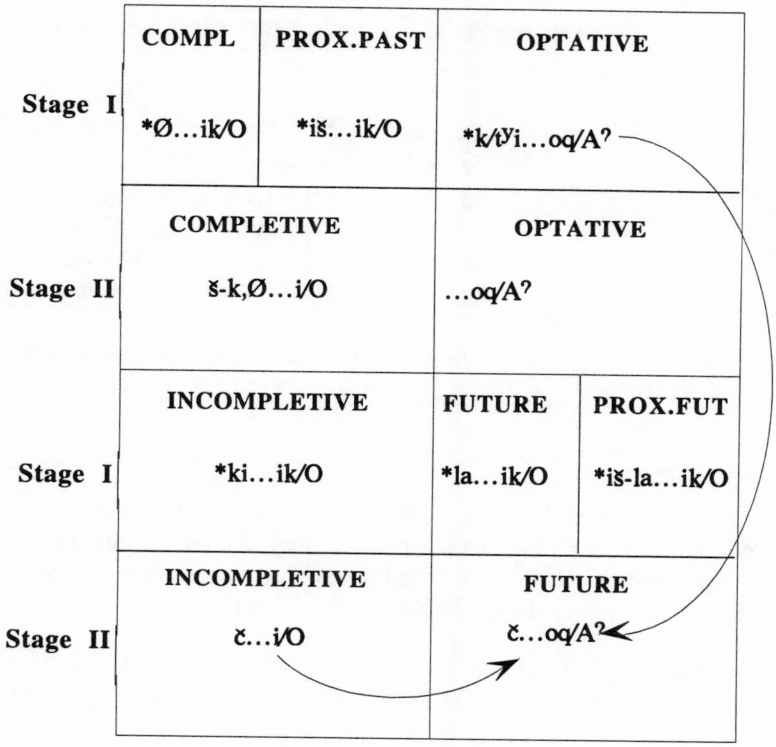

	COMPL	PROX.PAST	OPTATIVE	
Stage I	*Ø...ik/O	*iš...ik/O	*k/ʸi...oq/Aʔ	
Stage II	COMPLETIVE š-k,Ø...i/O		OPTATIVE ...oq/Aʔ	
Stage I	INCOMPLETIVE *ki...ik/O	FUTURE *la...ik/O	PROX.FUT *iš-la...ik/O	
Stage II	INCOMPLETIVE č...i/O		FUTURE č...oq/Aʔ	

Figure 6.10. Influence of the INCOMPLETIVE and the OPTATIVE on the FUTURE in Jakaltek.

Chuj

Chuj has two main dialects, one from San Mateo Ixtatán, and the other from San Sebastián, and both are very interesting to the comparatist for what they say about the common language.[1] Unfortunately, since I only have sufficient data from San Mateo, *Chuj* will here refer to the San Mateo Ixtatán dialect, unless stated otherwise.

COMPLETIVE and PROXIMATE PAST

Perhaps the most interesting fact about Chuj is that the COMPLETIVE and the PROXIMATE PAST preserve the common language intact; it is the only Mayan language that does so. It is this system which is antecedent to all the Mamean, K'iche'an, and Q'anjob'alan languages heretofore discussed, as shown in Figure 6.11.

	COMPLETIVE		PROXIMATE PAST	
	Common	Chuj	Common	Chuj
3SG	*...ik	...i	*iš...ik	š...i
2SG	*...at	ač...i	*iš-at...ik	š-ač...i
1SG	*...in	in...i	*iš-in...ik	š-in...i
3PL	*...eb⁷	...eb	*iš...eb	š...eb⁷
2PL	*...eš	eš...i	*iš-eš...ik	š-eš...i
1PL	*...o⁷ŋ	oŋ...i	*iš-o⁷ŋ...ik	š-oŋ...i

Figure 6.11. Comparison of the COMPLETIVE and PROXIMATE PAST in Common Mayan and Chuj.

INCOMPLETIVE

The etymology of the INCOMPLETIVE ¢- is not completely clear, although there is some evidence that, earlier in the history of Chuj, the marker was š- < *č-, since the morpheme š- can be found in highly restricted uses with the meaning INCOMPLETIVE. Hopkins (1967:120) says that

> š occurs in both positive and negative expressions, but is limited in positive expressions to (1) those in which *tah uncertainty* appears in

---

[1]My brief work with the San Sebastián dialect suggests that it has a rather more complicated system of tense and aspect than the San Mateo dialect. My first inclination is to hypothesize that most of its complication is best explained in terms of innovation and not conservation.

verbal suffix position +1 and (2) inflections of the verb *čih to say* used for direct and indirect quotations.

It is also used as the aspect marker of the negative in the INCOMPLETIVE, as shown in Figure 6.12.

	INCOMPLETIVE	
	Positive	**Negative**
3SG	s...i	ma-š...lax
2SG	¢-ač...i	ma-š-ač...lax
1SG	¢-in...i	ma-š-in...lax
3PL	s...eb⁷	ma-š...lax eb⁷
2PL	¢-eš...i	ma-š-eš...lax
1PL	¢-oŋ...i	ma-š-oŋ...lax

Figure 6.12. Evidence for a pre-Chuj *š- < *č-* INCOMPLETIVE marker.

These are precisely the circumstances that would lead one to look for displacement—where the old morpheme, in this case *š-*, was displaced by a new, innovative morpheme, *¢-*. The proposition is therefore this: that *š-* is an old morpheme, cognate with the other Q'anjob'alan languages' INCOMPLETIVE *č-*, owing to the fact that it is very common for *čC* to become *šC*, as attested in the 3SG of Jakaltek as explained above. Assuming that deaffrication first took place in the Chuj 3SG, it is easy to explain by Watkins' Law how it would then have spread upward through the paradigm. This would mean, of course, that there is still some vestige of the original Common Mayan **ki-* as marker of the Chuj INCOMPLETIVE: **ki- > *či- > č- > š-*. The etymology of the new *¢-* still awaits explanation.

OPTATIVE

The OPTATIVE has undergone a shift, in which the reflex of the Common Mayan **-oq* has been fronted so that it is capable of co-occurring with all TENSE/ASPECT markers:

¢-ok-in-way-í	'would that I sleep!'
ok-in-way-í	'(I hope) I slept!'
⁷iš-ok-in-way-í	'(I hope) I just slept!'

For the 1PL IMPERATIVE, in 1972 I recorded a form *k-oŋ-el-ok,* 'let's go out,' whereas in 1989 the form was *k-oŋ-way-í,* 'let's sleep' with the final OPTATIVE

-*ok* having been replaced by the declarative *í-*. My inclination is to consider the initial *k-* as I have treated the initial *oq-* in the Q'anjob'al FUTURE: as coming from the suffix -*ok* < *-*oq*, with the subsequent replacement of the marked OPTATIVE by the unmarked DECLARATIVE.

FUTURE

Figure 6.13 shows the FUTURE to be marked by *ol-:* I propose that the change from **la-* to *ol-* was the result of reinforcing the **la-* with *ok* < *-*oq*, as follows:

$$*-oq + *l(a)- = *oql- > ol-$$

This is almost the same as Q'anjob'al's *oq...oq* FUTURE, except that the **la-* was augmented, and not merely displaced.

	FUTURE			
	Intransitive		**Transitive**	
	Common	**Chuj**	**Common**	**Chuj**
3SG	**la...ik*	?ol...i	**la-s...O*	?ol-s...A?
2SG	**l-at...ik*	?ol-ač...i	**l-a...O*	?ol-a...A?
1SG	**l-in...ik*	?ol-in...i	**l-in...O*	?ol-in...A?
3PL	**la...eb?*	?ol...eb?	**la-s...eb*	?ol-s...eb?
2PL	**l-eš...ik*	?ol-eš...i	**l-e...O*	?ol-e...A?
1PL	**l-o?ŋ...ik*	?ol-oŋ...i	**la-ko...O*	?ol-ko...A?

Figure 6.13. Comparison of the FUTURE in Common Mayan and Chuj.

It will be recalled that the FUTURE is postulated as having the suffixes *-i/-O* in the common language, and not the OPTATIVE suffixes *-oq/-A?*. A striking piece of evidence supporting the claim that the -*i* < *-*ik* is conservative and that -*ok* is innovative in marking the FUTURE can be found in the statement by Hopkins (1967:123) that

> *ok*[1] is obligatory after underived intransitive verb roots or intransitive stems derived from non-verbal roots, if these are inflected for future inchoative [*?ol*]. The suffix *ok* may also occur after transitive verb roots derived in *w;* in this case, *ok* indicates doubt. In environments where both *i* and *ok* may occur, the use of *ok* rather than *i* indicates doubt.

---

[1]I modified the orthography to accord with the orthography in this book.

Thus, for example, the following forms are attested:

ol-pay-w-ok ŋal
FUT-dry.by.heat-ANTIPASS-SAPO maize
'he might dry maize'

ol-pay-w-i ŋal
FUT-dry.by.heat-ANTIPASS-SAPD maize
'he will dry maize'

It will be recalled that there are three versions of single-argument predication s: (1) intransitive verbs, (2) passive transitives, and (3) antipassive transitives, where intransitives are basic and unmarked. The *w* referred to above is the ANTIPASSIVE, which is a more-marked version of a single-argument verb. Since changes are introduced into grammatical systems in the less-marked categories, the OPTATIVE *-oq* > *-ok* displaced the *-ik* > *-i* of the FUTURE in the paradigm in the intransitive and the passive; but in the more-marked ANTIPASSIVE, the *-i* hangs on, with the *-ok* retaining its modal sense. It should not be surprising, therefore, to find the change not having totally affected the most-marked category of the paradigm.

Finally, owing to the same kind of markedness reversal found in Q'anjob'al (but significantly, not in Jakaltek, for example) Chuj, like Q'anjob'al (see page 158), innovated by replacing the transitive suffix *-A* with *-Aʔ*.[1] All of these changes are recapitulated in Figure 6.14.

Summary of Chuj

Chuj is a particularly interesting language since it is conservative in so many regards. If Chuj is not a direct reflection of the original system per se (as with the COMPLETIVE), it at least conserves of traces of the original system (as in the marked portions of the INCOMPLETIVE, or as in the conservation of *š-*, or the conservation of the FUTURE *la-* > *ol-*). Again, any discovery of Chujean Colonial documents would greatly help the general understanding of the history of Chuj, and would likely go a long way toward confirming or disproving the suggestions made in this section.

---

[1]My data are incomplete regarding whether the transitive marker is *-A* or *-Aʔ* in the COMPLETIVE and RECENT PAST. My guess is *-Aʔ*.

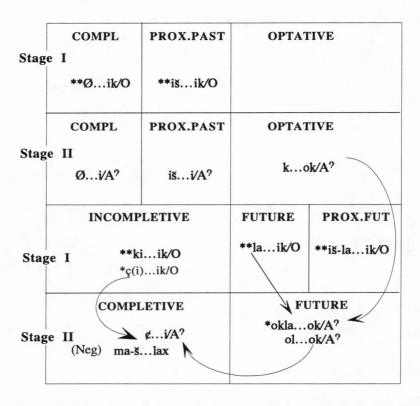

Figure 6.14. Summary of changes in the COMPLETIVE, INCOMPLETIVE, OPTATIVE, and FUTURE in Chuj.

Chapter 7. Choltí and Chorti'

Kaufman (1974) says that Choltí, a Colonial language recorded by Morán in 1695, is extinct—that it is related to modern Chorti', thus belonging to the same unique subgroup, but ultimately stemming from different ancestors. Careful comparison of the Colonial Choltí grammar with that of modern Chorti', however, shows that Choltí is "extinct" only in the same way that other Colonial languages discussed heretofore are extinct: they are no longer spoken, but are ancestors of their modern descendants. Thus, just as Colonial Kaqchikel is the ancestor of modern Kaqchikel, so Choltí is the ancestor of modern Chorti'. The reasons for this revision of Kaufman's view are not outlined here directly, but are the warp and woof of the following discussion, since the only way to describe the development of the grammatical system of Chorti' is to assume a Choltí-like ancestral system. Even if Choltí were not attested, many of the elements of Choltí grammar would best be postulated as ancestral to Chorti'. In fact, were the name 'Choltí' not so well established, it could appropriately be called 'Colonial Chorti',' in keeping with the established norms of this book.[1]

Choltí

Progressive, Incompletive, and Future

Perhaps the comparatist's main interest in this subgroup are the remarkable chains of displacement, both from the common language to Choltí, and from Choltí to Chorti'. Of further confirmatory interest is the fact that, despite a developmental history substantially different from any heretofore attested, the grammars of Choltí and later Chorti' are clearly a logical product of the same system common to all other Mayan languages. For example, given the original system, the inferred developmental pattern consists first of a displacement of the reflex of the original *ki- INCOMPLETIVE by a morphological version of the PROGRESSIVE, forcing displacement of the original INCOMPLETIVE to the category FUTURE, which further forces displacement of the original *la- FUTURE, restricting its meaning to a NEGATIVE FUTURE.[2] Similar chains of displacement based on the same postulated system can be found going both from Common Mayan to Choltí and from Choltí to Chorti'.

---

[1]Note that Chorti' has changed its *l*'s to *r*'s—hence *Chorti'* and not *Choltí*.
[2]For a more complete description of this process, see below.

A more detailed understanding of these phenomena rests on a description of how the Common Mayan INCOMPLETIVE *ki- changed to š- (which later was displaced to the category FUTURE) in the first place. Recall that the Q'anjob'alan INCOMPLETIVE č- is a reflex of Common Mayan *ki-. Similarly, the INCOMPLETIVE š found in Tzeltalan and Cholan, as shown below, is also proposed to be a reflex of the Common Mayan INCOMPLETIVE *ki—with this explanation: Tzeltalan and Cholan changed the *k to č, as in, e.g., Kaqchikel *kam* 'die', and Tzotzil, and Choltí *čam*. Thus, the INCOMPLETIVE *ki- would inevitably have become *či- in these languages. Furthermore, there is generally a strong tendency in Mayan languages in this linguistic area to syncopate the vowel, and to deaffricate the č to š before a consonant, as seen in the Tzotzil example, *nič'anab > *ničnab > nišnab?* 'brothers' (Anonymous 1812:19), though this particular change is not a regular change in the language. Such deaffrication occurred in the Jakaltek INCOMPLETIVE (see Chapter 5), where in 3SG *či* changed to č, and then to š, because it precedes the bare, consonant-initial root of the transitive verb. Because the Tzeltalan and Cholan languages suffix the absolutive pronoun, it follows that the *č- which would have preceded the stem of the verb would have similarly deaffricated to š- throughout the entire paradigm.[1] According to this scenario, Common Mayan *ki- became

---

[1] I should point out that I have found three instances in Choltí where č-C did not become š-C: *očk'in* 'sun to set,' *učtes* 'to give drink,' and *ločte* 'garabato' (Morán 1695). It should be pointed out that it is easy to find instances of č-C in Tzotzil dictionaries, however, as in e.g., *čučbe mul* 'incriminate' (Laughlin 1975:126), despite the fact that there are other irregular instances of such change, as in, e.g, *nič'anab > *ničnab > nišnab?* 'brothers,' as pointed out above. The probable reason for such inconsistencies might be found in Meillet (1967:47–48):

> The regularity of correspondences does not exclude the existence of special treatments. In a sentence words are found in various positions and under various conditions. The regularity of treatment comes often from the fixture of a median form among those varying according to the position in the sentence. But there are particular cases where forms pronounced more rapidly or carelessly are more usual than others, and from this result of accessory words.

Other instances of such deaffrication can be found in the ABS2SG pronouns of Ixil and Awakatek, where Common Mayan *at changed to ač. There are occurrences, of ač- changing to a š-: *ha-š-wit* 'you just slept' (Awakatek) and *yolon-aš* 'you spoke' (where historically aš < ač was an Ixil prefix). These examples of Meillet's "special treatment" help confirm the supposition that the closely locked, preverbal *č- also became dissimilated to š- in Choltí, particularly in view of the fact that the changing of č-C to š-C is an irregular sound change, but one that occurs frequently in the Mayan languages.

š- through the intermediary step *či- > *č- in Choltí and, as will be seen below, in Tzeltalan and Tojolab'alan as well.

As pointed out earlier, in Choltí š- no longer marks the INCOMPLETIVE but rather the FUTURE. What does mark the INCOMPLETIVE is the split-ergative form *wal* ERG-VIN-*el* and *wal* ERG-VT-ABS:

wal u-kaši-el[1]
CONT ERG3SG-come.back-NOMLZR
'he is coming back'

wal u-kol-o
CONT ERG3SG-save-SAPD
'he is saving him'

It seems reasonable to suppose that Choltí's INCOMPLETIVE has the same etymological pattern as that of Poqomchi' discussed earlier, where it was shown that the INCOMPLETIVE came from a syntactic, progressive construction, where raising had been lost:

Poqomchi':	kʔahčiʔ nu-wir-ik	'I am sleeping'
Choltí:	wal u-wan-*el*	'he is sleeping'
Tzeltal:	yak-on ta aʔt *el*	'I am working'
Tojolab'al:	van-on way *el*	'I am sleeping'[2]

The advent of Choltí's INCOMPLETIVE-né-PROGRESSIVE caused the chain displacement referred to above. First came the new, "split-ergative" INCOMPLETIVE based on an old PROGRESSIVE, a process I have already documented in Colonial Poqomchi' (p. 143). Second, the newly acquired INCOMPLETIVE took over the category originally occupied by the š- INCOMPLETIVE, with the consequence that the š- INCOMPLETIVE was displaced to the category of FUTURE as seen in Figure 7.1.

š-ka-toh-oʔ[3]

---

[1] I am not sure if the verb is *kaši-* or *kʔaš-*.

[2] In this regard, I might point out that Tojolabal's PROGRESSIVE uses the suffix -*Vlh* with single-argument predications. This is an innovation from Common Mayan times which was shared with Tzeltalan and Cholan, thus providing another reason for subgrouping these languages. This innovation does not occur in Chuj, so it does not support Kaufman's (1974) proposed Chuj-Tojolabal subgrouping.

[3] I am not sure whether the form is -*toh-o* or -*toh-o* ?, as there was no marking of glottal stops in the Colonial documents. We would, however, expect it to be *toh̲o* ? if it was influenced by the OPTATIVE, and it almost surely was, since we have

FUT-ERG1PL-pay-DAPO
'we will pay it'
š-kaš-i-k-on
FUT-ERG1PL-come.back-SAPD-OPT-ABS1PL
'we will come back'

Such movement from the INCOMPLETIVE to the FUTURE, it will be recalled, is an *attested* fact from Colonial Poqomchi' to the modern language, as well as from Colonial to modern K'iche'.[1] Third, the newly formed š- FUTURE, based on the original PRESENT š plus the OPTATIVE *-ik < *-oq*, displaced what was apparently the original **la-* FUTURE. That displacement caused the **la-* FUTURE to specialize, taking on a negative semantic value. It is instructive to see what Morán says concerning this NEGATIVE FUTURE:

> Se haçe con esta particula *el*, que significa prohibision. Y es de notar que siempre que se usa desta particula se ha de ablar con el verbo de preterito, y no de futuro, aunque la oracion sera de futuro: *a Ɛale au otot* 'hissiste tu cassa; *el-a-Ɛale au otot Ɛonahel* 'no haras otra tu casa.' ...Y no diremos... *el a Ɛalen*, sino *el a Ɛale* que equiuale a esta *ma xa Ɛalen.*

> [[The negative future] is made with this particle: *el*, which means prohibition. And it is important to note that with this particle the verb must always be used in the preterite and not the future, even though the sentence has the meaning of future: *a-kʔale aw-otot* 'you made your house'; *el-a-kʔale aw-otot konahel* 'you will not make your house.' ...We would never say *el-a-kʔalen*, but *el-a-kʔale* which is equivalent to saying *ma š-a-kʔalen.*]

From this source, two inferential facts emerge: (a) the so-called "second FUTURE" in *el-* is like the PRETERITE in not having the reflex of the OPTATIVE **-oq* as part of its formation (as postulated for Common Mayan), and (b) *el-* is a NEGATIVE FUTURE, exactly equivalent to the POSITIVE FUTURE plus the negative marker, *ma*. Thus, the specialized *le-* FUTURE is an excellent candidate to be a vestige of an earlier FUTURE. It is significant that the Colonial author said that the old *le-* FUTURE was based on the "preterite" and not on the FUTURE, further justifying the Common Mayan reconstruction of the *la-* FUTURE without the OPTATIVE **-oq* and *-Aʔ*. Figure 7.1 graphically summarizes

---

a reflex of the Common Mayan OPTATIVE **-oq* with intransitives.

[1]It also occurred in Tzeltalan.

the above-described chain displacement.[1]

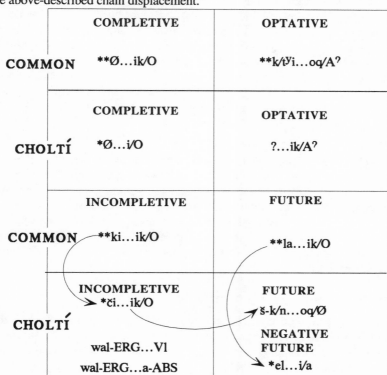

Figure 7.1. Displacement in the INCOMPLETIVE and the FUTURE in Choltí.

It is not clear precisely what the OPTATIVE was in Choltí since no clear description was given in the grammar, although in the modern language Chorti', the paradigm compared with Common Mayan is as follows:

Common	Choltí	Gloss
*tʸi-war-oq	wayn-ik	'would that he sleep'
*k-at-war-oq	wayn-ik-et	'would that you sleep'
*k-in-war-oq	wayn-ik-en	'would that I sleep'
*ki-war-eb?	wayn-ik-ob?	'would that they sleep'
*k-eš-war-oq	wayn-ik-oš	'would that you-guys sleep'
*k-o?ŋ-war-oq	wayn-ik-on	'would that we sleep'

---

[1] I have not included the PROXIMATE PAST or the PROXIMATE FUTURE in this formulation.

Observe that the prefixes have been lost, with a concomitant change of *-oq* to *-ik*. This prefixal loss in the OPTATIVE has been observed to occur many times in Mayan, as for example in Awakatek and Q'anjob'al, where the language innovates by taking zero for its OPTATIVE prefix, while the FUTURE is influenced either by the original prefix of the OPTATIVE (e.g., in Awakatek) or by the prefix of the INCOMPLETIVE (e.g., in Choltí). Although there is no secure attestation of the OPTATIVE in the Colonial documents, it seems inevitable that the language had something like the modern OPTATIVE listed above.

From Choltí to Chorti'

The changes that occurred from ancestral Choltí to modern Chorti' are as surprising as they are interesting. They are surprising because leveling has left so few distinctions in the modern language, and they are interesting because they once again show instances of chain displacement, which seems to be the hallmark of the kind of change occurring in Choltí. One change, which is a continuation of a pattern begun earlier in Choltí, effects change elsewhere in the paradigm, and the newly effected change causes another change, and so on.

Loss of INCOMPLETIVE/ COMPLETIVE/ FUTURE

The most profound change occurred with the loss of the *wal* in the INCOMPLETIVE, which resulted in the loss of the distinction between COMPLETIVE, INCOMPLETIVE, and FUTURE in the transitive verb. Thus, in today's language the Chorti' speaker can say

in-šur-i akb?i	'I cut it yesterday'
in-šur-i sahmi	'I cut it today'
in-šur-i ehk?ar	'I cut it tomorrow'

where the tense/aspect distinction is only syntactical (adverbial) and not morphological.

Whereas in Colonial times, to say 'I believe it,' one might have said *'wal in-kub?-u,'* in modern times the presence of *wal > war* means PROGRESSIVE: *war in-šur-i* 'I am cutting it.' In Colonial times to say 'God will save you,' the form *xuƐolo et [š-u-kol-o? et]* was used (Morán 1720),[1] whereas in Chorti' no such future marker exists. For transitives, then, all inflectional affixation dealing with time and aspect has been lost except in the OPTATIVE and NEGATIVE, to be discussed below.

---

[1] I am assuming that the glottal was in this form, since the reflex of the Common Mayan *-oq* > *-VƐ [-Vk]*, is for the FUTURE in the intransitives: *xƐaxiƐ en [š-kaš-ik en]* 'caere.'

With intransitives the old Choltí markers of tense and aspect have similarly been lost, but unlike the transitives, the intransitives maintained the distinction between the COMPLETIVE and INCOMPLETIVE—not by a special aspectual prefix, as one would expect, but by the development of a new pronominal set, a striking innovation. The new set has characteristics from both the ERGATIVE and the ABSOLUTIVE set. Note the distinction between the INCOMPLETIVE and the COMPLETIVE:

COMPLETIVE INTRANSITIVE		INCOMPLETIVE INTRANSITIVE	
wayan	'he slept'	a-wayan	'he sleeps'
wayan-et	'you slept'	i-wayan	'you sleep'
wayan-en	'I slept'	in-wayan	'I sleep'
wayan-ob?	'they slept'	a-wayan-ob?	'they sleep'
wayan-oš	'you-guys slept'	iš-wayan	'you-guys sleep'
wayan-on	'we slept'	ka-wayan	'we sleep'

COMPLETIVE/INCOMPLETIVE TRANSITIVE

u-šur-i	'he cut(s) it'
a-šur-i	'you cut it'
in-šur-i	'I cut it'
u-šur-i-ob?	'they cut it'
i-šur-i	'you-guys cut it'
ka-šur-i	'we cut it'

For the transitive verb, 'cut' is a good translation because there is no distinction between PAST, PRESENT, and FUTURE action. For the intransitive Chorti' verb, however, there *is* a distinction in aspect that is made not by temporal/aspectual affixation, but by a differentiation of pronominals, which is a highly innovative means of expressing aspect.

The emergence of this new pronominal set for the INCOMPLETIVE INTRANSITIVE is perhaps best explained in contrasting Choltí with Chorti', as shown in Figure 7.2. Note that first, *wal* was lost, thus potentially leaving no distinction between the TRANSITIVE INCOMPLETIVE, TRANSITIVE COMPLETIVE, and INTRANSITIVE INCOMPLETIVE. And, as shown above, the distinction between the COMPLETIVE and INCOMPLETIVE for transitives *was* lost, but for the INTRANSITIVE INCOMPLETIVE, with the loss of *wal,* the distinction was recreated by the invention of an entirely new pronominal series.

The provenance of this series seems to be due to a markedness reversal and a subsequent chain of displacements. In the INTRANSITIVE INCOMPLETIVE, the old form for ERG2PL, *i,* was displaced by a combination of two forms, *oš,* which marks 2PL in the INTRANSITIVE COMPLETIVE, and *i,* which marks 2PL in the TRANSITIVE COMPLETIVE/INCOMPLETIVE. These forms taken together yielded *iš,* a form which qualifies as "degrees of the same kind" since both parent forms, *oš* and *i,* are instances of 2PL. With the emergence of *iš,* the newly displaced *i* moved into the less-marked category ERG2SG, displacing the preexisting *a,* which in turn moved to the less-marked category ERG3SG, replacing the previously occurring *u,* as demonstrated in Figure 7.3.

	3SG		2SG		3PL		2PL	
	Choltí	Chorti'	Choltí	Chorti'	Choltí	Chorti'	Choltí	Chorti'
COMPL INTRANS	Ø	Ø	et	et	ob?	ob?	oš	oš
INC INTRANS	wal u	a	wal a	i	wal u...ob?	a...ob?	wal i	iš
COMPL TRANS	u	u	a	a	u...ob?	u...ob?	i	i
INC TRANS	wal u	u	wal a	a	wal u...ob?	u...ob?	wal i	i

Figure 7.2. Pronominal sets for Choltí and Chorti' for both the transitive and intransitive COMPLETIVE and INCOMPLETIVE.

		2PL (2PL)	2PL (2SG)	2PL (3SG)
INC INTRANS	Chorti', Choltí	oš	et	Ø
COMPL INTRANS	Chorti', (Choltí)	iš (wal i)	i (wal a)	a (wal u)
INC TRANS	Chorti', Choltí	i (wal i)	a (wal a)	u (wal u)

Figure 7.3. Displacement in the Choltí and Chorti' pronominal sets.

Although the first-person pronouns remained untouched by the shift, the other pronouns were changed by chaining, resulting in a totally new pronominal series, unlike any pronominal series in the other Mayan languages. Surely a more thorough understanding of the complex pressures that prompted the emergence of the new form *iš,* and the subsequent emergence of the new paradigm, would be an important theoretical insight. But the outline of the emergence of this paradigm shown above is likely to be on target.

A second observation regarding the above schema is that the unmarked sign for single-argument predications, *-ik > -i,* took over the old marker for double-argument predication, *-O > -a.* Given the structural relationship between the two forms, such a change is not surprising.

The Negative in Common Mayan, Choltí, and Chorti'

One of the most interesting comparative facts of the history of Choltí-Chorti' can be found in the negative, for it is in the comparison of the negative with the positive that many otherwise recondite facts of the language come into focus.

It was pointed out earlier that the shift from the common language to Choltí saw the preservation of the old POSITIVE FUTURE, *la-,* and the Choltí NEGATIVE FUTURE preserved as *el-.* Although there are no instances of the form with intransitives in Choltí, there are nonetheless some instances of it with transitives of the CVC type, and it seems to have preserved the original suffixal morphology (*-ik > -i* and *-O > -a*) along with a vestige of the original *l: el...i/a.* The reason for this shift—the POSITIVE FUTURE moving to the NEGATIVE—is that a new FUTURE based on the prefix from the INCOMPLETIVE (*š-*) and on the suffixes from the OPTATIVE (*-oq > -ik* and *-Aʔ > -Aʔ*), yielding *š...ik/Aʔ,* displaced the original FUTURE, which took over the office of signaling NEGATIVE. Although not attested, analogical thinking suggests that a reflex of the old NEGATIVE of Common Mayan times, *ma la...ik/O,* might have been further displaced to mark the NEGATIVE of the Choltí OPTATIVE.

Now, a look at the same system as it moves from Choltí to Chorti' reveals the same series of changes. The old form marking the POSITIVE (but this time in conjunction with the NEGATIVE marker—*mi-š...ik/iʔk*) came to mark the NEGATIVE FUTURE, because a new form (the INCOMPLETIVE, as happened in K'iche', incidentally) took over the semantic territory of the POSITIVE FUTURE. Furthermore, with the displacement of the new form, the old Choltí NEGATIVE FUTURE (*el-*) took over the function of marking the NEGATIVE OPTATIVE. All this is apparent in Figure 7.4.

The fact that influences similar to the ones attested here in Choltí-Chorti' can be found to have occurred in other, different languages, some occurring in geographically contiguous languages, but others clearly occurring independently, offers solid evidence for the paradigmatic system proposed for the system of the common language. Otherwise, no explanation for the recurrence of such changes — particularly those in geographically non contiguous areas — is immediately apparent.

There is not enough information available to explain the change of the Common Mayan *la-* FUTURE to the *el-* FUTURE of Choltí, nor the change of the NEGATIVE FUTURE *el-* to the NEGATIVE OPTATIVE *ila-* in Chorti', but there are enough similarities both in form and certainly in function to require the supposition that it is the same morpheme.

Note that the NEGATIVE OPTATIVE takes the same pronominal series as was used for the INCOMPLETIVE:

Chorti'
OPTATIVE

INTRANSITIVE	TRANSITIVE
wayn-ik	u-šur-i?k
wayn-ik-et	a-šur-i?k
wayn-ik-en	in-šur-i?k
wayn-ik-ob?	u-šur-i?k-ob?
wayn-ik-oš	i-šur-i?k
wayn-ik-on	ka-šur-i?k

'may he sleep'	'may he cut it'
'may you sleep'	'may you cut it'
'may I sleep'	'may I cut it'
'may they sleep'	'may they cut it'
'may you-guys sleep'	'may you-guys cut it'
'may we sleep'	'may we cut it'

NEGATIVE OPTATIVE

INTRANSITIVE	TRANSITIVE
ila a-wayan	ila u-šur-i
ila i-wayan	ila a-šur-i
—	—
ila a-wayan-ob?	ila u-šur-i-ob?
ila iš-wayan	ila i-šur-i
ila ka-wayan	ila ka-šur-i

'may he not sleep'	'may he not cut it'
'may you not sleep'	'may you not cut it'
—	—
'may they not sleep'	'may they not cut it'
'may you-guys not sleep'	'may you-guys not cut it'
'may we not sleep'	'may we not cut it'

One more observation regarding the negative is in order. For negating the now very general INCOMPLETIVE, the form *ma?ači* is used. It will be recalled that the form for the old INCOMPLETIVE for the Tzeltalan and Cholan languages was *š-* (from which the Choltí prefixes for the FUTURE were derived), which, as suggested above, was apparently derived from Common Mayan *ki-*, via an intermediate form *či-*. Given the conserving character of the negative in the rest of Chorti' history, it is plausible that the *či-* of *ma?ači-* might be the preservation of that postulated intermediate form: *ki-* > *či-*.

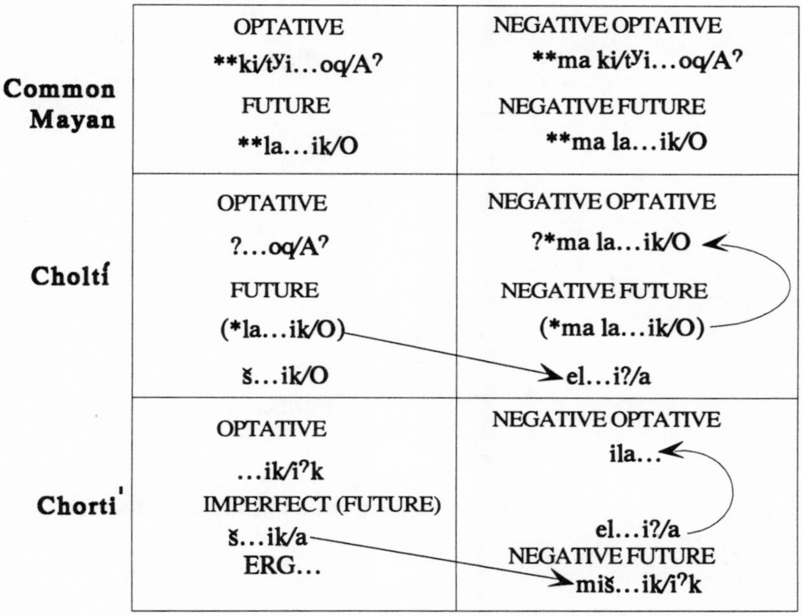

Common Mayan	OPTATIVE **ki/t^{y}i...oq/A? FUTURE **la...ik/O	NEGATIVE OPTATIVE **ma ki/t^{y}i...oq/A? NEGATIVE FUTURE **ma la...ik/O
Choltí	OPTATIVE ?...oq/A? FUTURE (*la...ik/O) š...ik/O	NEGATIVE OPTATIVE ?*ma la...ik/O NEGATIVE FUTURE (*ma la...ik/O) el...i?/a
Chorti'	OPTATIVE ...ik/i?k IMPERFECT (FUTURE) š...ik/a ERG...	NEGATIVE OPTATIVE ila... el...i?/a NEGATIVE FUTURE miš...ik/i?k

Figure 7.4. History of the OPTATIVE and the FUTURE from the Common Mayan to Choltí to Chorti'.

The Fate of the Common Mayan Suffixes *-ik*, *-O*, *-oq*, and -A?

As frequently happened in other Mayan languages, the Common Mayan *-ik* was reduced to *-i* in Choltí, as for example in *wiš-i-en* 'I went.' The *-oq* came to be *-ik*. The unrounding and raising of the vowel might have occurred from analogical influence from the unmarked *-i*. Although no glottal stop is included in the Choltí writing system, it was surely a part of the language, as for example in -A?, as evidenced by the fact that it was preserved in Chorti' as shown below.

In modern Chorti' the unmarked *-i* < *-ik* and *-k* < *-oq* took over the more marked *-a* < *-O* and -A? < -A?. The whole system can be given as in Figure 7.5.

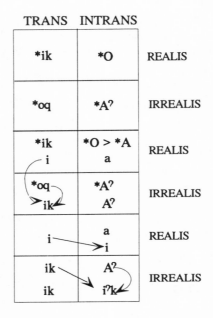

Figure 7.5. Markedness reversal of the Common Mayan suffixes in Choltí
and Chorti'.

Summary of Choltí/Chorti'

In the context of the reconstruction proposed in this book, Choltí is
particularly interesting for several reasons. The first is its ancestral relationship
to Chorti', requiring the resubgrouping from a lateral to a lineal relationship.
The second is the almost slavish following of the paradigm here proposed for
the system of TAMV in the Mayan languages. As shown below, (1) the
NOM-VOICE (CONTINUATIVE) moved wholesale into the INCOMPLETIVE; and (2)
NOM-VOICE (the directionals) also replaced NOM-MOOD. The grammar of Francisco
Morán reports nothing of what might be expected from Common Mayan
NOM-MOOD—only the construction with the directionals found in NOM-VOICE
(see page 77). Furthermore, as shown in Figure 7.6, the original INCOMPLETIVE,
which was displaced by the CONTINUATIVE, moved to the FUTURE, and the
original FUTURE was displaced to become a negative future. This remarkable
language has grammatical categories that are essentially one step ahead of,
say, the conservative K'iche', in its progression (by influence) toward the
grammatical FUTURE:[1]

---

[1]ABS-VOICE: The grammar (Morán) states that "los absolutos raras beses se

*...Vт-on/ow-ik [ABS]	*Vın DV-oq [ABS] [?] [?]	*Vın-ik [ABS] paxi en [paš-i en] 'I came back'	*ki/tʸi-Vın-oq [ABS] [?] [?]
*...Vт-on/ow-ik [ABS]	*Vт DV-oq [ERG&ABS] ? [?]	*Vт-O [ERG&ABS] Dios ucolo et [Dios u-kol-o et] 'God saved you'	*ki/tʸi-Vın-A? [ERG&ABS] ? [?]

ABS-VOICE	ABS-MOOD	COMPLETIVE	OPTATIVE
NOM-VOICE	**NOM-MOOD**	**INCOMPLETIVE**	**FUTURE**

*...Vın-NOMLZR [ABS] ? [?]	*DV Vın-oq [ABS] ? [?]	ki-Vın-ik [ABS] yual paxiel en [wal paš-i-el en] 'I fell'	*la-Vın-ik [ABS] xpaxic en [š-paš-i-k en] 'I will come back'
*...Vт-passive-ik [ERG&ABS] jual en ti caz te [wal en ti kas te] 'I am cutting wood'[1]	*DV Vт-DV-A? [ERG&ABS] xchic on tu yilal Dios [š-čik on t-uy-ilal Dios] 'we will go see God'	*Vт-O [ERG&ABS] yual in-cana [wal in-kan-a] 'I want it'	*la-Vт-O [ERG&ABS] xcatoho [š-ka-toh-o] 'we will pay it'

Figure 7.6. Summary of changes in TAMV from Common Mayan to Choltí to Chorti'.

---

usa en esta lengua." [...the absolutives are rarely used in this language.]

[1] The grammar is apparently in a state of flux with respect to the continuative. The representative form given above is the most conservative:"Quando se antepone las cossa de qe se abla se pone la actualidad *iual* con la vultima particula de pronombre primitibo *natzen*, y queda *en*, que junto con *iual* dira *iual en*. Y entonses no se pone a la cossa vna particula *ti* de la qual se ussa en este modo de ablar, vg. *caz ti iual en*, pero si se antepone a la cossa el *jual en*, se le pone la particula *ti*, y dira *jual en ti caz te*. Aora corte este palo: *cal jual en, jual en ti cal.*" [When the thing spoken of is preposed, the continuative *wal* [CONTINUATIVE] with the final particle of the primitive pronoun *naɟen* {'I'}, leaving *en* [ERG1SG], which, with *wal* will be *wal en*. And then it is not necessary to put with the thing spoken of the particle *ti* (used in this mode of speaking: *kas te wal en* [cut.wood CONTINUATIVE ABS1SG 'I am cutting wood']), but if *wal en* is preposed, the particle *ti* is used: *wal en ti kal* [CONTINUATIVE ABS1SG PREP cut 'I am cutting it'].]

Equally as interesting are the innovations accompanying the shift from Choltí to modern Chorti'. One of the most compelling is the innovation of an entirely new pronominal series which, as shown above, is a combination of the ERGATIVE and ABSOLUTIVE series, so that there is an ABSOLUTIVE series marking the COMPLETIVE, an ERGATIVE series marking transitive verbs, regardless of aspect or tense, and an ERGATIVE/ABSOLUTIVE series which marks the intransitive INCOMPLETIVE. This innovation resulted from a remarkable series of displacements, first of the original ERG3PL *i* by *iš* < *oš* + *i* and second of the ERG2SG *u* by the ERG2SG *a.*

Chapter 8. Tzeltalan

It is more difficult to give as secure an outline of the history of Tzeltalan from the common language to its first colonially attested state as was given of the languages heretofore discussed because Tzeltalan had changed substantially by Colonial times. But building on what *is* known of the manner of change of those earlier discussed languages, hypotheses that might otherwise be speculative become more secure, and suppositions more confident, because several patterns of change have already been established. There is good reason to believe that Tzeltalan followed suit.

Pre-Tzeltalan COMPLETIVE and PROXIMATE PAST

As a case in point, consider the COMPLETIVE, comparing the paradigms of pre-Tzeltalan with Common Mayan:

Common Mayan		pre-Tzeltalan	
COMPLETIVE	PROXIMATE PAST	COMPLETIVE	
**war in	**iš-in way-ik	*n-in way-ik	'I slept'
**war at	**iš-at way-ik	*n-at way-ik	'you slept'
**war ik	**iš-way-ik	*u-way-ik	'he slept'

On the face of it, there seems to be little connection between the two systems, but at a deeper level the connection is there. Consideration of the modern K'iche'an COMPLETIVE as compared with Common Mayan hints at where to look for the provenance of the Tzotzilan *n-.

Common Mayan		Modern K'iche'	
COMPLETIVE	PROXIMATE PAST	COMPLETIVE	
*war in	*iš-in way-ik	š-in way-ik	'I slept'
*war at	*iš-at way-ik	š-at way-ik	'you slept'
*war ik	*iš-way-ik	š-way-ik	'he slept'

Because the modern K'iche'an COMPLETIVE *š* comes from Common Mayan PROXIMATE PAST *iš* by way of markedness reversal, it is possible that Tzeltalan had a parallel history, particularly in light of the fact that the word in both Colonial Tzotzil and Tzeltal for PROXIMATE PAST (literally, 'past time of today') is *naš.*[1] Based on what has already been attested in K'iche'an, it is proposed that the *n-* of Common Tzeltalan comes from the PROXIMATE PAST *naš.* Even though the precise etymology of *n-* is not clear at this time, this hypothesis is strengthened by the observation that in Q'anjob'al there is (a) a form *mayal* meaning 'past time of today,' and (b) a prefix for past time *ma-š-,* which would be structurally identical to the Tzeltalan *na-š-* meaning 'past time of today.' Furthermore, if the prefix signaling the COMPLETIVE, *n-,* indeed has to do with the PROXIMATE PAST, *naš*—and it seems reasonable to presume that it does, in light of what happened in other Mayan languages—then this provides even more evidence that the distinction between the PROXIMATE PAST and the COMPLETIVE went back to Common Mayan times.

Tzeltalan, however, has a complication that did not exist in K'iche'an. There are two morphemes marking the COMPLETIVE, one co-occurring with PERSON—1st and 2nd (in this case, **n-* as discussed above)—and the other (**u-*) with NONPERSON—3SG. K'iche', by contrast, only had *š-* as a general COMPLETIVE. Such a distribution—PERSON VS. NONPERSON—is usual for TENSE/ASPECT marking in Mayan languages. While the above seems to be a reasonable hypothesis to explain where *n-* came from, the provenance of *u-* is less certain, although there is the suggestion that earlier there were two paradigms: a PROXIMATE PAST based on *n-,* and a DISTANT PAST based on *u-,* with the *u-* coming from *wo,* the root for 'yesterday.'

Finally, note that the Tzeltalan form, **u-,* and not the Tzotzilan form, *i-,* has been chosen to be the common form:

Common Tzeltalan	Colonial Tzotzil	Colonial Tzeltal	
**u-way-i	i-way-i	u-way	'he slept'
**n-at-way-i	n-a-way-i	u-way-at	'you slept'
**n-in-way-i	n-i-way-i	u-way-in	'I slept'

I chose *u-* over *i-* because "it seems more plausible for *u-* to become unrounded than the reverse" (Robertson 1987b:430).

Pronominal Affixation

For Common Tojolab'al-Tzeltal-Choltí I reconstruct the ABSOLUTIVE pronouns as prefixes to accommodate the prefixed first- and second-person singular pronouns of Colonial Tzotzil, *i-* < **in-* and *a-* < **at-,* respectively.[2] Recall

---

[1]It should not escape our notice that reflexes of **iš* mean PROXIMATE PAST in Q'anjob'alan, Mamean, and K'iche'an.

[2]Note that Kaqchikel similarly reduced **-at-C* and **-in-C* to *-a-C* and *-i-C.* The

that in Common Mayan, it was proposed that the ABSOLUTIVES were suffixed with participles and imperatives, and prefixed to verbs with TAMV (p. 53). In some language groups, such as Mamo-K'iche'an, prefixation became the predominant mode of pronominal inflection, so that in Colonial K'iche' (Anonymous 1793), for example, there exist only fossilized remnants of suffixation:

Colonial K'iche'[1]

oh	[ox]	'would that he go'	he	[x-e?]	'would that they go'
ohat	[ox-at]	'go!'	hix	[x-iš]	'go (pl)!'
ohin	[ox-in]	'would that I go!'	ho	[x-o?]	'would that we go'

On the other hand, in the Cholan and especially the Yukatekan subgroups, suffixation of the ABSOLUTIVE set came to predominate in verbal inflection, ASPECT/TENSE/MOOD included. Thus, first Yukatekan, then Cholan, and then neighboring Tzeltal and Tojolab'al, and finally certain bordering Tzotzil dialects all came to suffix the ABSOLUTIVE in the context of ASPECT/TENSE/MOOD, regardless of whether the verb was participial or inflectionally conjugated.[2] It is therefore likely that suffixation in Tzeltal was influenced by contiguous, suffixing Chol, which in turn was first influenced by the likely innovator of the whole business, Yukatekan. With Tzotzil, those dialects that are most removed from Tzeltal are those that have the most prefixation. A comparison of Zinacantan Tzotzil, Huixtán Tzotzil, and Tzeltal suggests a way by which suffixation may have originally developed in Tzeltal, at least in transitive verbs:

Zinacantan:	l-*a*-y-il	COMP-*ABS2SG*-ERG3SG-see	'he saw you'
Huixtán:	n-*a*-y-il-*ot*	COMP-*ABS2SG*-ERG3SG-see-*ABS2SG*	'he saw you'
Tzeltal:	la-y-il-*at*	COMP-ERG3SG-see-*ABS2SG*	'he saw you'

In both Zinacantan Tzotzil and Tzeltal, ABS2SG occurs only once in the expression, prefixed as *a-* < **at* in Zinacantan, and suffixed as -*at* in Tzeltal. In Huixtán, on the other hand, it occurs twice, once as a prefix *a-*, as in Zinacantan, and once as a suffix -*ot* < **at,* as in Tzeltal. With these data it seems reasonable to suggest that Zinacantan represents the initial stage and reflects the common language; that Huixtán represents an intermediate stage;

---

change was variably going on in Colonial times, as recorded in the grammars, so that today Kaqchikel, like Tzotzil, has the reduced *i-* and *a-* for ABSOLUTIVE first- and second-person singular.

[1]The orthography has been normalized.

[2]This suffixation of the ABSOLUTIVE extended even to the Mamean language, Ixil, which was obviously deeply influenced by Cholan.

and Tzeltal, the final stage. Because Huixtán has the redundancy of being marked twice for ABS2SG, it would be a simple step to lose the initial prefixation in favor of the final suffixation that is common to the Lowland Languages. The above scenario is suggested as a possible method by which the Lowland Languages could have changed from prefixing to suffixing languages.

One other difference between Tzeltal and Tzotzil must be accounted for, and that is that Tzotzil has two markers for the INCOMPLETIVE *(n-/i-)*, whereas Tzeltal has but one marker *(u-)*. This difference might be explained by the assumption that *u-* was generalized when the suffixation of the ABSOLUTIVE took place. Furthermore, Watkins (1962:90) has amply demonstrated that

> it is 3sg. which will tend to impose its form on the rest of the paradigm irrespective of the form of the 2sg. or another person, owing to the peculiar functional position of the 3sg. as 'la personne zéro,' 'la non-personne,' as Benveniste has put it in his very significant study of the problem in general linguistics.

Thus, the *u-*, occurring in the context of 3 SG, came to mark the INCOMPLETIVE in all persons, taking over the *n-*.

The INCOMPLETIVE in Tzeltalan

The INCOMPLETIVE in Tzeltalan is *š:*

Colonial Tzeltal			Colonial Tzotzil		
xpazot hon	[š-pas-ot hon]	'I am made'	ximuy	[š-i-muy]	'I descend'
xpazot at	[š-pas-ot at]	'you are made'	xamuy	[š-a-muy]	'you descend'
xpazot	[š-pas-ot]	'he is made'	xmuy	[š-muy]	'he descends'

As suggested earlier in the discussion of the negative of Chuj and Choltí, the INCOMPLETIVE *š-* comes from the INCOMPLETIVE **ki-* of the common language, with a probable intermediate stage of **č-* (which deaffricated to become *š-*). That such deaffrication is possible can be found in the Tzotzil example, *nič²anab* > **ničnab* > *nišnab²* 'brothers' (Anonymous, 1812:19).

The FUTURE in Colonial Tzeltal (Anonymous, n.d. [Confecionario...]), which is marked by the INCOMPLETIVE *š-* coupled with the morpheme *to* 'later,' postposed to the verb, has obviously been deeply influenced by the INCOMPLETIVE:

Colonial Tzeltal

xpazot hon to   [š-pas-ot-on to]   'I will be made'

xpazot at to	[š-pas-ot-at to]	'you will be made'
xpazot to	[š-pas-ot to]	'he will be made'

We have often seen such influence (INCOMPLETIVE on the FUTURE), as for example in modern K'iche', in Poqom, and in Choltí.

The FUTURE and the OPTATIVE in Tzeltalan

As will be demonstrated below, it is postulated that, like K'iche' or Chorti', Tzeltalan had an even earlier FUTURE influenced by the OPTATIVE. But, unlike K'iche'an and Chorti', the OPTATIVE changed dramatically from Common Mayan times, and this change must be taken into account to understand what took place in the FUTURE. To get an idea of this change, observe the paradigm for the OPTATIVE, for instance, in Colonial Tzeltal, with verbs of both single and double arguments:

muy-uk	'would that he ascend'
muy-uk-at	'would that you ascend'
muy-uk-on	'would that we ascend'
muy-uk-ik	'would that they ascend'
muy-uk-eš	'would that you-guys ascend'
muy-uk-otik	'would that we ascend'
aka-s-pas	'would that he do it'
?	
la-x-pas	'would that I do it'
aka-s-pas-ik	'would that they do it'
?	
la-x-pas-otik	'would that we (INC) do it'

With single-argument predications it is clear that the *-uk* comes from the OPTATIVE *-oq* of the common language, and it is also clear that the original prefix *ki-* was lost, as happened in Awakatek and Choltí. But it is not immediately clear where the *la-* of FIRST PERSON and the *aka-* of THIRD PERSON come from. A comparison, shown in Figure 8.1, between Tojolab'al and Colonial Tzeltal will help clear this up.

Although my data are incomplete for Tojolab'al, there are enough pieces of the paradigm to suggest some interesting relationships between Tzeltalan and Tojolab'al. First, in both languages the OPTATIVE has *a* to mark THIRD PERSON, and *la-* to mark FIRST PERSON. While it is possible that these strikingly specialized paradigms are attributable to chance or to independent developments, or even to borrowing, the singular character of these forms suggest rather that Tojolab'al and Tzeltalan shared a common period of development.[1]

Single-Argument Predication
Tojolab'al Col. Tzeltal

	Tojolab'al	Col. Tzeltal
3SG	a...uk	...uk
2SG	an	...an
1SG	la...uk-on	...uk-on
3PL	?	...uk
2PL	...an-ik	...anik
1INC	la...uk-otik	...uk-otik
1EXC		

Double-Argument Predication
Tojolab'al Col. Tzeltal

	Tojolab'al	Col. Tzeltal
3SG		ako-s...
2SG	...a	...o
1SG		la-x...
3PL		
2PL	...a-ik	...ik
1INC	la-h...tik	la-x...tik
1EXC		

Figure 8.1. Paradigms comparing the OPTATIVE in Tojolab'al and Colonial Tzeltal.

---

[1]Kaufman (1974) has proposed that, together, Tojolabal and Chuj form a separate subgroup, stemming from Common Mayan. Over the years my work on these languages has led me to separate Chuj from Tojolabal, grouping Chuj with Q'anjob'alan, and Tojolabal with Tzeltalan (Robertson 1977a). This study, which includes the investigation of the Colonial grammars of Tzeltal and Choltí, along with modern data from Tojolabal, only reconfirms my earlier proposed subgrouping. In fact, when beginning this study I had reconsidered, thinking possibly that the similarities in the pronominal systems of Tojolabal and Tzeltalan, for example, might have been all attributable to borrowing, and not commonly innovated, thus allowing for the possibility that Tojolabal might be an isolate. But as the data unfolded, I found it not only convenient for this study, but necessary for straightforward explanation, to put Tojolabal into the Tzeltalan subgroup.

The appearance of this innovation is rooted in the history of *a* and *la*. There was apparently a historical *a* which marked some kind of FUTURE, likely a PROXIMATE FUTURE, as well as the PROXIMATE PAST. In Choltí, for example, there is another, heretofore unmentioned FUTURE marker *a*, which has almost an OPTATIVE sense: *a tuch £a* "que se (os) manifieste" (Morán 1695).[1] Furthermore, Smailus (1973) reports that in Colonial Chontal of Acalán, there is an *a* of a PROXIMATE PAST and PROXIMATE FUTURE.[2] Similarly, it will be recalled that Colonial Poqomchi' has a PROXIMATE PAST and FUTURE in *a* (likely borrowed from Choltí) that is functionally equivalent to Mamo-K'iche'an *mi-*. It is likely, therefore, that Common Tojolab'al-Tzeltal-Chol had some kind of PROXIMATE FUTURE or even OPTATIVE paradigm in *a*.

Furthermore, recall the evidence for the **la-* FUTURE of Common Mayan times. The FUTURE in Ixil is *la-;* in certain embeddings in Awakatek it is *l + č-* (from **la-k*); in Chuj, it is *ol-;* and, as has been noted, there is a negative future in Choltí, *el-*. Additionally, there is a negative future in Colonial Yukatek, *wi-l,* which contains an *l*.

Thus, there were apparently two FUTURE paradigms in Common Tojolab'al-Tzeltalan-Cholan, one in *a-* and one in *la-*. The two paradigms apparently collapsed, as shown in Figure 8.2.

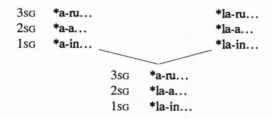

3SG	**a-ru...*		**la-ru...*
2SG	**a-a...*		**la-a...*
1SG	**a-in...*		**la-in...*

	3SG	**a-ru...*
	2SG	**la-a...*
	1SG	**la-in...*

Figure 8.2. Collapse of the two FUTURE paradigms of Common Tojolab'al-Tzeltalan-Cholan.

That such paradigmatic collapsing *is* possible can be seen in K'iche' of Nahualá (p. 129), although the collapse resulted in a different paradigmatic structure than what is proposed for Tzeltalan-Cholan.

This newly collapsed FUTURE was apparently displaced to occupy the semantic space of the OPTATIVE. To suppose a markedness reversal, however, there must be, by requirement, 'degrees of the same kind.' Such degrees of the same kind as occur, for example, in the FUTURE of Q'anjob'al, where it is

---

[1]The orthography is not normalized.

[2]Instances of the PROXIMATE FUTURE are not readily available in the text, but they can be found, as e.g., *a-ček-t-es-b²e-n-on-lal* 'you will show me (all your idols).'

visibly attestable (*oq-in-way-oq* 'I will sleep'), with the Common Mayan **-oq* prefixed. Careful consideration of the FUTURE in Tojolab'al reveals the same state of affairs, where the old Common Mayan **-oq* > *-ok* has been prefixed, and subsequently fricatized to become *-oh:* This is demonstrated in Figure 8.3.

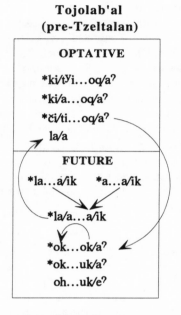

Tojolab'al
(pre-Tzeltalan)

Figure 8.3. Displacement and markedness reversal in the OPTATIVE and the FUTURE of Tojolab'al.

With a stage similar to that which exists in Tojolab'al, pre-Tzeltalan was then ready to replace the **ok...ok* FUTURE with the INCOMPLETIVE, as seen in Figure 8.4. This explanation presupposes, of course, a common history for both Tojolab'al and Tzeltalan, where vestiges of the old FUTURE appear in the OPTATIVE. This, in addition to all the other similarities between the two languages, strongly suggests that a shared history is not only plausible but highly likely.

From the Colonial to the Modern Tzeltalan Languages

Several factors must be taken into consideration in explaining the shift from the Colonial to the modern Tzeltalan languages. First, for the COMPLETIVE, there is a general pattern where the **u-* that originally marked 3SG ultimately comes to mark intransitive verbs, such as, in late Colonial Tzeltal. Second, there is a general tendency for the original inflectional morpheme *n-*, in FIRST- and second-person COMPLETIVE to be replaced by the transitive verb *lah-*, meaning 'finish, complete,' where *lah-* passes from a lexeme to a morpheme. Third, following a tendency that is almost universal in Mayan, the Tzeltalan group of languages augmented the INCOMPLETIVE with a morpheme taken from the PROGRESSIVE. Finally, Tzeltal underwent a striking instance of a change based on "degrees of the same kind," related to the notion of markedness reversal, where the INTRANSITIVE COMPLETIVE and the TRANSITIVE INCOMPLETIVE were both reduced to zero.

Pre-Tzeltal

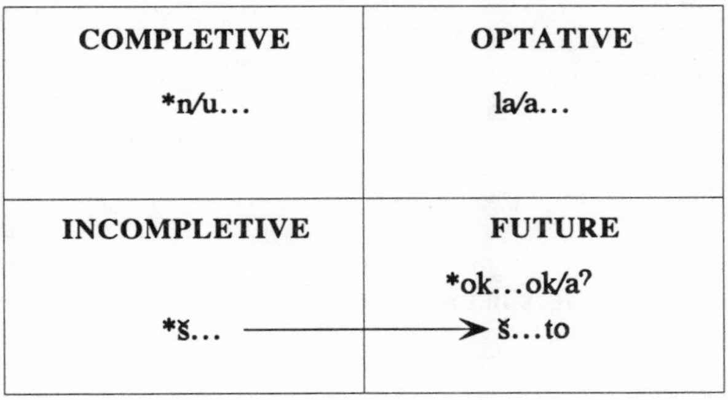

COMPLETIVE	OPTATIVE
*n/u...	la/a...
INCOMPLETIVE	**FUTURE**
	*ok...ok/a$^{?}$
*š... ⟶	š...to

Figure 8.4. Replacement of the FUTURE by the INCOMPLETIVE in pre-Tzeltalan.

Figure 8.5 reveals three stages. Stage I of the chart below preserves the original system, as exemplified by Zinacantan, with the change **u- > i-* in third-person. In Stage II, represented by Huixtán, *lah-* comes into third-person *and* first- and second-person in transitive verbs, the details of which are given below. Finally, by Stage III, as represented by late Colonial Tzeltal, the reflex of **u- > u-* moves from third- to first- and second-person, resulting in a system which distinguishes PERSON (Stage I) to one that distinguishes verb type (Stage III)

The data from the two stages are given below. Stage I is represented by a reconstruction of Common Tzeltal/Tzotzil and otherwise conservative Zinacantan[1] which, although it replaced the original **n-* by *la-*, maintains the original system:

Common Tzeltalan		Zinacantan	
*u-way	'he slept'	i-way	'he slept'

---

[1]The form *l-a-s-mah* is not attested, but has been filled in, based on other paradigms. The data are from Bricker (1977).

*n-at-way	'you slept'	l-a-way	'you slept'
*n-in-way	'I slept'	l-in-way	'I slept'

*u-s-mah	'he hit him'	i-s-mah	'he hit him'
*n-at-s-mah	'he hit you'	l-a-s-mah	'he hit you'
*n-in-s-mah	'he hit me'	l-in-s-mah	'he hit me'

	Stage I Zinacantan		**Stage II** Huixtan		**Stage III** Late Colonial Tzeltal	
person	Vin	Vt	Vin	Vt	Vin	Vt
3	*u i	*u i	i	⎰ lah ⎱ i	u	l(ah)
1,2	*n l	*n l	n	⎰ lah ⎱ n	u	l(ah)

Figure 8.5. Three stages in the change of Tzeltalan showing replacement in the INCOMPLETIVE.

In Huixtán[1] *lah-* has virtually displaced the *i-* < **u-* in transitive verbs, although only *i* can be found in intransitives, as in, e.g., *la-s-pas* 'he did it' vs. *i-b?at* 'he went.' Furthermore, although there are more instances of the old *n-i-* and *n-a-* of FIRST and SECOND PERSON in transitive verbs, those pronouns are being lost in favor of the suffixed pronouns, although in intransitive verbs they are the only forms:

Hiuxtán

intransitive		transitive	
i-b?at	'he went'	i-s-ve?	'he ate it'
		la-s-pas	'he did it'
n-a-b?at	'you went'	n-i-y-ak?-b?-un	'he gave it to me'
n-i-b?at	'I went'	lah-y-ak?-b?-un	'he gave it to me'

The *lah-* is always present in the context of FIRST and SECOND PERSON if the prefix *i-* (FIRST PERSON) and *a-* (SECOND PERSON) are not present, as seen in the above example; otherwise the forms are *ni-* and *na-*.

---

[1]The data from Huixtán are taken from Cowan (1968, 1969).

From Colonial to Modern Tzeltal

By Colonial Tzeltal times, the *u-* had taken over the **n-*, but by late Colonial times, as with Tzotzil, *lah-* replaced the *u-* in transitive verbs, just as *lah-* is active in Tzotzil transitives, as seen in Figure 8.6.

person	Common Vin	Common Vt	Colonial Vin	Colonial Vt	Late Colonial Vin	Late Colonial Vt
3	*u	*u	u	u	u	lah
1, 2	*n	*n	u	u	u	lah

Figure 8.6. Three stages showing replacement of the COMPLETIVE in Tzeltal.

The data for Colonial and Late Colonial Tzeltal are taken from an anonymous *Confeçionario* dating probably from the late eighteenth century. The grammar, however, has two parts, one that is surely a copy of an earlier grammar, and another that must be a later addition of Catholic liturgy. The discrepancy between the parts is significant—the earlier grammar has no COMPLETIVE in *lah-*, for example, while the later liturgical text does. In any case, the grammar apparently provides snapshots of both an earlier and a later stage of pre-Modern Tzeltal.

COMPLETIVE/INCOMPLETIVE with TRANSITIVE/INTRANSITIVE

The changes in the COMPLETIVE described above are important because the very parameters of the paradigm are changing with a logically given, newly formed paradigm emerging. The newly formed paradigm is based on the oppositions COMPLETIVE/INCOMPLETIVE and TRANSITIVE/INTRANSITIVE, where the latter was never historically significant in connection with the former. The changes associated with the new paradigm are at first glance somewhat unexpected: the loss of the INCOMPLETIVE with intransitive verbs, *u,* and the COMPLETIVE with transitive verbs, *š;* and the simultaneous preservation of the inverse—the COMPLETIVE with transitive verbs, *u-,* and the INCOMPLETIVE with intransitive verbs, *š-,* as shown in Figure 8.7.

It is important to note that this remarkable change is not only attested in the Colonial documents, but also evident from internal reconstruction, in consideration of the negatives. In *Tzeltal: Language Learning Guide* (n.d.:11), for example, the language learner is to 'use *maš* in the present tense' for the negative with vowel-initial verb stems: *maš k-aʔiy s-tohol* 'I don't understand.'

Furthermore, the negative imperative takes the form *ma-meš-aw-il* 'don't look at it,' where again the earlier *š-* of the INCOMPLETIVE is present vestigially. The negative marker, or what is taken to be the negative marker, includes the original INCOMPLETIVE *š-* on the intransitive verb. In this regard, recall that Chorti' maintains a negative FUTURE (which originally came from the IN-COMPLETIVE, incidentally) in *š-*. Thus, it is clear that the *š-* was historically there, even though it is no longer present in the modern language.

Tzeltal

	COMPLETIVE INTRANSITIVE	INCOMPLETIVE INTRANSITIVE
Late Colonial	u-muy-on	š-muy-on
Modern	Ø-muy-on	š-muy-on
	'I descended'	'I descend'

	COMPLETIVE TRANSITIVE	INCOMPLETIVE TRANSITIVE
Late Colonial	la-k-il	š-k-il
Modern	la-k-il	Ø-k-il
	'I saw it'	'I see it'

Figure 8.7. Summary of changes of the COMPLETIVE and INCOMPLETIVE from Late Colonial Tzeltal to Modern Tzeltal.

The evidence is compellingly at hand, therefore, both in historical documents and in the internal reconstruction of the language, given the four logical possibilities—COMPLETIVE INTRANSITIVE, COMPLETIVE TRANSITIVE, INCOMPLETIVE INTRANSITIVE, and INCOMPLETIVE TRANSITIVE—that the markers *la-* and *š-* were lost exactly in the COMPLETIVE INTRANSITIVE and in its opposite, the INCOMPLETIVE TRANSITIVE.

It is not enough, however, simply to observe that the change took place, for as Watkins (1973:101) has rightly stated, it is the comparatist's task "to demonstrate precisely how it is possible...to pass from one system at one point in time to another system at a later point," or, in other words, to demonstrate how it was possible for Tzeltal to have changed in precisely the way it did.

The hypothesis for our already observed change, the loss of the markers in opposite ends of the paradigm, can be given in terms of "degrees of the same kind," or markedness reversal. In this case the paradigm is built on two oppositions, (1) TRANSITIVE/INTRANSITIVE and (2) COMPLETIVE/INCOMPLETIVE, both of which belong to the same category, which has to do with CONTINUITY (or its absence; see p. 31). For example, the chief characteristic of transitive predicates in Mayan is the calling forth of two arguments, where the action described by the verb identifies the type of continuity that exists between the two arguments. As Peirce (1.361) puts it, "the first is agent, and the second patient, the third is the action by which the former influences the latter. Between the beginning as first, and the end as last, comes the process which leads from first to last." Thus, in the Tzeltal verbal complex *la-h-man* 'I bought it,' one sees a continuity between the two arguments 'I' and 'it,' as defined by the action 'buy,' with the former influencing the latter. Similar continuities exist in all transitive verbs of Tzeltal, and in all of Mayan. Intransitives lack such continuity simply because such verbs do not call up two arguments.

The notion INCOMPLETIVE has nothing to do with the connection of arguments to the verb—since only the verbal action itself is at issue—but references, rather, the idea of *continuity,* which is particularly obvious in the comparison between the INCOMPLETIVE and the COMPLETIVE. In the INCOMPLETIVE *š-,* one sees unbounded continuity, where there is neither first nor last, whereas with the COMPLETIVE *la-* one sees boundedness—a beginning and an end. Compare, for example, *k-il* 'I see it' in the INCOMPLETIVE with *la-k-il* 'I saw it' in the COMPLETIVE. The difference between the two notions of *seeing* is the difference between an unbroken, repetitive connectivity, one instant of seeing merging imperceptibly into the next, and on the other hand, a fact of having seen, a *fait accompli*—a semelfactive act, the exact replication of which is impossible. Thus, in general, there is a connectivity inherent in transitive verbs, and a similar connectivity found in the INCOMPLETIVE, and both are therefore degrees of the same kind, resulting in the paradigmatic potential for opposites to act similarly. In this case, the unmarked INTRANSITIVE COMPLETIVE and its exact opposite, the TRANSITIVE INCOMPLETIVE, act similarly, both losing their marks. This is another instance of a markedness reversal, where in this case the most marked becomes formally like the least marked.

The Tzeltalan INCOMPLETIVE

The last significant change to be discussed results from an already-discussed process of change in Mayan languages: the augmentation of the INCOMPLETIVE by a marker, usually the PROGRESSIVE. In Tzotzil, for example, the INCOMPLETIVE *š-* was augmented by *ta-,* which may well be related to the Mamean INCOMPLETIVE *ǯa·n-,* as discussed by Robertson (1987b:442).

Cowan (1969:14) distinguishes between the original aspect *š-* and its augmented counterpart *t(a)-š-* by naming the former TIMELESS and the latter INCOMPLETIVE. Delgaty and Sánchez (1978:394), on the other hand, call the first the INDEFINITE (TIEMPO INDEFINIDO) and the second PRESENT-FUTURE (PRESENTE-FUTURO). The so-called INDEFINITE seems to be more restricted in its range of reference than the PRESENT-FUTURE. The INDEFINITE "indicates that the action is ongoing. By itself this tense is seldom used, but is rather combinatory with other morphemes whose combination makes further tenses" (Delgaty 1978:394 [my translation]). The augmented *t(a)-š-* is very common, on the other hand, and has a referential range broad enough to take in either the present or the future. In fact, "to distinguish future from present action, very often an adverbial or adverbial phrase is used...."

Tzeltal was similarly augmented, but in this case with the morpheme *yak,* which is used as the PROGRESSIVE. Whereas it often happens that the PROGRESSIVE takes over the INCOMPLETIVE (as happened in Choltí, for example), it sometimes happens that the PROGRESSIVE simply augments what is already there. Laughlin (1975:382) says that in Tzotzil *yak* means 'continue or keep' doing something. In the modern language "they rarely occur separately" (Robertson 1987b:442–443).

Summary of Tzeltalan

Tzeltalan underwent significant changes by the time of the Conquest—more than most of the other languages heretofore discussed. Nonetheless, based on the kinds of changes observed in Mamean, K'iche'an, and Q'anjob'alan, it seems fairly certain that Tzeltalan underwent a similar change: namely, that the appearance of the *n-* in the COMPLETIVE has its source in the form *niš,* which means PROXIMATE PAST, or 'past time of today.' One of the most noteworthy changes has to do with the appearance of the *la-* as a PERSON marker, and *a-* as a NONPERSON marker in the OPTATIVE. It is noteworthy because a similar occurrence of morphemes can be found in Tojolab'al, whose FUTURE is marked with *-oh* < **-oq.* Assumedly, the paradigm *la-/a-* is derived from the Common Mayan FUTURE *la-* and PROXIMATE FUTURE *a,* which ended up moving to the OPTATIVE via markedness reversal. Therefore, Tzeltalan and Tojolab'al had a common history, separate from Chuj.

Finally the changes from the Colonial to the modern languages are interesting because of the overwhelming evidence they provide to support the reality of markedness reversal, where both the least- and the most-marked members of the paradigm—COMPLETIVE INTRANSITIVE and INCOMPLETIVE TRANSITIVE—lost their formal marking. These changes are summarized in Figure 8.8.

Tojolab'al

The discussion has already partially treated Tojolab'al, showing the probable provenance of its FUTURE and OPTATIVE. Briefly, remember that Tojolab'al shares with Tzeltalan the OPTATIVE, except that in Tojolab'al the OPTATIVE has *a/la* in both transitive and intransitive verbs, while in Colonial Tzeltal *a/la* exists only in the transitives. Further, there is the Tojolab'al FUTURE, the category from which the *a/la* was proposed to have been displaced. For Tojolab'al it is proposed that a new FUTURE was formed, where **ok* was preposed, exactly as OPTATIVE *oq* is preposed, as attested in Q'anjob'alan: *oq-in-way-oq* 'I will sleep.'

Q'anjob'al	pre-Tojolab'al	Tojolab'al
oq...oq	*ok...ok	oh...uk
oq-at...oq	*ok...ok-at	oh...an
oq-in...oq	*ok...ok-in	oh...uk-in

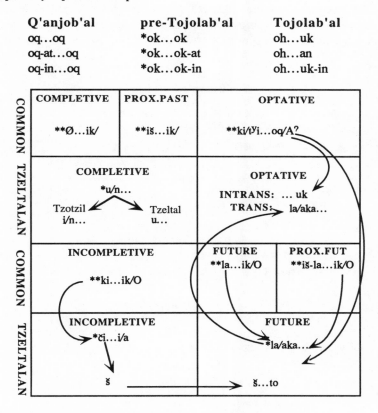

Figure 8.8. Summary of changes in the TAMV of Tzeltalan.

The pre-FUTURE then changed as follows. First, before consonants, *ok-* became *oh-* as happened regularly in all the languages of Tojolab'al, Tzeltalan, and Cholan: Common Mayan ERG1PL *qa > ka > *k > *h/__C*. Second, *-ok-at* became *-an,* which was a change unique to Tojolab'al.[1] Third, *-ok* became *-uk,* possibly on analogy with the other verb-complex suffixes that

---

[1]For a more thorough discussion, see Robertson (1980:58-59).

became high vowels, such as *tik* for 1 PL, which likely came from **tak* <
*taq.

The INCOMPLETIVE in Tojolab'al, as in Tzeltalan and many of the other
Mayan languages, was apparently augmented by the PROGRESSIVE—in this
case *wa* < *wan.* It will be recalled that Q'anjob'al, like Tojolab'al, augmented
the newly acquired FUTURE suffix by prefixing the suffix from Common
Mayan **-oq,* yielding *oq...oq* (degrees of the same kind). This set up a
markedness reversal, where the reflex of the transitive **-A?* was moved to the
less-marked INCOMPLETIVE (see p. 158). Similarly, Tojolab'al's displacement
drove the original FUTURE *la-* to the INCOMPLETIVE, as well as to the OPTATIVE,
as shown in Figure 8.9.

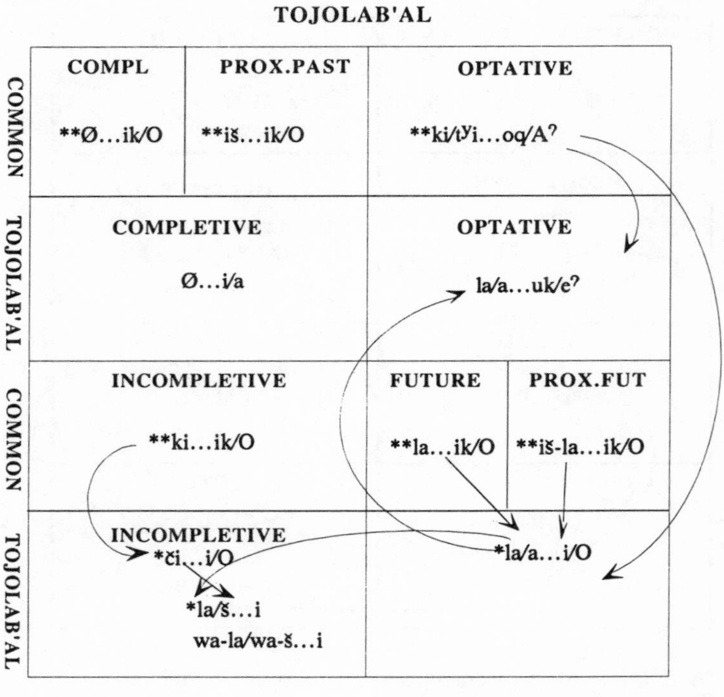

TOJOLAB'AL

Figure 8.9. Summary of changes in the TAMV of Tojolab'al.

Chapter 9. Yukatek Maya

If K'iche' is the best candidate for the most conservative of the Mayan languages, Yukatek is the likely candidate for the most innovative, owing to its unrelenting transformation of the grammatical system from simple to split ergativity.

Colonial Yukatekan

The overall explanation of the changes from the common language to Colonial Yukatek has a scope consistently broader than the other Mayan languages discussed heretofore. Perhaps more than any other language, it requires consideration not just of the familiar single-predication system, but also of the system discussed in Chapter 2 involving two predications, which includes MOOD (ABS-DV and NOM-DV) as well as VOICE (relative clause formation—RELATIVE VOICE—and nominalization—NOMINATIVE VOICE).

Following is a brief overview of what happened from Common Mayan to Colonial Yukatek. First, as in Q'anjob'alan, raising was lost, causing a marker of RELATIVE VOICE (*ow-ik*) to be extended to the category of NOMINATIVE VOICE, eliminating voice in nominalization. Second, as in Choltí and Poqom, a syntactic construction from the PROGRESSIVE (a subset of NOMINATIVE VOICE) took over the INCOMPLETIVE, beginning the significant change to split ergativity referred to above. Third, another form of the PROGRESSIVE—a verb-final construction, demonstrably from Common Mayan times—took over the INCOMPLETIVE. Fourth, the NOMINATIVE VOICE (originally from the RELATIVE VOICE, as explained above) once again took over the INCOMPLETIVE, thus removing the INCOMPLETIVE two steps from the common language. Finally, just as the NOMINATIVE VOICE took over the INCOMPLETIVE, so the NOM-DV analogously took over the FUTURE. Note that vestiges of the old *la-* future can be found in the NEGATIVE FUTURE, much like what happened in Choltí. The five steps outlined above are summarized in Figure 9.1.

Voice: Replacement of NOMINATIVE VOICE by RELATIVE VOICE

The discussion of the change from the common language to Colonial Yukatek will begin by comparing what happened in Q'anjob'alan with Yukatekan in the paradigm of RELATIVE and NOMINATIVE VOICE. It will be recalled that in Q'anjob'al, which lost raising, two concomitant changes took place (p. 83.). First, the system of nominalization changed from the Common Mayan (K'iche'an-type) system, where the nominative subjects of both transitives and intransitives were raised from the secondary predicate to the primary predicate, to a system where those subjects remained with the secondary predicate. Second, with that change, the old marker for relative clauses, *Vn-i,* came to mark the transitive verbs in the NOMINATIVE VOICE, as shown in Figure 9.2.

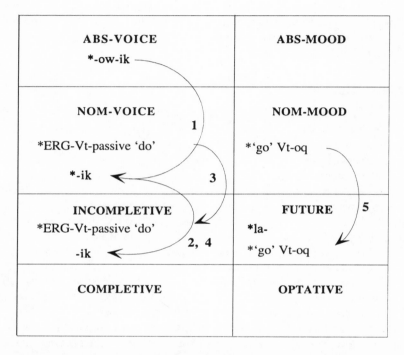

Figure 9.1. Summary of changes of TAMV from Common Mayan to Colonial Yukatek.

A comparison of these Q'anjob'alan data with data from Colonial Yukatek suggests a similar shift for Yukatek: that, like Q'anjob'alan, prehistoric Yukatek lost raising, causing the subjects to remain with the secondary predicates, and causing the old marker for RELATIVE VOICE to come to mark NOMINATIVE VOICE. In this case the common language RELATIVE VOICE marker, **ow-ik,* was reduced to **-ik.*[1] Thus, in Colonial Yukatek (as with Q'an-

---

[1]It might be that the form was **-Vn-ik* in the common language, and not **-ow-ik* for RELATIVE-VOICE (ABS-VOICE). In K'iche'an the ANTIPASSIVE is *-on-ik,* and *-ow-ik* for RELATIVE VOICE, whereas in Q'anjob'alan it is the opposite: *-Vn-i* for RELATIVE VOICE, and *w-i* for ANTIPASSIVE. More comparative work has to be done to work it out. At this point, all I can say is that the system of the common

job'alan's *-Vn-i)*, the same suffix (*-ik* in the case of Yukatek) marked both
RELATIVE and NOMINATIVE VOICE:[1]

> Juan kambes-*ik* Pedro
> John teach-SECONDARY Pedro
> '(it is) John (that) teaches Pedro'

> ¢'o'ok *in*-kan-*ik* payalči
> finish ERG1SG-learn-SECONDARY pray
> 'I finished learning to pray'

Chuj

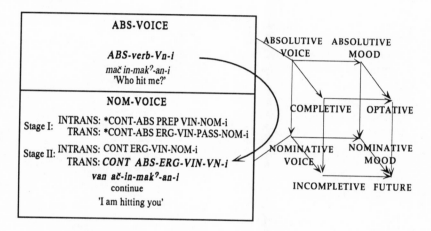

Figure 9.2. Paradigm showing the influence of ABSOLUTIVE VOICE (relative
clause marker) on NOMINATIVE VOICE (incompletive marker) in Chuj.

Note that the difference between the relative and nominal constructions
above is not in the suffix *-ik,* for they both have it, but in the presence or
absence of the ERGATIVE pronoun, where the relative has no ERGATIVE, but
where the formerly nominalized clause does. Again, note that Q'anjob'al,
independently of Yukatek, underwent an identical change, where the relative
clause has no ERGATIVE pronoun, but where the "nominalized" clause does:[2]

> a-naq §-'il-on-i

---

language may be like that of K'iche'an.

[1]This is taken from Gates' summary of San Buenaventura (1694).

[2]It is noteworthy in this regard that Q'anjob'alan *-i* comes from the Common
Mayan * - *ik.*

it's-he COMP-see-RELATIVE-<*-**ik**
'(it is) he (that) sees him'

láan ač-*in* -maqʔ-on-i
CONT ABS2SG-ERG1SG-hit-RELATIVE-<*-**ik**
'I'm hitting you'

In Yukatek, however, the changes in grammar are both broader and deeper than the changes in Q'anjob'alan—broader because the changes apply to analogically extended constructions, and deeper because they entered into the paradigm of COMPLETIVE/INCOMPLETIVE. Consider, for example, the following examples (Coronel 1620):

bal u-chum a-hatz'ic a-chuplil[1]
[bal u-čum a-haȼʔ-ik a-čuplil]
what ERG3SG-CAUSE ERG2SG-whip-OPT ERG2SG-wife
'Why do you beat your wife?'

bal u-chum a-hatzʔci
[bal u-čum a-haȼʔ-k-i]
what ERG3SG-CAUSE ERG2SG-whip-AFF-SAPD
'Why did you beat her?'

bal u-chum ta-haȼʔci
[bal u-čum t-a-haȼʔ-k-i]
what ERG3SG-CAUSE PROX.PAST-ERG2SG-whip-AFF-SAPD
'Why did you beat her (today)?'

bal a-haȼʔic a-čuplil
[bal a-haȼʔ-ik a-čuplil]
what ERG2SG-whip-SAPD ERG2SG-wife
'With what do you beat your wife?'

The -*ik* extended itself analogically from the simple RELATIVE and NOMINATIVE VOICE in Q'anjob'alan to include questions beyond 'who,' such as 'why,' 'when,' 'where,' etc. In Yukatek the change goes far beyond the Q'anjob'alan changes, but the change in Q'anjob'al is in the direction that Yukatek so fully expanded on.

---

[1]The data here are from a copy of a copy of Juan Coronel's *Arte, en lengua Maya, México, 1620*. The first copy was made by some unknown person for a Mr. Wilkinson, from the original, and William Gates then made his "corrections," including some reanalysis of morpheme boundaries with the addition of some hyphens.

Replacement of the INCOMPLETIVE by the NOMINATIVE VOICE

In Yukatek Maya, the INCOMPLETIVE was twice taken over by forms originally found in the NOMINATIVE VOICE; the first shift was apparently like that of Choltí and Poqom, and the second shift innovatively used a syntactic construction present in Common Mayan, but unique to Yukatek as an INCOMPLETIVE marker. Thus, by Colonial times the INCOMPLETIVE had apparently undergone two changes. The first is only indirectly attested, by external comparison and by internal reconstruction. It would have been something like the following for single- and double-argument predications:

*PRED in-way-el
PRED ERG1SG-sleep-NOMLZR
'I am sleeping'

*PRED in-haȼ⁷-ik-eč
PRED ERG1SG-whip-SAPD-ABS2SG
'I am whipping you'

The justification for postulating such unattested INCOMPLETIVE forms are twofold, one external and the other internal. First, the postulated pattern is virtually identical to that of Choltí and Poqom, as a result of the replacement of the forms of the INCOMPLETIVE by the NOMINATIVE VOICE. Second, the pattern of the above forms is attested in the NEGATIVE INCOMPLETIVE of Colonial Maya. The negative is likely a more archaic form because of the conservative nature of the negative already demonstrated in the shift from Common Mayan to Choltí to Chorti', and from Colonial to Modern Tzeltal. Beltrán (1746) says this of the negative INCOMPLETIVE in Yukatek:

> Este es el proprio lugar de un precissa advertencia, y es, que la negativa *ma,* que es *no* causa los efectos siquientes. El primero, que antepuesta a los verbos activos *no absolutos,* los muda en *ic,* en presente, è imperfecto de indicativo, como *ma a tacic a takin,* no guardes tu dinero: y aunque no muda à los absolutivos: pero les quita el *cah,* y se antepone el Pronombre, como *ma a nacal,* no subas.

> [This is the appropriate place for a necessary remark, which is, that the negative *ma,* which means 'no,' causes the following effects: first, that when placed before *nonabsolutive* transitive verbs, it changes them to *ik* in the present, and the imperfective of the indicative, as *ma a-tak-ik a-tak⁷in* 'you don't save your money,' and even though it does not change to the absolutive, it does lose the *kah,* with the prefixation of the [ergative] pronoun, as *ma a-nak-al,* 'you don't ascend.']

As can be seen in the above quotation, the negative in Colonial times preserves what must be taken as an old PROGRESSIVE, or at least a form very similar to that found in, say, Choltí (Morán 1695) or Poqom:

Choltí:
ywal in uixnel   'actualmente me voi'
[wal in-wišn-el]   'I'm going now'

ywal in-chohben Dios   'actualment amo a Dios'
[iwal in-čohben Dios]   'now I love God'

Colonial Yukatek (negative):
ma a nacal   'no subas'
[ma a-nak-al]   'you don't go up'

ma a tacic a takin   'no guardes tu dinero'
[ma a-tak-ik a-tak²in]   'you don't save your money'

The positive of the INCOMPLETIVE, however, as explained by Beltrán above, takes the verb *kah,* 'to do, make,' which appears *last* in the sentence, as shown in the single-argument predication listed below, which is apparently the innovative form that replaced the original Choltí-like form discussed above:

nacal in cah
[nak-al in-kah]
ascend-NOMLZR ERG1s-do
'I ascend'

For transitives, on the other hand, Coronel (1620) says that "it is the same, except that the patient is always mediated by the preposition *ti,* as, *cambezah incah ti palalob* 'I teach the boys.' These exemplify the forms used to express the idea of the INCOMPLETIVE in the earliest Colonial times.

An understanding of the origin of this Yukatekan sentence-final verb form for the INCOMPLETIVE grows from a comparison of syntactically cognate forms in other Mayan language families which similarly prepose the dependent verb to the sentence-final independent verb 'to do, make.' In the other non-Yukatekan languages the meaning is PROGRESSIVE. Because of its wide distribution, this particular construction was apparently a part of the common language:

Ixil:
vat-a²m n-i-b²an-e²
sleep-NOMLZR INC-ERG3SG-do-AFF

'he is sleeping'

q'os-el-in n-i-b'an-e'
hit-NOMLZR-ABS1SG INC-ERG3SG-do-AFF
'he is hitting me'

Awakatek:
wa·t-l na-in-b'an
sleep-NOMLZR INC-ERG1SG-do
'I am sleeping'
a-mak-l-e'n na-in-b'an
ERG2SG-touch-PASS-NOMLZR INC-ERG1SG-do
'I am touching you'

Cunén K'iche':
war-a·m n-u-b'n-o
sleep-NOMLZR INC-ERG3SG-do-AFF
'he is sleeping'

u-ču-·-p-i·k q'a·q' n-u-b'n-o
ERG3SG-extinguish-PASS[infix]-extinguish-SAPD fire INC-ERG3SG-do-AFF
'he is extinguishing the fire'

As pointed out above, the syntactic structure of these forms requires (1) the raising of the logical subject of the secondary verb to the subject position of the primary verb, and (2) the passivation and (3) the nominalization of the secondary verb to fill the office of the object of the primary verb. However, unlike any other syntactic construction in Mayan, this nominalized object is *preposed* to the sentence-final primary verb, which always has the meaning 'to make, do.'[1] This nearly pan-Mayan construction is cognate with the INCOMPLETIVE found in Colonial Yukatek Maya, given the fact that the primary verb is found in sentence-final position with the meaning 'to do, make.' But because Yukatek Maya ultimately lost the Common Mayan transitive verbal forms for NOMINATIVE VOICE in favor of RELATIVE VOICE, the logical object of the secondary clause was separated from the rest of the sentence by the preposition *ti*, as in **cambezah incah ti palalob** 'I teach the boys.' This

---

[1]This almost makes me want to believe that sometime in the pre-prehistory of Common Mayan, the language was of the type SOV (subject-object-verb), and that this particular verb-final syntactic form is a fossilized remnant. Otherwise, I am not quite sure how to account for this verb-final construction in what is otherwise a strongly verb-initial family.

insertion of the preposition is obviously innovative when compared to the rest of the examples given above.

Figure 9.3 shows the three stages of the INCOMPLETIVE discussed above, with the reminder that by Stage 2, Yukatek Maya had lost the NOMINATIVE VOICE of the transitive, having been replaced by the old PROGRESSIVE marker.

	Common	Pre-Yukatek (from PROGRESSIVE)	Col. Yukatek
Intrans	**ki-ABS-Vin-ik	*PRED ERG-Vin-Vl	Vin-Vl ERG-kah
Trans	**ki-ABS-ERG-Vt-O	*PRED ABS-ERG-Vt-ik	Vt ERG-kah ti Nobj

Figure 9.3. Change in the INCOMPLETIVE from Common Mayan to pre-Yukatek to Colonial Yukatek.

Colonial Yukatek Maya FUTURE

The evolution of the Yukatekan FUTURE from Common Mayan times holds particular interest because of its relationship to other important changes in the system. One of those changes has to do with a conservative negative, as has been seen so often up to this point; in this case it preserves at least a remnant of the Common Mayan *la-* FUTURE. Beltrán (1746) says this with regard to the Colonial Yukatek Maya FUTURE:

> And if the particle *wil* is added to [the negative] *ma,* it causes a special effect, which is that the verb is in the preterite perfect, without changing to *ik,* and has a future sense, without the particle *b?i·n,* as *ma wil a-kambesah,* 'you will not teach ' (Beltrán 1746)

This comment by Beltrán is strikingly similar to what Morán (1695) said about the NEGATIVE FUTURE in Choltí:

> Note the second future is made with the particle *el,* which signifies prohibition. And it should be noted that this particle is always used with the preterite, and not the future, despite the future meaning: *a-k?ale aw-otot* 'you built your house,' *el a-k?ale aw-otot konahel* 'you will not make another (your) house.'

It is significant that, apparently independently of each other, these two grammarians found it important enough to note that the NEGATIVE FUTURE was based on the so-called preterite (COMPLETIVE), with the reflexes of the suffixes *-ik* and *-O,* and *not* on the reflexes of the OPTATIVE, *-oq* and *-A?.* It is further significant that *l* figures prominently in both futures; *wil* in Colonial Yukatek Maya, and *el* in Choltí. This is more evidence supporting the reconstruction of the Common Mayan FUTURE as **la...ik/O,* which is *not* based on the OPTATIVE suffixes **-oq* and **-A?*.[1] Thus, the claim is strengthened that reflexes of the OPTATIVE, commonly found associated with the FUTURE in other Mayan languages, were not a part of the FUTURE of the common language, but resulted instead from influence of the OPTATIVE on the FUTURE.

The POSITIVE FUTURE in Colonial Yukatek is, for single-argument predications, *b?i'n Vn-Vk-ABS,* as seen in the example *b?i'n nak-ak-en* go ascend-OPT-ABS1SG 'I will ascend (go up),' and for double-argument predications, *b?i'n Vt-Vb,* as seen in the example *b?i'n ¢ik-ib* go obey-OPT 'he will obey it.' Likely etymologies for these two morphologies are these: the *-Vk* is a reflex of the OPTATIVE **-oq* of the common language, although it has acquired the innovative characteristic of being vowel harmonic with the root vowel. The vowel harmonic *-Vb* of *b?i'n ¢i-kib* comes from the vowel harmonic, Common Mayan OPTATIVE **-A?*. Apparently the form *b?i'n,* with rising (unstable) tone, came from the root **be·h-Vn,* which is likely a denominal from 'road.' Furthermore, this form apparently came from the old Common Mayan NOM-DV, of which the Colonial Yukatek Maya FUTURE is a direct reflex.

As might be apparent by now, there was a chain of changes where the NOM-DV displaced the FUTURE, and where the FUTURE survived only in the negative. The chain is summarized in Figure 9.4.

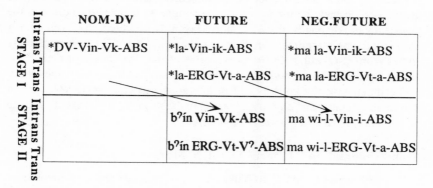

Figure 9.4. Chain displacement in the FUTURE and NEGATIVE FUTURE of Colonial Yukatek.

Thus, although it is not clear precisely what the origin of the *wi* of the negative FUTURE might have been, it is well within the theory propounded here to explain the *l* as a trace of the Common Mayan **la-* FUTURE. Common Mayan **-O* was apparently reduced to *-a*.

---

[1] Recall that such a reconstruction is further bolstered by the appearance of a restricted future in Awakatek, *l...,* which is also free of the OPTATIVE.

The COMPLETIVE in Colonial Yukatek Maya

Up to this point, the discussion has pointed out the changes relative to the INCOMPLETIVE and FUTURE as influenced by the NOMINAL and RELATIVE VOICE, but the COMPLETIVE remains to be discussed. First, note that the Colonial language there made a distinction between the PROXIMATE PAST (past time of today) and the COMPLETIVE, a distinction similar to that of Colonial K'iche'an (p. 176) and Mamean (p. 98), Choltí (p. 189), and probably Tzeltalan (p. 183). For example, Coronel (1620) said, "And if it is the preterite of the present day, it [the verb] is always changed, and to change it you prepose the letter *t,* which denotes being in the present day, as *bal u-chum ta-haȼ'ki* 'why do you whip him today?' " Although the etymology of the *ti,* meaning 'past time of today,' is not clear, it *is* clear that this is another instance of the grammatical category PROXIMATE PAST, thus providing further evidence of the antiquity of this grammatical category.

One of the chief differences between Colonial Yukatek Maya and the common language is the fact that the reflexes of Common Mayan *-ik* and *-O* are restricted to signaling only the COMPLETIVE. All of the Colonial grammars, for instance, list for the preterite (COMPLETIVE) *-i* for single-argument predications, and *-ah* for double-argument predications. The etymology of these so-called preterite markers is clear enough. As happened so often in the other Mayan languages, the Common Mayan *-ik,* which was originally a marker of single-argument predications, became *-i.*[1] The *-ah* apparently comes from *-O,* although the provenance of the final *h* is not clear. The reason *i* and *ah* took the additional sense of COMPLETIVE is obvious: they were replaced in the INCOMPLETIVE by *-Vl* of the PROGRESSIVE and *-ik* of VOICE. With that replacement, *i* and *ah* only appeared in the COMPLETIVE, where they came to be reinterpreted as a markers of that aspect.

From Colonial to Modern Yukatek Maya

The shift from Colonial to Yukatek Maya involves fewer changes than some of the other languages discussed, but the changes were indeed far-reaching. By way of review, recall that the shift from the common language

---

[1]There is a strong propensity for *-ik* to change to *-i,* partly because, as a single-argument predication, it is less marked in its Interpretant but more complex in its sign than its double-argument counterpart, *-a.* On the other hand, note that we have assumed that the *-ik* of RELATIVE VOICE, because it is the reduction of a double-argument predication to a single argument, is a conservation of the Common Mayan *-ik.* The change from *-ik* to *-i* happened among the Q'anjob'alan languages only in Poqomam of K'iche'an and in Choltí; it tends to remain in K'iche'an (although *-ik* > *-i* and *-oq* > *-o* in Tz'utujil) and to be lost in Mamean.

to Yukatek Maya saw the replacement of the original *ki-* of the INCOMPLETIVE by the NOMINATIVE VOICE, as happened in Chol, for example. It will be further recalled, however, that the NOMINATIVE VOICE was taken over by the RELATIVE VOICE, such that -*ik* appears in Yukatek transitives. In this regard, pre-Yukatek is virtually identical to Choltí:

Choltí:	**wal in-wan-el**	'I am sleeping'
pre-Yukatek:	**PRED in-wen-el*	'I am sleeping'
Choltí:	**wal in-kubu**	'I am believing it'
pre-Yukatek:	**PRED in-haȼʔ-ik*	'I am hitting it'

Next, this unattested form was replaced by a construction that includes the verb [*kah*] 'to do, make,' as in, for example, *nakal in-kah* 'I climb.' This form, however, was lost in modern Yukatek Maya, being replaced by the entire series of forms found in the NOMINAL/RELATIVE VOICE; there is no single form which means INCOMPLETIVE, but as pointed out by Bricker (1986:viii), there is a whole series of aspect markers in the modern language:

> Yukatek Maya does not have tenses as such. Instead, it has a system of aspectual inflection that indicates whether an action has been completed or not, whether it is just beginning or ending or has been in progress for a while. The perfective form of the verb refers to completed action. The imperfective stem refers to actions or events in the past, present, or future that have not been completed. Completed actions are restricted to the past.... The following aspect words or particles govern the imperfective stem of both transitive and intransitive verbs:

> **k** [incompletive, habitual]
> **t(áan)** [durative]
> **cʔ(óʔok)** [terminative]
> **hóʔopʔ** [inceptive]
> **yàan** [compulsive]

In Modern Yukatek the old distinction of the INCOMPLETIVE, so much a part of the systems heretofore analyzed, has been replaced by a whole range of morphemes, more specialized than before but nonetheless much broader than that of the common language. The change in question saw the NOMINAL construction totally replace the Colonial Yukatek Maya form INCOMPLETIVE in *kah,* so that today the INCOMPLETIVE consists of many different aspectual markers, as explained above.

Recall that in the common language the NOMINATIVE VOICE was aspect-like since the primary predicate modifies the verbal action of the secondary predicate. For example, in Common Mayan, the NOMINATIVE VOICE involved such meanings as, roughly translated, 'I continue/finish/begin…with sleeping, 'I continue/finish/begin…with your-being-hit,' and so on.[1] In many of the languages observed up to this point, there have been instances in which the PROGRESSIVE, in particular, took over or at least influenced the INCOMPLETIVE. In Yukatek Maya, however, it was more than just a *part* of the NOMINATIVE VOICE that took over the INCOMPLETIVE; it was the entire range of nominalized constructions that took over the aspectual category INCOMPLETIVE.

Finally, it should be noted that the old Common Mayan OPTATIVE *-A?* for transitive verbs was replaced by *-eh,* even by Beltrán's time (1746):

Para la tercera conjugacion sea la primera regla, que todos sus verbos son de una sylabal, y activos, e activo…, y el futurose forma añdiendo al cuerpo del vero una vocal simil á la del verbo; y luego una *b,* v.g. *mol* recoger, *bin in molob* lo recogerè; *tal,* tocar; *bin in talab,* lo tacarè….

Esto es, lo que enseña el R. Fr. Gabriel, no lo niego: pero es cierto, que ya el uso está corriente de otro modo: pues al futuro solo se le añade un *e* diciendo: *bin in tzicé,* obedeceré.

For the third conjugation [CVC transitives] the first rule is that all its verbs are of one syllable and active…, and the future is formed by adding to the body of the verb a final vowel that is like the verb, as in *mol,* 'to gather,' *bíin in molob,* 'I will gather it,' *tal* 'touch,' *bíin in talab,* 'I will touch it,' and so on with the others…

This was explained by Father Gabriel, and I do not deny it, but it is true that nowadays the use has changed to another form: that is, in the future, only an *e* is added, thus: *bíin in mole?*

The change referred to by Beltrán has run its course so that in modern Yukatek Maya the form is *e.*

As for the COMPLETIVE, the intransitive verb has *h* as a prefix, whereas the transitive has *t.* These markers are best explained as having come from the Colonial language's *t,* which, as will be recalled, meant PROXIMATE PAST (p. 208). The *h* of the intransitive, which no longer is spoken except in the most conservative dialects, apparently came from the *t,* which was historically always juxtaposed to the intransitive verb, which almost always was consonant-initial. There is a phonological process in Mayan where the first of two *t*'s optionally becomes *h,* as in the following:

---

[1]Other syntactic constructions existed, which are less aspectual, such as 'I help you with its-being-eaten,' but Yukatek Maya emphasized the aspectual portion of the construction.

t-u y-óok⁷ot̯ tah háarana   COMP-ERG3SG ERG3SG-dance.TRANSTVZR jarana
t-u y-óok⁷oh̯ tah háarana   'he danced the jarana'

It is reasonable to assume that the old *t-* first became *h-* before the intransitive, *t*-initial stems, and subsequently spread to the remaining verbs. The reason the *t-* remained to mark intransitives is because the ERGATIVE pronouns are vowel-initial; and because they precede the stem of intransitives, the *t* remained unchanged as a marker of the COMPLETIVE with transitive verbs.

Summary of Yukatek Maya

The major points of interest regarding Yukatek Maya include the following observations. First RELATIVE and NOMINATIVE VOICE both have the same marker, which is precisely the state of affairs in Q'anjob'al. This is attributable to the fact that RELATIVE VOICE is unmarked with respect to NOMINATIVE VOICE, and as a consequence, the unmarked influenced the marked. Second, after being taken over by RELATIVE VOICE, the NOMINATIVE VOICE took over the INCOMPLETIVE; as a consequence, the same markers that are found in the RELATIVE VOICE are also found in the INCOMPLETIVE with transitive verbs:

leti⁷ loš-*ik*   'it is he who hit you'
k-u-loš-*ik*   'he hits you'

Third, since the NOMINATIVE VOICE took over the INCOMPLETIVE, the Common Mayan structure for nominalization exists essentially unchanged in the Yukatek INCOMPLETIVE for intransitives, as in *k-u-wen-el* 'I sleep.' Fourth, Colonial Yukatek, like Choltí, likely has a remnant of the original Common Mayan FUTURE **la-* in the form *wil: wil a-kambesah,* 'you will not teach.' The morphology is not based on the OPTATIVE. Fifth, the PROXIMATE PAST of Colonial times, *t-,* became the COMPLETIVE of modern Yukatek. Note that in the intransitive construction, where *t* was juxtaposed to the intransitive stem, it became *h:*

h-wèeni   'I slept'
t-u-loš-ah   'he hit him'

Finally, it is assumed that originally only the PROGRESSIVE of the NOMINATIVE VOICE took over the INCOMPLETIVE. Later, as attested in Colonial times, the INCOMPLETIVE was again taken over by another PROGRESSIVE, *kah;* then, in modern times the whole range of the NOMINATIVE VOICE took over the IN-COMPLETIVE, such that today, there are a series of constructions which all belong to the split-ergative INCOMPLETIVE ASPECT.

These things taken together reconfirm our supposition that while K'iche' is the candidate for the least-changed language from Common Mayan times, Yukatek Maya may well be the most-changed.

Chapter 10. **Huastec**

Huastec[1]—spoken in Mexico roughly in a triangular area between Tampico to the north, San Luís Potosí to the west, and (north of) Vera Cruz to the south—is the only Mayan language that is not geographically contiguous with all the other Mayan languages. It is clearly descended from the original TAMV system, and is undoubtedly related to the Cholan-Tzeltalan subgroup. Two historical factors that occur commonly in Mayan language history contributed to its modern configuration: first, influence from the PROGRESSIVE on the INCOMPLETIVE (page 93), which was very significant in Huastecan prehistory, and second, the loss of RAISING (page 80).

As regards the influence from the PROGRESSIVE on the INCOMPLETIVE, one is struck by how similar Huastec is to Choltí. It will be recalled that the original Common Mayan system for NOM-VOICE (p. 77.) is postulated to have had the following system:

INTRANSITIVE: *primary.verb-ABS PREP (*t^{y}i) VIN+NOMLZR

TRANSITIVE: *primary.verb-ABS PREP (*t^{y}i) ERG+VT+PASS+NOMLZR

This system can be compared to Choltí and Huastecan:

INCOMPLETIVE
INTRANSITIVE

PROG	*PROG-ABS PREP VIN-el	'to be verb-ing'	(Common West-Mayan)
INC	*PROG-ABS PREP VIN-el	'I (verb)'	(Common West-Mayan)
INC	yual in uuanel	'I sleep'	(Choltí)
	[wal in wan-el]		
	ABS1SG-VIN-NOMLZR		
PROG	yak-on ta way-el	'I am sleeping'	(Tzeltal)
	PROG-ABS1SG PREP sleep-NOMLZR		
INC	ya-x-way-on	'I sleep'	(Tzeltal)
	PROG-INC-sleep-ABS1SG		
PROG	ešom t-in-way-el	'I am sleeping'	(Huastec)
	PROG PREP-ABS1SG-sleep-NOMLZR		
INC	in-way-el	'I sleep'	(Huastec)
	ERG1SG sleep-NOMLZR		

---

[1]The Colonial data are from Tapia Zenteno (1767). The modern data are from the Chinampa, Vera Cruz dialect of Huastec.

TRANSITIVE

	*PROG-ABS PREP ERG-VT-el	'I (verb) it'	(Common West-Mayan)
INC	yual in-cana	'I want it'	(Choltí)
	[wal in-kan-a]		
	PROG ERG1SG-want-THEME		
PROG	yak-on ta pas	'I am making it'	(Tzeltal)
	PROG-ABS1SG PREP make		
INC	ya-h-pas	'I do it'	(Tzeltal)
	PROG-ERG1SG-cure		
PROG	ešom u-kʔap-u-l	'I am eating it'	(Huastec)
	PROG ERG1SG-eat-THEME-NOMLZR		
INC	u-kʔap-al	'I eat it'	(Huastec)
	ERG1SG-eat-NOMLZR		

The relationship between the syntagmatic PROGRESSIVE and the paradigmatic INCOMPLETIVE is compelling. Here, as with virtually all the other Mayan families, the PROGRESSIVE has deeply influenced the INCOMPLETIVE. In the case of Choltí, the INCOMPLETIVE partially preserves the Common Mayan PROGRESSIVE (p. 77.), including the split-ergative use of the ERGATIVE as the subject of an intransitive, and the -*Vl* NOMINALIZER. In the transitive verb, however, the PROGRESSIVE marker simply displaced the old INCOMPLETIVE marker, thus obviating the markers for PREPOSITION, PASSIVE, and NOMINALIZATION. Although the PROGRESSIVE was not recorded in the Choltí grammar, it is likely that it existed as a fairly conservative reflex of the system in the common language, since it exists in modern Chorti'.

There is also a PROGRESSIVE influence on the INCOMPLETIVE in Tzeltal, but of a different nature. As with Choltí's transitive verbs, the marker for the PROGRESSIVE simply replaced the reflex of the old INCOMPLETIVE; with INTRANSITIVES the PROGRESSIVE augmented the old INCOMPLETIVE (p. 93). Here, the INCOMPLETIVE *š-*, which is from Common Mayan *kV-*, was augmented by the PROGRESSIVE marker *yak*, with strict maintenance of the original ERGATIVE/ABSOLUTIVE case-marking system. Notice that with the PROGRESSIVE in the transitive, both RAISING and the PREPOSITION of Common Mayan times were lost.

Huastec also shows evidence of a profound but different kind of PROGRESSIVE influence on the INCOMPLETIVE. In this case the old nominalizer -*Vl* moved by influence from the PROGRESSIVE and was reanalyzed as a marker of the INCOMPLETIVE. For transitive verbs there was a concomitant loss of the markers of PASSIVIZATION and any split-ergative case marking, as happened in Tzeltal and Choltí.

Perhaps the most striking changes took place with the reanalysis of the PREPOSITION. With INCOMPLETIVE transitive verbs, the *tV* of the syntagmatic

PROGRESSIVE construction influenced the non-third-person objects, resulting in a system of forms like that in figure 10.1.[1]

	Subj.	Object 3	2	2 P	1	1 P
Common Mayan		**ru	**at-ru	**eš-ru	**in-ru	**oʔŋ-ru
pre-Huastec		*ru	*ta-at-ru	*ta-eš-ru	*ta-in-ru	?*wa
pre-Colonial	3	*in	*ta-t-in	*ta-š-in	*ta-n-in	*ta-wa
Colonial		in	ta-t-i	ta-š-i	ta-n-in	ta-wa
Chinampa		in	titi	tiši	tin	tu
Common Mayan		**a	—	—	**in-a	**oʔŋ-a
pre-Huastec		*a	—	—	*ta-in-a	?*wa
pre-Colonial	2	*a	—	—	*ta-n-a	*ta-wa
Colonial		a	—	—	ta-n-a	ta-wa
Chinampa		a	—	—	tin	tu
Common Mayan		**nu/qa	**at-nu	**eš-nu	—	—
pre-Huastec		*nu/ka	*ta-at-nu	*ta-eš-nu	—	—
pre-Colonial	1	*u/i	*ta-t-u	*ta-š-u	—	—
Colonial		u/i	ta-t-u	ta-š-u	—	—
Chinampa		u/i	tutu	?	—	—

Figure 10.1. Paradigm illustrating the influence of the PROGRESSIVE on the INCOMPLETIVE in Huastecan.

It is to be reemphasized that the loss of raising caused the same problem for Huastec transitive verbs as it caused for those of Q'anjob'alan, Yukatek, and Mam, as discussed on page 81. Q'anjob'alan and Yukatek compensated by bringing down the marker for ABS-VOICE (Q'anjob'alan was *-Vn-i*). Huastec's solution was conceptually the opposite of what Mam did. Whereas Mam used the ERGATIVE set of pronouns to mark the transitive object as well as the intransitive subject (page 176), Huastec used the ABSOLUTIVE to mark the transitive object and intransitive subject, thus losing the effect of nominalization. The distinction that used to be carried by nominalization, however, was newly made by the old preposition *ti,* and by the fact that the old NOMINALIZER *-Vl* was brought down from the intransitive verb. These changes are witnessed by the following forms:

ešom t-in kʔap-ul
CONT PREP-ABS1SG eat-NOMLZR

---

[1]For transitive verbs the distinction between SINGULAR/PLURAL subject was ultimately lost, except for first person: *u* = 'I', and *i* = 'we.' Furthermore, SINGULAR/PLURAL objects are apparently not significant in Huastecan.

'I am eating'

ešom u-kʔáp-al
CONT ERG1SG eat-NOMLZR
'I am eating it'

As for the category FUTURE, it seems reasonable that it was influenced at various times by the OPTATIVE and by the NOM-MOOD in the following way. First, in Huastec, as in Q'anjob'al, the OPTATIVE influenced the FUTURE, and furthermore, like Q'anjob'al, Chuj, and Tojolab'al, the reflex of *-oq* was prefixed to the intransitive verb and then generalized to the transitive (see page 189).[1] Thus, in the NOM-MOOD, the OPTATIVE, and the FUTURE, the prefix *k-* can be found:

leʔakič k ʔin ka ʔahtin
would.that <*-oq ABS1SG sing
'would that I sing'

leʔakic k-u ahatna
would.that <*-oq ERG1SG-sing
'would that I sing it'

Another important influence was that of the NOM-MOOD on the FUTURE. As in Yukatekan (p. 207), the word for 'to go' in its several conjugations came to mark the FUTURE:

neʔč t-in way-al
go PREP-ABS1SG-sleep-NOMLZR
'I will sleep'

neʔč k-u kʔápu
go <*-oq-ABS1SG-sleep
'I will eat it'

Summary of Huastec

Despite the fact that Huastec has been outside the influence of the other Mayan language for hundreds of years, it is clear that it, like the rest of the Mayan languages, descended from the Common Mayan system of TAMV proposed herein. A summary is given in Figure 10.2.

---

[1]Note that it is possible that the prefixing could have first taken place in the OPTATIVE and then influenced the FUTURE.

There are many reasons to group Huastec with Western Mayan: (a) siblings-in-law have reflexes of *b?al* (male speaking to male), *mu?* (female to male or male to female), and *hawan* (female to male), which *all* Western Mayan languages share (Robertson 1984c:372), (b) palatalization of Common Mayan *k* occurs in both groups, (c) the obvious and pervasive influence of NOM-VOICE on the INCOMPLETIVE affected Huastec as well, (d) The -*Vl* nominalizer is present as in both groups, and (e) in general the need to postulate something like Western Mayan Choltí in Huastec's derivation from the common language makes subgrouping Huastec with the Western Mayan languages defensible. To say that Huastec comes directly from Common Mayan seems less defensible: Clearly, all of the above traits were not conservative, and it is doubtful that Huastec would have made them all up by itself in its isolated, northern existence.

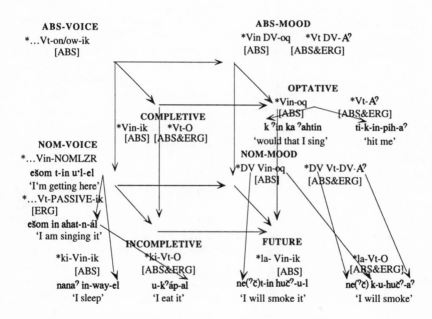

Figure 10.2. Summary of changes in the TAMV of Huastec.

Chapter 11. Summary

The application of the comparative method to the TAMV of the Mayan languages has had two distinct but related consequences. First it results in a deeper understanding of the nature of language and of language theory. Second, it results in a more complete compassing of Mayan synchrony and diachrony. The December 1989 issue of *Language* contains a curious juxtaposition of views regarding the role of historical linguistics in linguistic theory. On one hand, Sarah Grey Thomason (1989:920) editorializes that "historical linguistics had lost its central place in the discipline...by about 1965" to what she calls the "traditional central areas": "phonology, morphology, and (sentence level) syntax," and this despite the fact that "in a recent survey of linguists' specialties, historical linguistics ranked second after syntax."[1] On the other hand, in the same issue, Calvert Watkins (1989:798), in his Presidential address to the Linguistic Society of America, claims that "historical linguistics is alive and well, and must be integrated into a holistic theory of human language," but with the warning that "to remove the historical dimension from the study of human language would have consequences as serious as removing the historical dimension from the study of man."

Although in recent years historical linguistics seems to be increasingly but unwisely ignored by university curricula with their attendant texts, by the editors of some important journals, and by linguists in their submission of articles, nonetheless its vitality and relevance to linguistic theory persistently and stubbornly reemerges. Even in Thomason's "traditional central areas," the light shed by the comparative historical method on phonology, morphology, and syntax, and especially on their role in linguistic theory, is in many cases megawatts beyond the modest enkindling generated by mere synchronic inquiry. If linguists genuinely see the object of their work to be the illumination of the nature of language, then they will sooner or later submit to their understanding the propositions of the comparatist's with their theoretical implications, for in the careful explanation of language change the very constitution of language necessarily unfolds.

The theoretical implications regarding the nature of language that result from the careful comparison of Mayan TAMVs are difficult to ignore. First, one of the primary assumptions of this book—that grammatical systems are hierarchically structured—has been borne out with such thorough repetition that Peirce's (5.265) injunction that scientific explanation "should not form a

---

[1]I assume that the linguists in question are members of the Linguistic Society of America.

chain which is no stronger than its weakest link, but a cable whose fibers may be ever so slender, provided they are sufficiently numerous and intimately connected" seems amply accounted for. Indeed, the millennia-old, hierarchically defined Mayan structure represented in this book either in two dimensions by

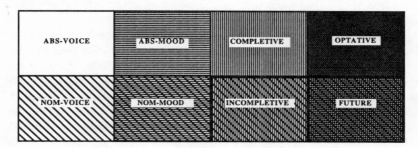

or in three dimensions by

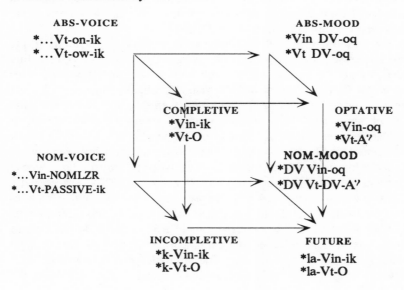

has predicted the flow of grammatical change so consistently in each of the language families as to provide strong evidence for the reality of such a relationship among the grammatical categories.

Furthermore, the theoretical assumption of categorial markedness finds confirmation in the flow of language change. The shifts from NOM-VOICE to INCOMPLETIVE to FUTURE, or OPTATIVE to FUTURE, or NOM-MOOD to FUTURE ABS-VOICE to NOM-VOICE—all help to confirm the validity of the markedness relationships, both in their synchronic existence and in their diachronic implications, inherent in the structure of the common language. Additionally, the several attested instances of markedness reversal, particularly along the axis { ABS-MOOD—NOM-MOOD}, where the presence of the attendant degrees of the same kind help to account for changes that would otherwise remain outside the purview of linguistic accountability.

Perhaps one of the most important contributions to linguistic theory is the logical explanation of the genesis of split ergativity in Mayan as a possible model for change in other languages. Although it seems quite obvious now, given the rigors of the comparative method, that Common Mayan did not originally have split ergativity, it is easily shown that the seeds of its growth in the languages that later exploited it lie in the relative structure of the grammatical system of TAMV itself. It is clear that NOM-VOICE (p. 77), with its NOMINATIVE/ACCUSATIVE focus on the subjects of transitives and intransitives, along with its structural propensity to influence the INCOMPLETIVE, provided the impetus for the emergence of the split-ergative opposition COMPLETIVE-cum-ABSOLUTIVE/ERGATIVE VS. INCOMPLETIVE-cum-NOMINATIVE/ACCUSATIVE currently found in Yukatekan and Cholan.

As for the refinement of the common understanding of Mayan itself, the comparative research done in this book has helped in several ways, including the definition of the relationship between the several grammatical categories in Common, Colonial, and modern Mayan. Additionally, it has clarified the genetic relationship between the languages themselves; it has defined the nature of TENSE, ASPECT, MOOD, and VOICE in general, and for Mayan in particular, it has shown the provenance of split ergativity.

In summary, the history of TAMV in the Mayan languages has been given a reasonable interpretation in the context of *paradigmatic structure*, whose constituent parts are ABS-VOICE (p. 90), NOM-VOICE (p. 77), ABS-MOOD (p. 83), NOM-MOOD (p. 87), COMPLETIVE, INCOMPLETIVE, OPTATIVE, and FUTURE, as summarized as in Figure 11.1, where each line connecting the several points of the above cube is marked with a number from 1 to 12. Most of these numbers represent an influence that a less-marked member of the paradigm has had on a more-marked member. The discussion that follows will work backwards from 12 to 1, summarizing the languages and referencing the kinds of influences that have effected change in the history of Mayan.

Note that three lines—10, 11, and 12—converge on the FUTURE. All three, sometimes separately but most often together (particularly the OPTATIVE and INCOMPLETIVE) significantly influenced the FUTURE.

12. The INCOMPLETIVE has influenced the FUTURE at various times and in various families in the history of Mayan. One of the chief differences between Colonial and Modern K'iche', for example, is the total replacement of the FUTURE by the INCOMPLETIVE, so that today's FUTURE is no longer expressed grammatically, but is lexically given (p. 128). Q'eqchi' registers a similar Colonial-to-Modern influence (p. 153). Within this same K'iche'an language family, Poqomchi' exemplifies the influence of the INCOMPLETIVE on the FUTURE (p. 176). Similarly, in Jakaltek the INCOMPLETIVE marker influenced the FUTURE (p. 162). Another significant example is the shift in Choltí, where the INCOMPLETIVE influenced the FUTURE, relegating the original *l-*future to mark the NEGATIVE FUTURE. Finally, Tzotzil and Tzeltal, like K'iche', entirely lost the FUTURE, which was taken over by the INCOMPLETIVE (p. 171).

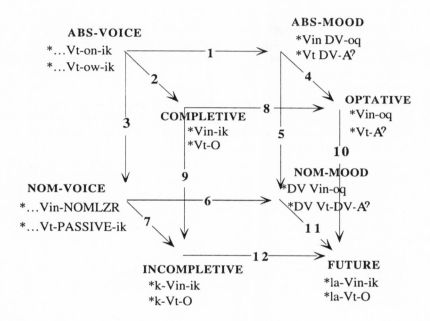

Figure 11.1. TAMV structure used in interpreting the history of the Mayan languages.

11. One of the most interesting influences of NOM-MOOD on the FUTURE was what happened in Mam, where the old Common Mayan ***-*Vl* NOMINALIZER, which replaced the reflex of ***-*oq* in the NOM-MOOD, came to mark the FUTURE, as in *(ok)-čin-bʔeˑt-el-e* (FUT)-ABS1SG-walk-FUT-clitic. Other telling examples can be seen both in Huastec (p. 216) and in Yukatek, in this case with the directional verb 'to go' (p. 207).

10. The influence of the OPTATIVE on the FUTURE has been strongly felt in the Mayan languages. Recall that the original Common Mayan FUTURE was ***la...ik/O**, which was subsequently replaced either partially or totally by the OPTATIVE ***ki/ȼ...oq/Aʔ**. Such influence is readily found in Mam (p.

105), Awakatek (p. 113), Colonial K'iche' (p. 128), Chuj (p. 166), Poqomchi' (p. 176), Colonial Q'eqchi' (p. 150), and Tzeltal/Tzotzil (p. 186).

9, 8. The influence of the COMPLETIVE on the INCOMPLETIVE or the OPTATIVE is diachronically rare, although the iconic relationship between *-*ik* and *-*oq* and *-*O* and *-*A*ʔ is highly significant, and was an important factor in the formation of the Common Mayan system. It is possible, however, that Huastec went from a split-ergative language to straight ergativity again when the ABSOLUTIVE from the INCOMPLETIVE came to replace the ERGATIVE that marked the intransitive verb.

7. The influence of NOM-VOICE on the INCOMPLETIVE has undoubtedly had more significant impact on the grammar of Mayan than any of the other relationships under discussion. That influence was almost universally some sort of augmentation from the PROGRESSIVE, as seen on page 93off, and can be classified as either morphological or syntactic; the syntactic influence precipitated the shift from a simple ERGATIVE/ABSOLUTIVE system to the richer system of split ergativity, commonly found in the modern Lowland Mayan languages. On the other hand, simple morphological influence occurred in Mamean, where in Mam the form *¢un-* (Reynoso 1644) changed to *¢in-* (modern—reduced to *n-* in normal speech; see page 102). Related to this form is the Awakatek progressive *¢aˑn:*

na-¢aˑn Waʔn taʔn čʔiˑw-aʔn
INC-CONT John PREP wait-NOMLZR
'John is waiting'

na-č-in-¢aˑn taʔn a-mak-l-eʔn
INC-INC-ABS1SG-CONT PREP ERG2SG-touch-PASS-AFF
'I am touching you'

Similarly, Awakatek augmented the Common Mayan INCOMPLETIVE **ki-* with *na*, which can be supposed to have been, at least in Common Mamean, something like *na, which when it shifted to the INCOMPLETIVE in its augmentative role was replaced by *¢Vˑn.*[1] In this regard, it is significant that the same *na-* marks the PROGRESSIVE in Poqom, which as postulated on page 144 has its source in the PROGRESSIVE.

The effect of the PROGRESSIVE on the INCOMPLETIVE is transparently obvious in Tzeltal, where for intransitive verbs the original NOM-VOICE keeps its pure syntax:

---

[1]One wonders if this is not related to the Yukatek *táan,* which has the same PROGRESSIVE function.

yak-on ta we$^?$-el
PRED-ABS1SG PREP eat-NOMLZR
'I am eating'

But for transitive verbs, the augmentation is morphological:

ya-š-tal-on
PROG-INC-come-ABS1SG
'I come'

Finally, as discussed on pages 145 and 171, Choltí's INCOMPLETIVE is best assumed to be derived from the NOMINATIVE VOICE's PROGRESSIVE. By the same token, Yukatek is similarly derived, as explained starting on page 203. It is also clear that the *-Vl* of the Huastec IMPERFECT came from NOM-VOICE.

6. The relationship between NOM-VOICE and NOM-MOOD goes back to Common Mayan times (see p. 90), as exemplified by the Colonial K'iche' example given below:

K'iche' (Anleo n.d.):

xbetihonok [š-b$^?$e-tixo-·n-αq]
COMP-go-teach-ANTI.PASS-SAPO
'He went in order to teach'

xbetihonel [š-b$^?$e-tixo-·n-*el*]
COMP-ABS3SG-go-teach-ANTI.PASS-NOMLZR
'He went in order to teach'

It is in precisely this relationship—between NOM-VOICE and NOM-MOOD—where the unmarked NOM-VOICE nominalizer *-·Vl*, replaced the more-marked *-oq* in Mam. It is of particular interest that the reflex of *-·Vl* became the marker for the FUTURE in Mam (p. 105), which further demonstrates the validity of the relationship between NOM-MOOD and FUTURE (line 11) discussed above. The influence of *-Vl* is also of great importance in Poqomchi'.

5. The relationship between ABS-MOOD and NOM-MOOD is apparent in the fact that most Mayan languages, starting with Common Mayan, show *-oq* in the intransitive and *-A$^?$* in the transitive in both ABS-MOOD and NOM-MOOD.

4. The relationship between ABS-MOOD and OPTATIVE is particularly interesting since it is subject to markedness reversal, where in Mam, NOM-DV influenced ABS-DV (p. 108), and in Awakatek, NOM-DV came to be associated with the COMPLETIVE and ABS-DV with the INCOMPLETIVE. Furthermore, Tzotzil has similarly replaced the reflex of the Common Mayan *-oq* with *-el*, which surely came from NOM-DV:

Kaliman s-hib² oč-el
Kaliman throw-ABS1SG enter- < **V·1*
'Kaliman threw it inside'

3. The relationship between ABS-VOICE and NOM-VOICE is one of the most interesting in all Mayan linguistic history. The shift from ABS-VOICE to NOM-VOICE occurred both in Q'anjob'alan (p. 83) and most probably in Yukatek (p. 206).

2, 1. So far as I know, no changes occurred in these relationships, although I would not rule out the possibility that the etymology of the Mam *n* in ABS-MOOD constructions, as shown below, is to be found in the ABS-VOICE.
ma-ṣi²-t-k²aṣ-u-²n
PROX.PAST-go-ERG3-eat(crunch)-THEME-DAPD
'he ate it (crunched it down)'.

Chaining

One of the most impressive occurrences revealed in Figure 11.1 is found in serial influences, where one change precipitates another. Such chained shifts happened both in Poqomchi' and in Choltí.

It will be recalled that Colonial Poqomchi' had two "present tenses" (INCOMPLETIVES) according to the grammarians (p. 143), one of which came down from the NOM-VOICE PROGRESSIVE. In modern Poqomchi', however, this same form has moved from the INCOMPLETIVE to the FUTURE (p. 176):

> *na-nu-wir-ik*
> PROG-ERG1SG-*sleep* -SAPD
> 'I sleep right now' (Colonial)

> *na-ni-wir-ik*
> FUT-AFF ERG1SG-*sleep* -SAPD
> 'I will sleep' (Modern)

The same lines of change determined the direction of the shifts of Choltí with different results. Like Poqomchi', Choltí moved what was originally a PROGRESSIVE to the INCOMPLETIVE, but unlike Poqomchi', the INCOMPLETIVE-né-PROGRESSIVE displaced the original PROGRESSIVE (*ṣ- < *ki-*) to the FUTURE. The FUTURE-né-INCOMPLETIVE then displaced the original **la-* future to the negative. All this is spelled out in Figure 11.2.

In the first chapter it was suggested that it would be the multitude of explanations which would naturally flow from a well-informed reconstruction which would constitute a kind of "cable whose fibers are ever so slender," but which are "numerous and intimately connected." The remarkable stability of the hierarchically defined, reconstructed Mayan system allows for a clear view of certain predispositions for change, as for example NOM-VOICE (PROGRESSIVE) influencing the INCOMPLETIVE, or the various influences on the FUTURE, including the INCOMPLETIVE, or the NOM-MOOD, or the OPTATIVE, and so on. These changes, effected in one form or another over and over again in the several daughter languages, demonstrate at once the overall unity of the Mayan TAMV system, and the effect of that system on the resulting daughter languages.

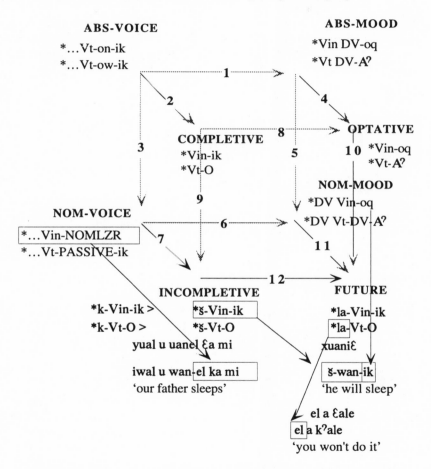

Figure 11.2. Common TAMV structure used to interpret changes in Choltí.

Bibliography

Anleo, Bartolome. n.d. Arte de la lengua Quiché. Box 55, Folder 7, William E. Gates Collection. Harold B. Lee Library. Brigham Young University, Provo, Utah.

Anonymous. n.d. Confecionario en lengua Tzeldal. Box 65, Folder 3, William E. Gates Collection, Harold B. Lee Library. Brigham Young University, Provo, Utah

Anonymous. n.d. Arte de lengua Giché Box 58, Folder 8, William E. Gates Collection, Harold B. Lee Library. Brigham Young University, Provo, Utah

Anonymous. n.d. (ca.1960). Tzeltal: Language learning guide, prepared especially for jungle training camp Yaxoquintela. Chiapas, Mexico: Summer Institute of Linguistics.

Anonymous. 1812. "Manuscrito en lengua Sotzil." In Fragmentos de idiomas Chaneabal, Zoque, Zendal, Chiapaneca. Box 64, Folder 1, William E. Gates Collection, Harold B. Lee Library. Brigham Young University, Provo, Utah

Anttila, Raimo. 1972. An introduction to historical and comparative linguistics. Toronto: MacMillan Co.

Beltrán, Pedro. 1746. Arte de el idioma Maya reducido a succintas reglas. Box 46, Folder 1, William E. Gates Collection, Harold B. Lee Library. Brigham Young University, Provo, Utah

Benveniste, Emile. 1946. "Structure des relations de personne dans le verbe." BSL #43: 1–12.

Bricker, Victoria Reifler. 1977. Pronominal inflection in the Mayan Languages. New Orleans: Middle American Research Institute, Tulane University.

Bricker, Victoria R. 1986. A grammar of Mayan hieroglyphs. New Orleans: Tulane University, American Research Institute.

Brinton, D. G., trans. 1884. A grammar of the Cakchiquel language of Guatemala. Philadelphia: McCalla and Stavely.

Campbell, Lyle. 1977. Quichéan linguistic prehistory. University of California Publications, Linguistics 81. Berkeley and Los Angeles: University of California Press.

Coronel, Juan. 1620. Arte, en lengua Maya. Box 46, Folder 2, William E. Gates Collection, Harold B. Lee Library. Brigham Young University, Provo, Utah

Cowan, Marion M. 1968. The verb phrase in Hiuxtec Tzotzil. *Language* 44:284–305.

✓ Cowan, Marion M. 1969. *Tzotzil grammar.* Norman, Okla.: Summer Institute of Linguistics.

◥ Day, Christopher. 1967. The Jacaltec language. Ph.D. dissertation, The University of Chicago.

Dayley, Jon P. 1985. *Tzutujil grammar.* University of California Publications, Linguistics 107. Berkeley and Los Angeles: University of California Press.

✓ Delgaty, Alfa Hurley Vda. de, and Agustín Ruíz Sánchez. 1978. *Diccionario Tzotzil de San Andrés con variaciones dialectales.* Vocabularios Indígenas no. 22. México: Instituto Lingüístico de Verano.

✓ England, Nora. 1983. *A grammar of Mam, a Mayan language.* Austin: University of Texas Press.

Gates, William E. n.d. Discussion on Choltí. Box 55, Folder 2, William E. Gates Collection, Harold B. Lee Library. Brigham Young University, Provo, Utah

Givón, Talmy, 1984. Syntax: *A functional-typological introduction.* Amsterdam and Philadelphia: John Benjamins Pub. Co.

✓ Guzmán, Pantaleon de. 1704. Compendio de nombres en lengua Cakchiquel. Box 36, Folder 5, William E. Gates Collection, Harold B. Lee Library. Brigham Young University, Provo, Utah

Head, Brian. 1978. "Respect degrees in pronominal reference." In *Universals of Human Language*, vol. 3, *Word structure*, ed. Joseph E. Greenberg. Stanford, Calif.: Stanford University Press.

Hopkins, Nicholas. 1967. The Chuj language. Ph.D. dissertation, University of Chicago.

Hopper, P. J., and S. A. Thompson. 1984. "The discourse basis for lexical categories in universal grammar." *Language*. 60, no. 4: 703–752.

Jakobson, Roman. 1971a. "Quest for the essence of language." In *Selected Writings*, vol. 2, 148–153. The Hague: Mouton.

Jakobson, Roman. 1971b. "Signe zéro." In *Selected Writings*, vol. 2, 211–219. The Hague: Mouton.

Jakobson, Roman. 1971c. "The relationship between genitive and plural in the declension of Russian nouns." In Selected Writings, vol. 2, 148–153. The Hague: Mouton.

Jakobson, Roman. 1971d. "Beitrag zur allgemeinen Kasuslehre: Gesamtbedeutungen der russischen Kasus." In *Selected Writings*, vol. 2, 23–71. The Hague: Mouton.

Kaufman, Terrence. 1974. Meso-American Indian languages. *Encyclopaedia Britannica*, 15th ed., vol. 11:956–963.

Kurylowicz, Jerzy. 1966. "La nature des procés dits 'analogiques.'" *Acta Linguistica* 5 (1945–1949):121–138. Reprinted in *Readings in linguistics*

II, ed. Eric P. Hamp, Fred W. Householder, and Robert Austerlitz. Chicago: The University of Texas Press.

Laughlin, Robert M. 1975. *The Great Tzotzil Dictionary of San Lorenzo Zinacantán*. Washington: Smithsonian Institution Press.

Martínez, Marcos. n.d. Arte de la lengua Utlateca o kiché. Box 57, Folder 6, William E. Gates Collection, Harold B. Lee Library. Brigham Young University, Provo, Utah

Meillet, Antoine. 1967. *The comparative method in historical linguistics*, trans. Gordon B. Ford, Jr. Paris: Librairie Honoré Champoin.

Mithun, Marianne. 1984. "The evolution of noun incorporation." *Language*, 60, no. 4:847–894.

Mondloch, James L. 1978. *Basic Quiché grammar*. Albany: State University of New York, Institute for Mesoamerican Studies.

Morales. n.d. Arte de lengua Cacchí. Box 43, Folder 9, William E. Gates Collection, Harold B. Lee Library. Brigham Young University, Provo, Utah

Morán, Fransisco. 1695. Arte en lengua Cholti que quiere decir lengua de milperos. Box 42, Folder 1, William E. Gates Collection, Harold B. Lee Library. Brigham Young University, Provo, Utah

Morán, Pedro. 1720. Arte breve y compendioso de la lengua Pokomchí de la provincia de la Verapaz. Box 52, Folder 8, William E. Gates Collection, Harold B. Lee Library. Brigham Young University, Provo, Utah

Morris, William, ed. 1975. *The American Heritage Dictionary of the English Language*. Boston: Houghton Mifflin.

Peirce, C. S. 1931–1966. *Collected papers*. Edited by Charles Hartshorne, P. Weiss, and Arthur Burks. Cambridge, Mass.: Harvard University Press.

Reynoso, Diego de. [1644] 1916. *Vocabulario de la lengua Mame*. Reprint with brief statement on the Mames by Alberto Mari Carreño. México: Departamento de la Secretaria de Fomento.

Robertson, John S. 1975. "A syntactic example of Kurylowicz's fourth law of analogy in Mayan." *International Journal of American Linguistics* 41, no. 2:140–147.

Robertson, John S. 1977a. "A proposed revision in Mayan subgrouping." *International Journal of American Linguistics* 43, no. 2:105–120.

Robertson, John S. 1977b. "A phonological reconstruction of the ergative third-person singular of Common Mayan." *International Journal of American Linguistics* 43, no. 3:201–210.

Robertson, John S. 1980. *The structure of pronoun incorporation in the Mayan verbal complex*. New York: Garland Press.

Robertson, John S. 1982. "The history of the absolute second person pronoun from Common Mayan to modern Tzotzil." *International Journal of American Linguistics* 48, no. 4:436–443.

Robertson, John S. 1983. "From symbol to icon: The evolution of the pronominal system of Common Mayan to modern Yucatecan." *Language* 59, no. 3:529–540.

Robertson, John S. 1984a. Toward a group theoretical definition of the universal deixis in kinship and in pronouns. Unpublished paper, Brigham Young University, Provo, Utah

Robertson, John S. 1984b. "An oppositional explanation of the shift from Common Mayan to the modern Chiapan pronouns." *Quaderni di Semantica* 5, no. 1:193–206.

Robertson, John S. 1984c. "Of day names, kin names and numerals: cultural affinities and distinctions among the Mayan languages." *Anthropos* 79:369–375.

Robertson, John S. 1984d. "Colonial evidence for a pre-Quiché, ERGATIVE 3SG *ru-"*International Journal of American Linguistics* 50, no. 4:452–455.

Robertson, John S. 1985. "A re-reconstruction of the ERGATIVE 1SG for Common Tzeltal-Tzotzil based on Colonial documents." *International Journal of American Linguistics* 51, no. 4:555–561.

Robertson, John S. 1986. "A reconstruction and evolutionary statement of the Mayan numerals from 20 to 400." *International Journal of American Linguistics* 52, no. 3:227–241.

Robertson, John S. 1987a. "The origins of the Mamean pronominals: A Mayan Indo-European comparison." *International Journal of American Linguistics* 52, no. 2:227-241

Robertson, John S. 1987b. "The common beginning and evolution of the tense-aspect system of Tzotzil and Tzeltal Mayan." *International Journal of American Linguistics* 53, no. 4:423-444

✓ Saenz de Santa María, Carmelo. 1940. *Diccionario Cakchiquel-Español.* Guatemala: Tipografía Nacional.

San Buenaventura, Gabriel. 1694. Arte de la lengua Maya, summarized by William E. Gates. Box 46, Folder 11, William E. Gates Collection, Harold B. Lee Library. Brigham Young University, Provo, Utah

Sapir, Eward. [1921] 1949. *Language.* New York: Harcourt, Brace & World.

Shumway, Neal O. 1985. *Tzutujil grammar.* Unpublished paper, Brigham Young University, Provo, Utah

✓ Smailus, Ortwin. 1973. Das Maya-Chontal von Acalan: Sprachanalysie eines Dokumentes aus den Jahren 1610/12. Ph.D. Dissertation, University of Hamburg.

Stewart, Steven Omer. 1978. Inflection in a grammar of Kekchí (Mayan). Ph.D. Dissertation, University of Colorado.

Tapia Zenteno, Carlos de. 1767. Notícia de la lengua huasteca. William E. Gates Collection, Harold B. Lee Library, Brigham Young University, Provo, Utah

Thomason, Sarah Grey. 1989. "The editor's department,"*Language* 65, no. 4:919-921.

Torresano, Estevan. 1692. Arte de lengua Cakchikel. William E. Gates Collection, Box 38, Folder 2. Harold B. Lee Library. Brigham Young University, Provo, Utah

Torresano, Estevan. 1794. Arte de lengua Kakchikel de Usso de. William E. Gates Collection, Box 38, Folder 3. Harold B. Lee Library. Brigham Young University, Provo, Utah

Utlan, Russell. 1978. "The nature of future tenses." In *Universals of human language*, ed. Joseph H. Greenberg, vol. 3:84–123. Stanford, California: Stanford University Press.

Villacorta, C. J. Antonio, and Flavio Rodas. 1927. *Manuscrito de Chichicastenango (Popol Wuj)*. Guatemala: Sanchez y de Guise.

Watkins, Calvert. 1962. *Indo-European origins of the Celtic verb*. Dublin: Dublin Institute for Advanced Studies.

Watkins, Calvert. 1970. "A further remark on Lachmann's Law." *Harvard Studies in Classical Philosophy* 74:55–56.

Watkins, Calvert. 1973. "Language and its history." *Daedalus* 102:99–111.

Watkins, Calvert. 1989. "New parameters in historical linguistics, philology, and culture history." *Language*. 65, no. 4:783–799.

Witkowski, Stanley R., and Cecil H. Brown. 1983. "Marking reversal and cultural importance." *Language* 59:569–582.

Zúñiga, Dionysio de. n.d. Pocomchí dictionary. Compiled by William E. Gates. William E. Gates Collection, Box 55, Folder 2. Harold B. Lee Library. Brigham Young University, Provo, Utah

Index